Hayek

Key Contemporary Thinkers

Published

Jeremy Ahearne, *Michel de Certeau: Interpretation and its Other*
Peter Burke, *The French Historical Revolution: The Annales School 1929–1989*
Simon Evnine, *Donald Davidson*
Andrew Gamble, *Hayek: The Iron Cage of Liberty*
Graeme Gilloch, *Walter Benjamin*
Phillip Hansen, *Hannah Arendt: Politics, History and Citizenship*
Christopher Hookway, *Quine: Language, Experience and Reality*
Douglas Kellner, *Jean Baudrillard: From Marxism to Post-Modernism and Beyond*
Chandran Kukathas and Philip Pettit, *Rawls: A Theory of Justice and its Critics*
Lois McNay, *Foucault: A Critical Introduction*
Philip Manning, *Erving Goffman and Modern Sociology*
Michael Moriarty, *Roland Barthes*
William Outhwaite, *Habermas: A Critical Introduction*
Susan Sellers, *Hélène Cixous: An Introduction*
Georgia Warnke, *Gadamer: Hermeneutics, Tradition and Reason*
Jonathan Wolff, *Robert Nozick: Property, Justice and the Minimal State*

Forthcoming

Alison Ainley, *Irigaray*
Sara Beardsworth, *Kristeva*
Michael Best, *Galbraith*
Michael Caesar, *Umberto Eco*
James Carey, *Innis and McLuhan*
Colin Davis, *Levinas*
Eric Dunning, *Norbert Elias*
Jocelyn Dunphy, *Paul Ricoeur*
Judith Feher-Gurewich, *Lacan*
Kate and Edward Fullbrook, *Simone de Beauvoir*
Adrian Hayes, *Talcott Parsons and the Theory of Action*
Sean Homer, *Fredric Jameson*
Christina Howells, *Derrida*
Simon Jarvis, *Adorno*
Paul Kelly, *Ronald Dworkin*
Carl Levy, *Antonio Gramsci*
Harold Noonan, *Frege*
John Preston, *Feyerabend*
Nick Smith, *Charles Taylor*
Geoff Stokes, *Popper: Politics, Epistemology and Method*
Ian Whitehouse, *Rorty*
James Williams, *Lyotard*

Hayek

The Iron Cage of Liberty

Andrew Gamble

Polity Press

Copyright © Andrew Gamble 1996

The right of Andrew Gamble to be identified as author of this work
has been asserted in accordance with the Copyright, Designs and
Patents Act 1988.

First published in 1996 by Polity Press in association with Blackwell
Publishers Ltd.

Reprinted 2004, 2007

2 4 6 8 10 9 7 5 3 1

Polity Press
65 Bridge Street
Cambridge CB2 1UR, UK

Polity Press
350 Main Street
Malden, MA 02148, USA

ISBN: 978-0-7456-0744-3
ISBN: 978-0-7456-0745-0 (pbk)

A CIP catalogue record for this book is available from the British
Library and the Library of Congress.

Typeset in 10½ on 12 pt Palatino
by Graphicraft Typesetters Ltd, Hong Kong

Printed and bound in Great Britain by
Marston Book Services Limited, Oxford

This book is printed on acid-free paper.

For further information on Polity, visit our website: www.polity.co.uk

For Tom, Corinna, and Sarah

While it may not be difficult to destroy the spontaneous formations which are the indispensable bases of a free civilisation, it may be beyond our power deliberately to reconstruct such a civilisation once these foundations are destroyed.

Hayek, *The Road to Serfdom*

There is simply no other choice than this: either to abstain from interference in the free play of the market, or to delegate the entire management of production and distribution to the government. Either capitalism or socialism: there exists no middle way.

Mises, *The Free and Prosperous Commonwealth*

Contents

Contents   ix

Preface

Hayek has long held a peculiar fascination for me, connected as he is with so many of the themes and problems which have interested me since I was a graduate student. Many of these obsessions appear in some form in these pages. David Held first suggested that I should turn some of my thoughts on Hayek into a book. I did not think it would take me as long as it has, and I am conscious of only having scratched the surface of some topics. The more I have explored Hayek, the more aware I have become of the complexity and range of his thought and the difficulty of some of the issues he raises, for which we lack answers. What I have tried to do here is to provide an assessment and a critical analysis of Hayek's achievement, to indicate some of the limitations of his thought, and to suggest why he is still relevant to us.

One of my particular interests in Hayek is his role in the ideological change in the British Conservative party in the 1970s. One of the origins of this book, as well as much other work I have done in the last fifteen years, is the article 'The Free Economy and the Strong State' published in the *Socialist Register* in 1979. The exploration of Hayek as an ideologue remains one of the central themes of the book. But I have also become interested in the contrast between Hayek the ideologue and Hayek the social scientist, and the extent to which he failed to develop many of his insights because of the ideological closures he imposed on his work. These ideological closures have also been responsible for Hayek not reaching a wider readership. It has been too easy to dismiss him as engaged in a forlorn project to restore the liberalism of an earlier era. I hope to have shown that there is great deal more to Hayek than that.

I have incurred many debts in the writing of this book. An invitation to a Liberty Fund symposium on the relationship between ideas, interests, and circumstances was very valuable at an early stage, and I particularly benefited from conversations with Arthur Seldon, David Willetts, John Burton, and Norman Barry among others about some of the general themes of the book. Others from whom I have learnt a great deal include Raymond Plant, Richard Bellamy, Martin Durham, Hilary Wainwright, Andrew Denham, Rodney Barker, and Jeremy Shearmur. David Miliband invited me to give a presentation on Hayek to an Institute of Public Policy Research seminar which produced a lively exchange, and I have also benefited from seminar discussions at Kobe, Strathclyde, Manchester, Cambridge, the London School of Economics, Edinburgh, and Nuffield.

I owe most of all to the Department of Politics and the Political Economy Research Centre at the University of Sheffield for providing such a stimulating environment in the last few years in which to think about problems of political economy. I am particularly grateful for specific help, comments, conversations, and encouragement from Anthony Arblaster, Tim Bale, Michael Harris, Gavin Kelly, Michael Kenny, Ankie Hoogvelt, David Marquand, Brian McCormick, James Meadowcroft, Tony Payne, and Matthew Sowemimo.

Andrew Gamble

Acknowledgements

The author and publishers wish to thank the following for permission to use copyright material:

Routledge and The University of Chicago Press for extracts from Hayek: *The Constitution of Liberty*. Copyright © 1960 by Routledge. Copyright © 1960 The University of Chicago Press.

Every effort has been made to trace all the copyright holders, but if any have been inadvertently overlooked the publishers will be pleased to make the necessary arrangement at the first opportunity.

1

Introduction: Rethinking Hayek

Every social order rests on an ideology.
Hayek, *Law, Legislation, and Liberty*

When Hayek died in Freiburg on 23 March 1992, the obituaries paid tribute to him as a central figure in the intellectual history of the twentieth century. But the nature of his achievement remains controversial. In the course of his long life – he was born in Vienna on 8 May 1899 – he contributed to many different academic disciplines – economics, political science, the history of ideas, philosophy, and psychology – without being identified exclusively with any one of them. He was always a polymath. Speaking of his time at the University of Vienna, he once said, 'In the University the decisive point was simply that you were not expected to confine yourself to your own subject.'[1] He followed this principle throughout his academic career. In a century of increasing intellectual specialization, Hayek moved firmly in the other direction.

This fact alone would make it difficult to assess his achievement. But what makes it even harder is that he had two intellectual personas. He was a patient, thorough, wide-ranging scholar, who emerged as one of the most important and original thinkers of the century, but also as one of the century's most renowned ideologues, a leading critic of all forms of socialism and collectivism and a passionate advocate of classical liberalism.

One of my purposes in this book is to argue that Hayek's reputation as an ideologue has for long been a barrier to a wider appreciation of his intellectual contribution to social science. This is hardly surprising. The two are hard to disentangle, because Hayek for the most part saw no reason to keep them apart. His ideological views flow from the same methodological assumptions as his scientific work, and his writings are all part of the same intellectual project.

This is not how many have seen him, however. One view of his career quite common among his critics is that he was a failed economist who abandoned serious academic work in the 1940s for extravagant ideological polemics against even mild forms of state intervention. Having begun as a theoretical economist who made some contributions to business cycle theory and monetary theory from the Austrian school perspective during the 1930s, Hayek then found himself on the losing side in two major theoretical debates: the first with Maynard Keynes over monetary theory and the causes of the Depression, the second with Oscar Lange over the feasibility of economic calculation in a socialist economy. The apparent failure of his research programme and the conversion of so many economists to the new Keynesian paradigm persuaded Hayek to abandon theoretical economics midway through his career and take up social and political theory. Starting with *The Road to Serfdom*, published in 1944, which warned that even mild government intervention and redistribution could lead to totalitarianism, he became an implacable critic of all forms of socialism and collectivism, setting himself the task of restating and reviving the principles of nineteenth-century political and economic liberalism which he believed were in danger of being forgotten.

The substance in this view is that there was a major change of direction in Hayek's career. In the 1930s he was a leading and respected member of the economics profession. Keynes's view of him (which Hayek himself quotes) was that 'of course he is crazy, but his ideas are also rather interesting'.[2] Outside the narrow circle of professional economists, he was little known. The publication of *The Road to Serfdom* changed all that. It made Hayek a celebrity, particularly in the United States. Lecture tours, radio debates, and newspaper articles expounding his views followed. He received great adulation in some quarters, but in the economics profession he was no longer regarded by most as a serious figure. The economics department at the University of Chicago even refused to consider him for a chair. Eventually the Committee of Social Thought at Chicago came to the rescue, and appointed him to a chair in social and political theory. This marked the end of his formal career as an economist.

His reception among political scientists and social and political philosophers was little better, however. He was ignored or belittled for many years as pedlar of an antiquated, reactionary creed. His greatest book, *The Constitution of Liberty*, published in 1960, was regarded as a grand folly, a last spasm of nineteenth-century *laissez-faire* liberalism, which the world had left behind. Hayek was seen as a Don Quixote fighting enemies which only existed in his imagination. George Lichtheim wrote in his review:

> With its remorseless extrapolation of the logic inherent in the liberal doctrine, its unflinching demonstration that individualism is incompatible with the vital needs of modern society, this massive work stands as both a timely warning to political philosophers and as an impressive monument to a myth.[3]

But Hayek was a more formidable figure than many of those who dismissed him in the 1950s and 1960s realized. In the 1970s and 1980s the ideology he had espoused for so long proved to be not so moribund after all, and by the 1990s new interest was beginning to be expressed in his economics, amidst realization that some of his insights had been neglected during the Keynesian and monetarist ascendancy of the previous forty years, and that he offered a way of thinking about economic co-ordination problems which had not been surpassed.[4]

The improvement in Hayek's standing was closely linked with the revival of the fortunes of economic liberalism and its renewed ascendancy as public doctrine in both Britain and the United States. Hayek became one of the main inspirations for many of the currents of thought which made up the New Right of this period. He also belatedly began to receive academic recognition and public honours. But this hardly amounted to full rehabilitation. The partisanship of his followers and his association with conviction politicians like Margaret Thatcher only helped confirm the earlier image of him as an ideologue rather than a serious thinker.

Rescuing Hayek from fifty years of ideological stereotyping is not an easy task, and Hayek himself is often of little help. In time, however, the ideological components of Hayek's work may fade, as his contribution to social science comes to be better understood. One of the arguments of this book is that some of Hayek's most important insights remain undeveloped in his writings because of the ideological closures he imposed on his work. Often his questions are more interesting than his answers. Critics of Hayek, feeling themselves to be in the presence of an ideological adversary, have often concentrated on rebutting his arguments or criticizing his assumptions, rather than exploring his questions. Hayek often gives his opponents little incentive to do otherwise. But in the last ten years this has begun to change. It used to be the case that Hayek was taken seriously only by those who were ideologically sympathetic to his position. This is no longer true. There is especial interest in his economics, particularly his theory of knowledge and his theory of spontaneous order, and the methodological assumptions which underlie them. Beyond this, there is also a new appreciation of the strengths as well as the limitations of Hayek's account of liberalism and modernity.

The first reason for rethinking Hayek is that the long ideological war of position in which he was involved throughout his life is over. Reflecting on Hayek is one way of reflecting on what was at stake in that struggle, and who had the better arguments. Hayek turns out to have been more right than wrong. Many of the earlier judgements of him were misplaced or misinformed. Hayek often had greater insight than his critics into the organization of modern society, even if some of his ideas are crudely expressed, or are expressed in such an extreme way that many who might otherwise have been sympathetic were led to reject them.

The second reason for rethinking Hayek is to assess his work as an account of the nature of modernity. Which of Hayek's insights into social and economic organization transcend the ideological controversies in which he was involved? Confident declarations at the end of the twentieth century that not merely ideology but history itself is over have focused renewed attention on the meaning of modernity and the claims which are common to all versions of the modern project. Hayek provides a particular account of modernity and its economic, social, and political dimensions, based on arguments about the nature and distribution of knowledge in society and the relationship between reason and tradition.

The scope of his work and the scale of his achievement need to be registered. He may well prove to be one of the last Western thinkers to attempt to rethink from first principles the nature of Western civilization and the institutions and rules which are central to it. What spurred Hayek to do this was his desire to resist the encroachment of collectivism and socialism. If Hayek had not had an ideological vision of the modern world, he might be remembered now only for a scholarly technical contribution to economics, but the wider implications of his economic ideas for theories of knowledge and social order would not have emerged. What makes him of interest to us, and far more than just an ideologue, is that, like all truly great social and political thinkers, his thought is full of contradictions and tensions, and is capable of many different interpretations.[5] He was operating at a level such that his insights in one field have implications which conflict with his assumptions or conclusions in other fields. Sometimes he himself was only partly aware of some of these implications, and sometimes he failed to develop them. But many of his ideas have a life beyond the particular ideological form he chose to give them, and raise general issues about the nature of modernity and social change which remain at the heart of contemporary social theory, even if many of his own answers are inadequate or flawed.

The Crisis of Liberalism

In order to understand Hayek's work, it is therefore necessary to explore his ideological as well as his intellectual formation. Hayek was eighteen years old at the time of the Bolshevik Revolution in 1917, thirty-one when Hitler came to power, thirty-three when Roosevelt launched his New Deal, and thirty-seven when Keynes published his *General Theory*. He lived just long enough to witness the opening of the Berlin Wall in 1989 and the collapse of communism in Russia in 1991. He lived through the whole of the short twentieth century between 1917 and 1991: the destruction of the liberal global economic order and its state system, the rise and collapse of totalitarian movements and regimes, the Great Depression, the Second World War, the establishment and subsequent weakening of United States hegemony, the disappearance of the European colonial empires, the long boom, the growth of the state, and the cold war with communism.

During the first half of this period, liberalism as a public doctrine was widely perceived to be losing ground in its battle with new collectivist doctrines whose common feature was that they justified an extended role for the state. The doctrine of liberalism as it had developed in the nineteenth century was generally regarded as having declining relevance to the circumstances of advanced industrial societies. In the 1930s the slogan 'Forward from Liberalism' expressed a sentiment shared by many different movements and parties. Liberalism was seen as belonging to an era that was past.

The ideological challenge to liberalism came not just from

totalitarian doctrines such as fascism and communism, but also from the programmes for social amelioration through state action which were increasingly adopted by parties of the Centre Right and Centre Left. As suffrages were extended and mass democracies created, so the pressure for increasing the scope and the scale of collectivist programmes of public provision in the fields of welfare, economic development, and military defence was intensified. The extension of democracy came to be seen as synonymous with the extension of the spending and regulatory powers of the state. Politicians became subject to the new discipline of winning support from the electorate and organized interests, making use of the new mass media. Old Liberal parties tended to be marginalized in a double sense. They were often slow to adjust to the requirements of the new mass politics, and they obstinately clung to their beliefs in the simple verities of free trade, balanced budgets, and *laissez-faire*. They were challenged by New Liberals, who developed liberal arguments to justify limited measures of intervention and redistribution, and by the collectivist wing of the socialist movement, which, in the new circumstances of an extended franchise, increasingly favoured using the agency of the state to achieve socialist goals.

The rise of collectivism as a public doctrine in the heartland of liberalism was the basic theme of A. V. Dicey's *Lectures on the Relation between Law and Public Opinion in England during the Nineteenth Century.*[6] Dicey argued that from around 1860 collectivist doctrines had begun to supplant individualist doctrines in their hold on public opinion, and that, as a result, legislation was increasingly reflecting collectivist principles, a trend he deplored. He pointed in particular to legislation on trade unions and social security. Individualist principles were everywhere on the defensive as the collectivist tide flowed in.

The anxieties of many liberals at the beginning of the twentieth century echoed the fears which had long been expressed by both conservatives and liberals about the dangers of democracy. The potential domination of the poor and the ignorant through the ballot-box appeared to threaten the maintenance of property rights and the rule of the wise and the best. Conservatives adjusted more readily to the challenge of mass democracy, seeking ways of mobilizing voters which could cut across class. Old Liberals found it much harder, partly because of their lack of sympathy with any form of collectivism.

The new collectivist doctrines could have taken a very long time to replace liberalism as the dominant public doctrine in Britain and the United States. But their triumph was speeded up by a series of cataclysmic events, in particular the two world wars and the Great Depression of the 1930s, which destroyed the liberal world order and undermined many liberal institutions. These events helped sustain claims that liberalism, whatever its merits, had simply become irrelevant as a guide to policy in increasingly interdependent and highly organized industrial societies.

The growing conviction in the first half of the twentieth century that the age of liberalism was over was reflected in two influential books of the 1940s, both written by citizens of the former Austro-Hapsburg Empire, who, like Hayek, ended up outside it: Karl Polanyi's *The Great Transformation* and Joseph Schumpeter's *Capitalism, Socialism, and Democracy*. Polanyi was a Hungarian, a socialist and an economic historian, Schumpeter an Austrian, a conservative and an economist. Both regarded the liberal order and liberal civilization of the nineteenth century as something that had passed away and could not be revived. Both saw the future as belonging to some form of collectivism or socialism.

Polanyi argued that the liberal order had finally come apart in the 1930s. The landmarks of this change were:

> ... the abandonment of the gold standard by Great Britain; the Five-Year Plans in Russia; the launching of the New Deal; the National Socialist Revolution in Germany; the collapse of the League in favour of autarkist empires. While at the end of the Great War nineteenth century ideals were paramount, and their influence dominated the following decade, by 1940 every vestige of the international system had disappeared and, apart from a few enclaves, the nations were living in an entirely new international setting.[7]

But Polanyi argued that the reasons for the disintegration of the liberal order went deeper. Nineteenth-century civilization was not destroyed by external attack or overthrown from within by social revolution; nor did it fall victim to some iron law of political economy, such as the falling rate of profit. The true reason, according to Polanyi, was different: it was the measures that society had been forced to adopt in order not to be annihilated by the action of the self-regulating market: 'the conflict between the market and the elementary requirements of an organised social life ... produced the typical strains and stresses which ultimately destroyed that society'.[8]

Polanyi argued that the market order was not a spontaneous, natural development, but the result of deliberate policy. It had given rise to great dynamism and progress, but at great cost, and socialist and conservative political movements had arisen to curb it. Polanyi thus traced the demise of the self-regulating market to the workings of the market order itself.

This was a conclusion with which Joseph Schumpeter was in substantial agreement, although his analysis of the causes was different. In *Capitalism, Socialism, and Democracy* he announced that the era of capitalist civilization was at an end. The future belonged to collectivism and socialism, in the sense of state ownership and control of the economy. Capitalism had undermined its own foundations. It had applied its utilitarian calculus of profit and loss to all the institutions which had protected its rise and given legitimacy to the social order. Capitalism now had to face its own rationalist weapons being turned upon itself. 'Can Capitalism survive ?', asked Schumpeter, replying: 'No, I do not think it can.'[9] The future industrial society would be collectivist, organized, and highly regulated. Polanyi and Schumpeter reflected a wide ideological consensus. Many liberals and conservatives hoped to avoid a full collectivization of society and the economy, but there was resigned acceptance of the need to extend further the powers of the state, in order to provide the security and the prosperity which would preserve the legitimacy of the social order. If liberals and conservatives did not help to reform market economies in this way, the initiative would pass to those advocating more drastic social change.

At the same time, however, as Polanyi and Schumpeter were making these predictions, Hayek was sounding a very different note. In *The Road to Serfdom*, published in 1944, he agreed that the trends were overwhelmingly pointing towards the triumph of collectivism and that liberals had become isolated. There was hardly anyone active in politics, he complained, who was not a socialist. But Hayek differed from Polanyi and Schumpeter in believing that there was nothing inevitable about this triumph of collectivism. It had come about through the ascendancy of a set of doctrines which were deeply flawed in their understanding of the basis of Western civilization and its success. Hayek claimed that the consequences of continued application of these doctrines would be so serious that they would be discredited, and there would be a return to the principles of classical liberalism.

Hayek's certainty was rooted in his conviction that the basic ideas of nineteenth-century liberalism did not constitute just another ideology. They were grounded in reality, and provided the only possible doctrine to guide policy in modern society. Hayek believed as firmly in scientific liberalism as any Marxist in scientific socialism. The ideas of classical liberalism were true and relevant, while all other doctrines were literally utopian. They had no relevance to the modern world, and if an attempt were made to put them into practice, the outcomes would be not only quite different from what was intended, but highly damaging as well.

The Liberty Crusade

In 1947 Hayek helped to found the Mont Pèlerin Society, a liberal international, composed of liberal intellectuals from many disciplines dedicated to the recovery of liberal principles and the overthrow of collectivism. It built on an initiative first launched in 1938 in Paris, Le Colloque Walter Lippmann.[10] At first, progress was slow. Although there was a recovery of liberalism and a decline in the appeal of collectivist ideas in many countries in the 1950s, there were few signs of a return to the old certainties of nineteenth-century liberalism. When Daniel Bell and others spoke of an end of ideology at the end of the 1950s,[11] they meant that the ideological battle between individualism and collectivism had lost its intensity. As Lipset put it:

> the fundamental political problems of the industrial revolution have been solved: the workers have achieved industrial and political citizenship; the conservatives have accepted the welfare state; and the democratic left has recognised that an increase in over-all state power carries with it more dangers to freedom than solutions for economic problems.[12]

Hayek believed that it was not enough to reach a compromise with the forces of collectivism, however. All the territory that had been lost must be reclaimed. Through his writings and other activities he played an important part in establishing independent research institutes and think-tanks, most significantly the Institute of Economic Affairs in Britain. Libertarian and liberal-conservative think-tanks and foundations grew rapidly in the 1970s and 1980s, in both Britain and the United States, and Hayek was universally recognized as the leading thinker and mentor of both libertarian and liberal-conservative strands in the New Right.[13]

The emergence of the New Right and the strength of the doctrines of neo-liberalism throughout the 1970s and 1980s and their espousal by influential political leaders and political movements in many countries signified the triumph of Hayek's lonely crusade. From a position of great isolation and apparent irrelevance in the 1940s, he found himself thirty years later the acknowledged leader of the new political orthodoxy, the intellectual guide of prime ministers and presidents, the icon of a rapidly growing worldwide political movement, and the recipient of numerous honours, including the Nobel Prize for Economics and the Companion of Honour. The award of the former was ironic on two scores: first, because he received it for economics, a discipline which no longer recognized him as one of its leading figures, and second, because he shared it with Gunnar Myrdal, an economist of a very different methodological and political persuasion.

As the veteran of so many intellectual and political battles during the twentieth century, Hayek was understandably jubilant in his last years. 'Surely', he declared, 'it is high time for us to cry from the house tops that the intellectual foundations of socialism have all collapsed.'[14] Like an Old Testament prophet, he had stood firm and had proclaimed his faith while many around him who once shared his values had deserted the cause in the name of pragmatism and realism. In retrospect, he came to see the period between 1848 and 1948 as what he called the 'socialist century'. But now it was over. The long wave of collectivism had spent itself. It had threatened, but in the end had not destroyed, the individualism that Hayek regarded as the foundation of Western civilization.

In the decades since 1948, the influence of socialism as a doctrine had waned, and socialist regimes had collapsed. The opening of the Berlin Wall in 1989 and the subsequent overthrow of Communist regimes throughout East and Central Europe, culminating in the downfall of communism in the Soviet Union in 1991, set the seal on the victory of liberalism. By the time of Hayek's death in March 1992, the cause to which he had been intellectually and politically committed since the 1920s appeared to have triumphed.

Vienna

An appreciation of Hayek's intellectual formation is crucial for understanding his thought, and it has received increasing attention in recent years. Friedrich August von Hayek was born into a well-established, well-connected Austrian family. His father was a doctor and a botanist, who never achieved his ambition of becoming a full university professor, but who instilled in his son the importance of science as a vocation. Through his mother, Hayek was related to Wittgenstein. He grew up during the last phase of the Austro-Hungarian Empire, at a time when Vienna was undergoing a remarkable burst of intellectual creativity in art, literature, music, science, philosophy, psychology, and economics.[15]

Hayek briefly served in the Austrian army in an artillery regiment on the Italian Front at the end of the First World War. He began his studies at the University of Vienna in November 1918. His main intellectual interest at this time seems to have been psychology, but he also had to think of a future career, so he enrolled for a law degree, in order to secure a qualification which would make him eligible to enter the legal profession or the civil service. What it also offered was a grounding in economics.

Despite the dislocations of the war, the University of Vienna still offered at this time a distinctive intellectual experience. This was crucial for Hayek's intellectual formation, and gave him a breadth of outlook which he never lost. Among the approaches he encountered which had a profound influence on his social theory were the Austrian school of economics based on the works of Carl Menger; Kantian philosophy and the particular kind of liberalism which was associated with it; and the positivism of Ernst Mach and Moritz Schlick (founder of the Vienna circle), in philosophy and psychology.

The Austrian school of economics influenced his choice of topics to study, but his fundamental methodological and theoretical assumptions came from the philosophical positions on knowledge and mind that he adopted at a very early age, and never abandoned. John Gray has argued convincingly that the key to Hayek's philosophical standpoint is to be found in *The Sensory Order*,[16] a work of psychology and philosophy which was drafted in the 1920s but not published until 1952.[17]

The Sensory Order is based on Kantian assumptions about knowledge. First, direct knowledge of the physical world is impossible. We cannot know the world as it is. Secondly, the order that is found in our experience is constructed by our minds. It follows that it is impossible to have a complete knowledge of the world or to stand outside the world. All knowledge is partial and immanent, because the mind is seeking to make sense of a reality of which it is itself part. The task of philosophy, therefore, is a modest one. It has to discover the limits of reason, rather than elevate reason above experience or lay claim to a knowledge beyond experience.

Such a view of knowledge makes theory and theory building an indispensable feature of the human condition. All human beings have to theorize. There are no facts and no knowledge which exist independently of theory, the constant activity of human minds to construct an order out of the myriad experiences presented to them. Science is the activity which seeks a set of deductive principles which can provide a more comprehensive understanding of the phenomena of experience.

In some versions of Kantianism, such as the praxeological theory of Ludwig von Mises, the theory building proceeds without any empirical reference at all. The deductive principles once arrived at are claimed to be axiomatically true, tools for understanding empirical phenomena, but not capable of being refuted by them. Hayek never subscribed to this position. The influence of Mach and, later, Popper led him to accept that within the framework of concepts established by scientific theories there was a wide area in which empirical testing of hypotheses was relevant.[18]

Many of Hayek's distinctive positions in social theory and liberal thought can be related to his Kantianism.[19] Like Kant, he rejects natural rights as a basis for justice, seeing justice as based instead on procedural arguments, drawing on the Kantian-inspired conception of the *Rechtsstaat*. Order in both science and society depends on the identification of rules and conditions which can be universalized. The establishment and enforcement of these general rules provide the criteria for defining the character of the outcomes without determining in detail what those outcomes are.

In *The Sensory Order* Hayek argues that the human mind is engaged in a continuous process of classification and reclassification of experiences, and that the complexity of the classifications tends to increase, as human beings learn new ways of understanding and ordering their experience. Hayek distinguishes between the physical order of external events and the sensory order of the human mind. The sensory order is a microcosm, part of the macrocosm of the physical order, because the way in which the mind works through the central nervous system is part of the physical order. Hayek argues that the possibility of knowledge of the macrocosm comes about because of the formation of a microcosm within it (the human mind) which is capable of reproducing enough aspects of the macrocosm to allow the microcosm to continue to exist. However, there are strict limits to what can be achieved. It is impossible for something to classify something else unless it has a greater degree of complexity. As a part of the physical order, the human mind is less complex than the order it is seeking to understand. This implies that the human mind can never fully comprehend itself. The knowledge we gain of the world is necessarily partial and limited, and is dependent on the fact that there are certain recurrent patterns and general abstract rules which the human mind can grasp and reproduce. The more developed the human mind becomes, the more complex the classification systems it uses, and the greater the congruence, it is assumed, between the physical and the sensory order.

From this philosophical theory of mind, Hayek derived a lasting concern with the conditions which make knowledge of both the social world and the natural world possible and the limits to that knowledge. His work in economics, and subsequently in social and political theory, was an attempt to work through the implications of his philosophical ideas. But these ideas were themselves developed through his engagement with one of the most powerful intellectual perspectives current in Vienna – the Austrian school of economics.

The Austrian School

The Austrian school was based on the work of Carl Menger (1840– 1921), professor at the University of Vienna from 1873 until his retirement in 1903. His two key books were *Grundsätze der Volkswirtschaftslehre* (1871), which was a seminal work in developing the subjective theory of value and the conception of marginal utility, and *Untersuchungen über die Methode der Sozialwissenschaftlichen und der politischen Ökonomie insbesondere* (1883), which launched the *Methodenstreit* between Austrian theoretical economics and the German historical school.

Hayek never met Menger personally, but he had already read the *Grundsätze* before entering university, where he attended the seminar of Friedrich von Wieser (1851–1926), one of the most important of the second-generation members of the Austrian school. Wieser was one of a number of economists, among them Eugen von Böhm-Bawerk, who were converted to Menger's doctrine and played a key role in developing and communicating his ideas as a new and distinctive school.

Hayek always revered Wieser as his first teacher.[20] But the more important intellectual influence upon him was Ludwig von Mises (1881–1973), a third-generation member of the school, who had been a member of Böhm-Bawerk's seminar.[21] Hayek began attending

Mises' seminar in the early 1920s, and this, more than anything else, appears to have been decisive in his intellectual formation. Wieser had inclined to Fabianism in his political views, offering a defence, for example, of progressive taxation. Hayek admits that his motive for studying economics was initially a Fabian desire to find ways to intervene in society to improve the position of the people. Mises shook him out of that. Hayek later wrote that it was insight into the economic problems of society that made him a radical anti-socialist. It was Mises who convinced him of what precisely those economic problems were.[22]

The importance of the Austrian school of economics for Hayek's intellectual development was that the school was part of the new mainstream in the development of economics as an international discipline; yet it also had distinctive characteristics which set it apart – in particular its methodological approach and its analysis of institutions. Menger, together with Léon Walras and Stanley Jevons, had been one of the pioneers of the marginalist revolution in economics in the 1870s and 1880s, which created the analytical basis for modern economic analysis. The marginalist revolution created a new paradigm for economics by breaking decisively with the labour theory of value of both classical political economy and Marxism. Economics became focused on the analysis of the problems of choice and allocation under conditions of scarcity, rather than the problems of the origins of the wealth of nations.

The Austrian school was noted not only for its part in developing the subjective theory of value, but also for its strong identification with political liberalism. Several leading Austrians, notably Böhm-Bawerk and then Mises, became prominent defenders of liberal capitalism against intellectual and political attack. The attack after 1880, in both Austria and Germany, came mainly from the rise of strong social democratic movements whose major intellectual influence was Marxism.

The Austrian school was hostile to Marxism on methodological as well as political grounds. Its position was formed in the fierce intellectual debate which became known as the *Methodenstreit* in the German-speaking world, and which was an important moment in the formation of the separate disciplines of economics, on the one side, and sociology, economic history, and political science on the other. The main contestants were Gustav Schmoller, representing the historical school, and Carl Menger representing the economic school. The debate began with Menger's book on the methodology of the social sciences, to which Schmoller wrote a sharp rejoinder. Menger then wrote a pamphlet in reply, which Schmoller refused to have reviewed in his journal. Followers of the two leading figures carried on the battle. The dispute was so bitter that it soon influenced academic appointments. Applicants strongly identified with one of the two factions found it impossible to get appointments at universities where the other faction was dominant.

The key issue in the *Methodenstreit* was the question of relativism. Was truth relative to the concepts formed in particular historical contexts, or were there certain concepts which were true in all times and all societies? But the dispute between the two schools also concerned broader issues of political economy. The arguments of the historical school provided justifications for policies of nationalism and protectionism, stressing the unique character of German institutions and German development. The Austrian school, by contrast, was universalist, which derived in part from its methodological individualism,[23] and in part from the tradition of German liberalism associated with Kant and the idea of the *Rechtsstaat* – a government of universal laws which prescribed strict limits for government intervention in civil society.

By coming under the influence of Mises, Hayek received a training as an economist which made him not just a supporter of marginalist economics, but also a committed liberal and an anti-socialist and anti-collectivist. Out of the political and intellectual battles with the historical school and with Marxism, several members of the Austrian school fashioned an uncompromising defence of capitalism and liberal institutions. Eugen von Böhm-Bawerk, for example, who was briefly Austrian Finance Minister before 1914, was the author of a noted critique of Marx's economics, *Karl Marx and the Close of his System,* which claimed (incorrectly) to have discovered fatal logical flaws between the first and the third problems in the construction of *Capital.* But the political character of Austrian economics was most clearly set by Mises, who developed a line of enquiry suggested by Böhm-Bawerk before his death in 1914. Mises offered no concessions to those fashionable trends of thought which sought accommodation with collectivism. By the time Hayek left Austria, he was fully inoculated against sympathy with interventionist or collectivist ideas, and equipped with a firm intellectual case.

London

Hayek received his doctorate in jurisprudence in 1921. Wieser gave him a letter of introduction to Mises, who found him a job as a temporary civil servant in the Office of Accounts. It was at this time that he began attending Mises' seminar. Other members of the seminar in the 1920s who later became famous economists included Gottfried Haberler (1900–), Fritz Machlup (1902–83), and Oscar Morgenstern (1902–77). In 1923–4 Hayek visited America at the invitation of Wesley Mitchell, where he learnt to speak fluent English and observed the theoretical naïvety of much American economics, but also its technical sophistication. On his return to Vienna, Hayek established with Mises an Institute for Business Cycle Research, and became its first director.

Hayek did not stay in Vienna for long, however. Lionel Robbins, who had been strongly influenced by some of the ideas of the Austrian school and had made several visits to Vienna, invited Hayek to the London School of Economics and Political Science as a visiting professor for 1931–2. Hayek made such an impression with his lectures[24] that he was subsequently offered the Tooke Professorship of Economic Science.

Hayek stayed at the LSE for eighteen years, finally leaving for a chair at the University of Chicago in 1949. This phase of his life was extremely important, because it is that of his principal contributions as an economic theorist, his participation in the debate on economic calculation under socialism, as well as the publication of *The Road to Serfdom* in 1944, which was to change the subsequent direction of his research programme.

At the LSE Hayek was part of a group of economists, including Lionel Robbins and Arnold Plant, who became noted for their opposition to the new thinking associated with Keynes for dealing with the problems of unemployment and the trade cycle. One of the motives Robbins had in bringing Hayek to London was to reinforce those members of the profession who were critical of Keynes's theories and their political implications. Robbins and Hayek formed a very close personal and professional bond, but drifted apart when Robbins was drawn into working for the state during the Second World War. As Hayek ruefully put it, 'Robbins and I became very close friends, we worked beautifully together, and from 1931 till 1940 we were thinking together and working together. Then I'm afraid he fell under Keynes' influence.'[25]

Hayek spent most of the 1930s patiently applying Austrian insights into the nature of the capitalist economy to problems of capital theory and the business cycle.[26] As with all Austrian economics, this research programme directed attention to the micro-foundations of economic behaviour. But it was sidelined by the rapid switch to the new macro-economic paradigm which Keynes created for economics in *The General Theory of Interest, Employment and Money*. Hayek was out of sympathy with Keynes's theoretical approach, and even more with what he believed to be its consequences for policy; yet he produced no major critique of it directly. What he did instead was to provide a critique of Keynes's liberalism by issuing a warning about the direction in which English liberalism was headed.

Living in England gave Hayek firsthand experience of the liberal tradition and liberal institutions which he so much admired. But it also made him fearful that the great achievements of English liberalism were in danger of being lost, just as the early promise of German liberalism had been lost in the avalanche of collectivist thought and the rise of socialist movements after 1880.

Hayek had not originally planned to stay in England for as long as he did, but the establishment of the Nazi regime in Germany in 1933 and the *Anschluss* with Austria in 1938 made return to the German-speaking world impossible. He became an exile. But although he took British citizenship in 1936, he never sought a career in public life in England, as he might well have done had he remained in Austria. Many other members of the Austrian school, including Menger himself, had been drawn into public service. But Hayek found himself confined to the life of a scholar. He would have preferred a life which combined academic and public work. Other exiles made the transition, but not Hayek.

Hayek developed a deep love of England and of English manners. (Only the mountains in the Austrian Tyrol, which he returned to every year, had a comparable emotional attraction for him.) He particularly admired the style of academic life in Cambridge, which he got to know well when the LSE moved there during the Second World War. Keynes obtained rooms for him at King's. He returned to London when the war was over, and shortly after left for the United States. The controversy aroused by *The Road to Serfdom* played only a small part in the decision; a more pressing reason for leaving England was his divorce and remarriage, which created difficulties for Hayek with many of his English friends. It finally severed his close friendship with Robbins, who felt that Hayek had behaved very badly towards his first wife. The two families had been near neighbours in the 1930s and knew each other well. Hayek and Robbins hardly spoke for ten years.

During his time at LSE, Hayek was mostly preoccupied with theoretical economics. But he was also drawn into the economic calculation debate (discussed in chapter 3). Economic calculation under socialism had been a major topic of discussion in both Wieser's and Mises' seminars in Vienna. In 1935 Hayek edited a book entitled *Collectivist Economic Planning* which brought together Mises' original 1920 article, which argued that economic calculation under socialism was impossible, articles by a number of Mises' critics, such as Oscar Lange and H. D. Dickinson, as well as contributions by Hayek and Robbins. Hayek wrote the introduction and the conclusion to the volume.[27] It seems to have been this renewed involvement in broad issues of political economy or what Schumpeter called *Sozial Ökonomik* that not only led Hayek to his most profound insight into the way in which economies function but also changed the course of his work. *Collectivist Economic Planning*, rather than *The Road to Serfdom*, is perhaps the true turning-point of Hayek's career.

The direct consequence of the rethinking of the methodological problems of studying economics which the calculation debate inspired was the seminal 1937 essay 'Economics and Knowledge',[28] regarded by many as his single most important work. In this essay he began to explore the character of knowledge in a market economy. He had realized that the concept of knowledge assumed by both Lange and Mises was fundamentally flawed, because it remained rationalist. Despite disagreements between them, both assumed that the function performed by the market could be understood intellectually, and therefore, in principle, improved upon. By rejecting the rationalist assumption that the mind could know itself and could therefore master reality, Hayek challenged the epistemological basis of all modern economics.

Hayek himself came to see the 1937 essay as 'the decisive point of the change in my outlook'.[29] It supplied him with the essential foundation from which he developed his political and economic views. Participation in the calculation debate reinforced his belief in the essential correctness of the economic principles of the founders of the Austrian school, particularly Carl Menger. Mises' argument was fundamentally correct, but its formulation conceded too much to the position it was criticizing. Returning to the anti-rationalist foundations of Austrian economics also meant recovering the anti-rationalism of the Scottish political economists and David Hume. Hayek began to see that anti-rationalism was a distinct position within economics and philosophy, from which to analyse modernity and to understand economic and political trends. An anti-rationalist outlook provided the only secure basis for the policy precepts of classical liberalism. Rationalism, or 'constructivism' as Hayek called it, led inexorably to socialism and collectivism. The infection of all modern ideologies, even liberalism, by rationalism meant that classical liberalism was being abandoned everywhere, even in England, its heartland.

The Turn to Politics

The issues raised in 'Economics and Knowledge' and *Collectivist Economic Planning* pointed to a very different research programme than the one on which Hayek was engaged.[30] It moved beyond the rather narrow, technical debates about the best way to understand economic fluctuations and the role of money to a consideration of the basic principles of social and economic organization, how order is created and sustained in society.

It also supplied an economic rationale from which to develop a searching critique of contemporary politics and policy. It was this critique on which Hayek was to embark during the Second World War and which led to the publication of his most famous book, *The Road to Serfdom*, in 1944. There was an element of accident about it. Because of his former Austrian nationality, Hayek was debarred from taking any active part in the war effort. The LSE moved to Cambridge, and most of Hayek's colleagues entered government service. Normal intellectual life was severely curtailed during the war, and Hayek, in the congenial surroundings of Cambridge, devoted his energies to an analysis of the forces which in his view had undermined Western civilization and brought it to the brink of catastrophe.

The Road to Serfdom was an extremely unusual book for a professional economist to write, even in the 1940s. It contained very little economics, and ranged widely over history and politics. Hayek undoubtedly saw it as a temporary diversion from his strictly economic research programme, although, as already indicated, this new direction was clearly signalled by the fundamental turn in his thought represented by 'Economics and Knowledge'. Like many academic authors whose books suddenly become bestsellers, Hayek was rather surprised and overwhelmed at the book's reception. He wrote many years later that after a time it began to irritate him, because the attention he received as its author prevented him from resuming his career as a professional economist. But he never did resume that career. The new research programme which 'Economics and Knowledge' had opened up increasingly preoccupied him.

What the success of *The Road to Serfdom* also gave him was a new mission. Denied the opportunity to work as a civil servant in either Austria or England, Hayek still desired a public role. His new research programme allowed him to emerge as a public intellectual, a crusader for liberty, a patron of think-tanks, a thinker who ranged widely over fundamental questions concerning Western civilization, but one who also could intervene in policy debates and write letters to *The Times*.

The idea for this new public role seems to have followed inexorably from the success of *The Road to Serfdom*. The book occasioned great interest, particularly in America. Hayek had not visited the United States since his trip in 1923–4, but now he received many invitations from there both to lecture and to write. He found that many of his views were misunderstood and had been distorted,[31] and persuaded himself that there was a greater need for a clear restatement of the fundamental principles of the liberal tradition than for detailed work on theoretical problems in the Austrian paradigm. Another factor in Hayek's decision to abandon his economic research programme was that in the 1940s the Keynesian revolution in economic theory was in full flood. Hayek had strong methodological objections to the macro-economics of Keynesianism, which now for a time became the dominant orthodoxy within economics. The Austrian school became increasingly marginalized, and although Hayek could have hung on as others did, he increasingly risked being seen as prisoner of an approach that had become outmoded. Looking back from the 1990s, it is easy to forget that, for a time, Keynes was credited with having achieved a Copernican revolution in economics, moving the whole basis of analysis and policy into a new era. The dominant textbooks of the 1950s and 1960s, most notably Paul Samuelson's *Economics*, proclaimed the new orthodoxy. Criticism, when it came, tended to accept many of the new methodological foundations that Keynes had established.

Hayek regarded the new economics as having serious flaws, not just as economic theory but also as political economy. Its great danger was that it failed to understand the true anti-rationalist foundations of a market order, and although most economists regarded themselves as liberals, Hayek argued that, in espousing rationalist models of the economy, they were assisting the currents of opinion that were steadily undermining these foundations and thereby threatening future prosperity.

At the age of forty-five, Hayek's life changed course. He resolved to spend his energies in an ambitious attempt to restate the principles of classical liberalism, as well as lend his support to a crusade for liberty. In order to win back ground lost to collectivism, liberals and individualists had to be prepared to find new ways to propagate their views, to win intellectual arguments, and to recapture the high ground of public debate. The series of catastrophes from 1914 to 1944 had seen the rise of totalitarian regimes and movements, the destruction of the liberal world order, and the collapse of faith in liberal principles and values. The defeat of Nazism, however, and the reconstruction of Western Europe and Japan under American leadership so as to contain the challenge of Soviet communism created a new confidence and momentum, of which Hayek and other liberals took full advantage.

Hayek never became a statesman like Keynes, and, although at times consulted by political leaders, never played an active part in helping to shape government policy from the inside. His efforts were devoted instead to trying to influence the climate of ideas within which politicians operated. The Mont Pèlerin Society, which continued to meet every year, the Institute of Economic Affairs, and the numerous other societies, political groups, and think-tanks with which Hayek became associated were the fruits of this activity.

Hayek's Project

In evaluating Hayek's intellectual contribution, there has been considerable debate over the extent to which his work reflects a unified, consistent theoretical approach. Some have argued that there were major changes, from his early writings, when he was influenced by Mises, to his writings after 1937, when he accepted many of Popper's ideas. There is evidence too that in the 1950s he incorporated into his thinking Michael Polanyi's concept of tacit knowledge. Despite such shifts of emphasis, however, several commentators on Hayek have argued that his fundamental epistemological and methodological position did not really change from the way in which he elaborated it in *The Sensory Order*,[32] and that there is an underlying consistency in Hayek which infuses both his economic writings and his later social and political theory.[33]

This fundamental theoretical consistency of his approach was masked by the shift in the focus of his writing and scholarship from economics to political theory. Changes of place – from Vienna to London to Chicago to Freiburg – played a part, but so too did Hayek's desire to be more than just an economist. His intellectual project came to involve much more than academic scholarship. Part of him wanted to play a public role, and when that proved impossible in a conventional way, the success of *The Road to Serfdom* gave him a different outlet as an ideological entrepreneur. Such a role carried dangers, however. It obscured what in the end was most important to him – his scientific contribution to the understanding of society.

In assessing and summarizing Hayek's intellectual project, his life divides into four principal periods. The first period, in Vienna, from 1899 to 1931, gave Hayek his basic intellectual formation in Austrian economics, in the philosophy of science, and in the theory of mind. Austrian economics made him a methodological individualist and a subjectivist; in his ethical philosophy he became primarily a consequentialist; while his study of psychology had a profound influence on his understanding of knowledge. These were foundations which Hayek later modified but never really abandoned.

The second period, in England, between 1931 and 1949, established Hayek as an academic professional economist, and also brought him into close contact with the intellectual and political traditions of English liberalism. He devised a research programme on the micro-foundations of capital and business cycles, which, although it had a distinct Austrian perspective in seeking to develop some of the concepts of Böhm-Bawerk's capital theory, was also orthodox in framing the research as a problem within general equilibrium theory. Hayek's breakthrough in 1937 led him to reject the concept of general equilibrium as the right framework for economic analysis, and instead to treat equilibrium and order as the result of the co-ordination of the plans of individuals which depended crucially on the information available to them. Hayek abandoned the assumption that the correct starting-point for analysis was the concept of a general equilibrium, arguing instead that it was necessary to begin with the plans of individuals and the distribution of knowledge in society. The achievement of order and equilibrium were the end result, not the starting-point, for the analysis. The correct procedure was to see by what institutional mechanisms co-ordination was achieved and maintained. When this approach no longer appeared central to the concerns of economics, following the shift to macro-economics which Keynes's *General Theory* encouraged, Hayek became more interested in the implications of an anti-rationalist critique of constructivism in social science and in rethinking the arguments for a liberal society.

The most important publication of his English period was *The Road to Serfdom*, which was born out of his respect for the English tradition and his fear that it was being lost because the English themselves no longer properly understood it.

In the third period of his career, between 1949 and 1969, first in Chicago, then at Freiburg, Hayek's reputation as an economist dwindled; but his reputation as a social and political philosopher was established with the publication in 1960 of *The Constitution of Liberty*, which even its critics recognized as a major accomplishment, and quite different in tone and scale from *The Road to Serfdom*. This was also the period in which he became increasingly active as a crusader for liberty, an organizer and patron of the movement that developed into the New Right of the 1970s and 1980s.

In the fourth and final phase of his career, between 1969 and 1992, Hayek enjoyed a return to public prominence, mainly as a result of the ascendancy of the New Right and retrospective assessments of the importance of his contributions. He continued to write and publish right up to the end of his life, his last major work being *The Fatal Conceit*, published in 1988. This period also saw the completion of the three-volume study *Law, Legislation, and Liberty*, which continued the themes and the argument of *The Constitution of Liberty*.

By the time of his death, Hayek had achieved most of the objectives he had set himself. He had produced the most comprehensive twentieth-century restatement of the principles of anti-rationalist liberalism. He had participated in the revival of anti-rationalist liberalism both as a doctrine and as a guide to public policy, and had witnessed the considerable triumphs it achieved during the 1970s and 1980s. Right at the end of his life came the opening of the Berlin Wall and the fall of communism. By the time he died, aged ninety-two, he could reasonably say that he had outlived all these major challenges to the liberal order, and had seen the tide swing back in liberalism's favour.

The Critique of Socialism

Hayek's intellectual project needs to be assessed both as an ideological critique of socialism and as a contribution to understanding the nature of modern society. The two are closely intertwined, but it is the argument of this book that they are also separable. Hayek always viewed socialism in its many guises as the greatest threat

to the survival of modern civilization. Underlying this critique is
the conviction that ideas matter. A vigorous defence and restatement of liberal principles was necessary to prevent the world becoming dominated by doctrines whose effects were harmful.

Hayek therefore came to see himself as engaged in a profound
battle with socialism. When he was young, he was drawn to socialism, particularly towards the idea of planning. But he soon moved
away. Hayek defined socialism as direction of economic activity in
accordance with some ideal of social justice. During the 'socialist
century' the favoured technique had been nationalization of the
means of production, distribution, and exchange. In the period
since 1948 nationalization and central planning had lost support,
and instead, the spending programmes and regulatory regimes of
the welfare state had become the characteristic features which
defined socialism.

Hayek's ideological vision of the identity and meaning of Western civilization is expressed through his critique of socialism. His
own deeper insights into the nature of modernity and the organization of society are arrived at through this critique. In the following chapters the essential features of this critique are examined, not
chronologically, but thematically.

Hayek's critique of socialism makes three key claims:

Socialism destroys the basis of morals, personal freedom, and
    responsibility.
Socialism impedes the production of wealth and may cause im-
    poverishment.
Socialism (sooner or later) leads to totalitarian government.[34]

These claims look like empirical hypotheses about the consequences
of implementing socialist policies. Hayek notes that, in fact, the
experience of socialist societies does provide evidence that these
are the consequences of socialism. Whenever there had been serious attempts to create socialist societies, they had resulted in less,
not more, social justice, less not more production, and a new despotism, once limits on state power had been weakened. But his
argument does not depend on empirical confirmation. He makes
his case against socialism primarily on a priori theoretical grounds.
The fact that social-democratic regimes in Western Europe have
not in practice paved the way for totalitarianism did not lead Hayek
to moderate his view that socialism always leads to totalitarian
government. Socialism always possessed that potential, because it

was fundamentally antagonistic to the only principles on which modern civilization could be based.

Chapters 2, 3, and 4 explore the critique of socialism which Hayek advances in relation to morals, markets, and politics, noting the distinctive epistemological and methodological position from which it is made and the particular understanding of modernity and politics which it entails. These chapters discuss the core concepts of the Hayekian system – spontaneous orders, justice, coercion, property, liberty, knowledge, evolution, rationalism and anti-rationalism, economic calculation, and the totalitarian tendencies of modern politics. Chapter 5 then examines Hayek's own ideological position in relation to other strands in contemporary liberalism and conservatism. Is Hayek best described as a liberal, a libertarian, or a conservative? Chapters 6 and 7 examine some of Hayek's policy proposals, particularly his constitutional ideas, his analysis of inflation, and his criticisms of the failures of the welfare state. Chapter 8 summarizes the account of modernity and the role of reason which emerges from these different strands of Hayek's ideological discourse, and discusses why Hayek matters, as well as the insights and limitations of his thought.

The grand narrative he offers may not ultimately be sustainable; the tensions and silences in his writings are often more interesting than his substantive claims. What is rewarding about reading Hayek is that he challenges many of the intellectual assumptions on which the ideological discourses and the social sciences of the twentieth century have been based, and rehabilitates an alternative way of conceiving social order. In doing so, he forces all of us to reflect upon our own assumptions and methods, and provides insights which are not dependent on his own, ultimately rather narrow, ideological vision, insights which are available for a range of purposes beyond those he could ever have imagined or desired.

2

Morals

We make our rational insight dominate over our inherited instincts. But the great moral adventure on which modern man has embarked when he launched into the Open Society is threatened when he is required to apply to all his fellow-men rules which are appropriate only to the fellow-members of a tribal group.

Hayek, *Law, Legislation, and Liberty*

At the root of Hayek's critique of socialism is his conception of Western civilization and the 'Great Society', a term used by Adam Smith. His claim that socialism destroys the basis of all morals, including personal freedom, and responsibility, which lie at the heart of this civilization, appears extravagant. One of the strengths of socialism has always been its moral critique of capitalism. It has been criticized more often for its lack of economic realism than for its lack of moral concern. Socialists have frequently applied moral criteria to the question of how the economy is organized and how economic agents behave. The tradition of ethical socialism has always sought to occupy the high moral ground, condemning capitalism for its disregard of morality and its encouragement of individual selfishness and greed. The moral economy of socialism is counterposed to the political economy of capitalism.

Hayek's attack is much more subtle, however, than at first appears. He does not mean that socialism is immoral in the sense of having no moral vision. In many passages he accepts that socialism is a moral doctrine. The problem, as Hayek sees it, is that socialism is not an appropriate moral doctrine for the Great Society which civilization has created.[1] It is applicable only to a much earlier stage of human development, the stage of primitive society, the long period of time in which human beings were hunter-gatherers. Socialism is an atavism. As such, it threatens the only basis on which the Great Society can function, because it introduces standards and criteria which are wholly inappropriate for life in the Great Society, however valuable they might have been for hunter-gatherers.

Underpinning these confident judgements is a particular conception of civilization and the Great Society, a meta-narrative about human history and progress. For Hayek and the Austrian school, the Great Society described by Adam Smith *is* modern society. There are no stages beyond it, or alternatives to it. Modernity has a precise meaning. The Great Society is not just one version among many: it is the only feasible one. The kind of moral, economic, and political rules and institutions that are appropriate to this society are not optional.

The problem with socialism, therefore, is that it is not a modern doctrine at all, even though it masquerades as one. Hayek's work is a sustained attempt to unmask its pretensions. Socialism is a deeply flawed doctrine for Hayek, because it is based on a series of fundamental intellectual errors which have grave practical consequences through their impact on policy. Since socialists do not understand the basis of modern civilization, they are constantly proposing policies which threaten its survival. Far from being a higher stage of civilization, socialism represents an unwitting regression to modes of thought and morality characteristic of primitive societies.

Evolution, Progress, and Civilization

To understand Hayek's argument, it is necessary to consider his meta-narrative about evolution, progress, and civilization. Central to Hayek's liberal vision is a contrast between primitive society, the society of the tribal band, and civilized society, which has culminated in the Great Society. The human species has spent almost the whole span of its existence in primitive society. Civilization has developed only during the last 8,000 years, and urban life only during the last 3,000. Hayek estimates that this means that civilization is the work of only a hundred generations of human beings.[2] Of even more recent origin is the transition to the Great Society and to modernity.

Civilization is a specific set of rules and institutions which have allowed societies to evolve to a point where this transition became possible. This set of rules and instituations was slowly constructed over many centuries and despite many setbacks. Hayek asserts that man's biological equipment failed to keep pace with his cultural and institutional innovation. As a result, many of his instincts and emotions are still better adapted to the life of a hunter than to life in civilization. This is why, according to Hayek, civilization has so often been regarded as unhealthy, unnatural, and artificial, and human beings have sought so hard to escape from its disciplines and its requirements.

For Hayek, human beings have become civilized against their basic instincts and emotions. In their hearts they remain socialists.[3] The process of civilization has been painful – the accumulation of traditions, rules, customs, practices, knowledge, and institutions which gradually set some human societies apart from primitive societies. Socialism, on the other hand, represents 'innate moral emotions and instincts acquired during 500,000 years' of experience in hunter-gatherer communities.[4] These emotions and instincts have to be suppressed for two reasons: first, in order to maintain a civilized society, and second, in order to sustain an economic order on which that society can depend.

Socialism threatens the survival of civilization because it encourages two moral instincts, solidarity and altruism, which Hayek argues are the two great obstacles to the development of the modern economy. The problem with both of them is that they suggest that there can and should exist a common purpose. Hayek speculates that in the tribal bands of the hunter-gatherers, achievement of a common purpose was vital to the survival of the group. Moral rules which enjoined both solidarity and altruism were the natural outcome. But in the Great Society, while organizations and small groups like families may still seek a common purpose, the pursuit of a common purpose for the whole society is an illusion, and a dangerous one at that. In an extended order, the practice of altruism is impossible. Altruism, says Hayek, can extend only to the known needs of known other people, or, as Adam Smith put it:

> It is not from the benevolence of the butcher, the brewer or the baker, that we expect our dinner but from their regard to their own interest. We address ourselves, not to their humanity but to their self-love, and never talk to them of our own necessities but of their advantages. Nobody but a beggar chooses to depend chiefly upon the benevolence of his fellow citizens.[5]

The morality required by the Great Society is one of individual freedom and responsibility. Over the course of many generations, according to Hayek, the 'good natural instincts' of the tribal band were gradually subdued by culturally developed rules of conduct which no longer concerned concrete ends and concrete needs of known people, but were purely 'abstract rules of behaviour having little to do with what our instincts told us to do'.[6] Such a society was held together by exchange, and depended for its effectiveness on the spread of instrumental orientations to action. Adam Smith again gave classic expression to this:

> Whoever offers to another a bargain of any kind, proposes to do this. Give me that which I want, and you shall have this which you want, is the meaning of every such offer; and it is in this manner that we obtain from one another the far greater part of those good offices which we stand in need of.[7]

Once such a system is established 'every man . . . lives by exchanging or becomes in some measure a merchant, and the society itself grows to be what is properly a commercial society'.[8]

Hayek illustrates his argument with some examples. The rise of the Great Society has been marked by frequent battles between two conceptions of morals: the instinctual morals of primitive society and the learned morals of the market order. The campaigns against usury and the moral opprobrium directed at money-lenders reflect the primitive moral instincts. From the standpoint of the Great Society, the money-lender is performing a valuable and indispensable social function. Money-lenders made the development of capitalism possible. Hayek's point is that applying moral principles derived from a different kind of society is inappropriate and foolish. The money-lender should be judged by the criteria of what is necessary for the survival of an impersonal market order on which all have come to depend for the satisfaction of their needs. What causes Hayek almost to despair is that even most anti-socialists are socialists when it comes to morals, because they affirm that altruism and solidarity are more fundamental moral values than those arising from exchange and the market-place. What few people understand or are prepared to accept is that the extended order is not an expression of our fundamental moral instincts but a denial of them. This follows from the kind of society that civilization has created: 'We are living in a society which exists only because we are capable of serving people whom we do not know.'[9]

Are civilized societies morally better than primitive societies? Hayek
does not tell us. In some moods he suggests not. We might all have
been happier to have stayed as hunter-gatherers. He does have a
notion of progress, but it is rather a truncated one. It has little of
the triumphalism or the certainty of nineteenth-century liberalism.
His justification for the Great Society is in terms not of its higher
morality but of its outcomes. The reason why civilization is better
than primitive society, for Hayek, is simply that it supports a larger
population. Progress is measured in terms of the number of addi-
tional human beings which industrial societies make possible. The
economic calculus is a calculus of life. Hayek argues that the way
in which the division of labour has evolved has favoured the poor
more than the rich, because it has made possible such a large increase in their numbers. Formerly, most of them would have per-
ished. The only way to deal with the problems which plague
industrial societies is to encourage the universal adoption of the
institutions and morality of the Great Society. Hayek brushes aside
the problem of over-population. Population growth, he believes,
will regulate itself.

The problem for Hayek's evolutionary account is one that recurs
throughout his writings. Civilization and the Great Society were
the result of unplanned development, not design. The moral rules
which the citizens of the Great Society have been obliged to learn
have been adopted not because anyone understood that these were
the most appropriate rules, but because the groups who by accident accepted them prospered and multiplied more than others.[10]
The process had to be like this, because the human race was civilized against its wishes. The process was one of cultural selection,
not human intelligence and design. The process of selection has
been ruthless and functional.[11] Hayek asserts, for example, that the
only religions which have survived into the modern era are those
which support property and the family. Yet, paradoxically, it seems
that in this modern era we can no longer rely on cultural selection
alone to do the job for us. Hayek implies that we now need understanding of the nature of the Great Society, so that we can safeguard it against the dangers that threaten it. What was spontaneous
process can now be preserved only through the conscious application, if not of planning, then at least of anti-planning.

The most important characteristic of modern civilization, for
Hayek, is its individualism, which comes from a number of sources,
in particular from Greece and Rome, with their new forms of
intellectual enquiry and new kinds of institutions, and from

Christianity, with its ethic of individual responsibility and individual salvation. Freedom, for Hayek, is not a state of nature, but an artefact of civilization. But although freedom has been created through a social process, it has not arisen because of human planning, design, or intention.

Such a conception of civilization and its gradual unfolding implies a notion of progress, the unfolding of human powers, the achievement of higher forms of human and social existence, and the emergence of a more differentiated and complex society.[12] But Hayek remains unsure as to whether the individualist civilization that has made the Great Society possible is an improvement or not. He frequently notes that it works only by imposing a severe discipline on all human beings, who must repress their instincts and the preferences learnt in the millennia spent hunting and gathering. The Great Society is therefore, in Hayek's account, against nature.[13]

Civilization for Hayek, like many before him, represents a thin crust. Its achievements are provisional and fragile. New generations have to learn the behaviour and values appropriate to the Great Society. But the crucial point for Hayek is that there is no going back. As Mises put it, the Middle Ages cannot be restored.[14] The Great Society has made possible the support of a population far in excess of the size sustained by any previous society. Hayek and Mises repeatedly insist that no other possible form of society could support the present size of the world population. Whether or not the Great Society is desirable or represents an improvement on what went before, the essential point is that there is no alternative to it. What is required, therefore, is an understanding of how the Great Society came into existence and what must be done to sustain its institutions and its values.

Hayek's meta-narrative about the origins of human societies needs to be understood in this context. It is the key to many aspects of his thought and to many of the tensions within it. His evolutionary stance is closely connected to his epistemology and his attack upon what he calls constructivist rationalism. Hayek always reasons in terms of dualities, and his system of thought can be set out in terms of some of the polarities within it.

evolutionary rationalism	constructivist rationalism
spontaneous order	organization
cosmos	taxis
catallaxy	economy
freedom	coercion

individualism   socialism
justice   social justice
abstract   concrete

Because one of Hayek's key arguments is that civilization arose
through a process of spontaneous, unplanned development, not by
design, he has no time for social contracts, states of nature, or any
of the other devices of rationalist liberalism. His own stance is
always anti-rationalist, in that he believes that human reason, although it has some influence, including an important influence on
events, is never in control. Human beings never have enough knowledge to control their own environment or to design a better one.
They can make small incremental improvements, but if they attempt planning on too grand a scale, they will fail.

Two Types of Rationalism

For Hayek there are two kinds of rationalism, which he calls 'evolutionary rationalism' and 'constructivist rationalism'. The former
is good, the latter pernicious. Though at times Hayek refers to
himself as an anti-rationalist, this does not make him an irration-
alist, but a particular kind of rationalist. Evolutionary rationalism
is concerned with understanding how civilization has developed
and what principles underlie it. An evolutionary rationalist might
propose a change to a particular rule, but the change would always
be cautious, incremental, and experimental. A constructivist rationalist would have no such inhibitions. Believing in the power of
human reason, a constructivist rationalist, according to Hayek, is
always prepared to sweep away existing institutions and practices
and propose the adoption of completely new, untried plans. This
hubris of human reason Hayek traces to the start of the modern
period, to Bacon and Descartes. They originated a tradition of
thought which is the source, he believes, of the intellectual errors
that have plagued the modern world and put at risk the survival
of its distinctive civilization.

Constructivist rationalists see human reason, human will, and
human intention in all human institutions and behaviour. They
therefore believe that human societies can be mastered by human
beings and be remodelled according to rational criteria. Human
societies can be organized so as to abolish social evils such as
poverty and violence. Modern consciousness assumes the possibility

of self-knowledge, and therefore that human reason can be deliberately applied in the cause of human progress.

This theory of liberty, in Hayek's view, received its fullest elaboration in France, in the flowering of Cartesian rationalism in the Enlightenment of the eighteenth century, the encyclopedists, Rousseau, the physiocrats, and Condorcet. This school had its English and American adherents too, from Bacon and Hobbes to the enthusiasts for the French Revolution – Godwin, Paine, Priestley, Price, and Jefferson. Attitude to the French Revolution is, in fact, a good indicator for Hayek of a thinker's soundness. No one who approved of the French Revolution could be considered a true liberal.

True liberals all subscribe to a different theory of liberty, which is mainly a British tradition, and which includes Mandeville, Hume, Smith, Ferguson, Paley, Tucker, and Burke among its most important early representatives. Although this tradition was largely a British affair, Hayek mentions Montesquieu and Constant as two Frenchmen who also belonged to it. In the nineteenth century, Tocqueville, Acton, and Menger were to continue it.

What distinguishes this tradition is a distrust of the powers of human reason, a recognition of the extent of human ignorance about the social and natural worlds, and therefore a stress upon the unexpected, unintended consequences of social action. Mandeville is a key figure in the development of this conception, and Hayek pays him a great deal of attention.[15] Mandeville's importance came from his exploration of the paradox that, instead of there being a direct relationship between private virtue and the achievement of the public good, the public good would be much better served if individuals indulged their private vices. This disjunction between moral behaviour of the individual and the welfare of the whole society had been explored by Machiavelli earlier in relation to statecraft. What Mandeville did, to the outrage of conventional moralists, but to the fascination of many later social theorists, was to begin to explore the possible disjunctions between individual behaviour and social outcomes.

Mandeville's insight could be used in a highly constructivist manner. But Hayek draws on him to reinforce his picture of human society as an enterprise which no individual or group of individuals can hope to understand fully, still less direct. An attitude of humility and caution is required before considering proposals for change. No attempt to operate a free society can be successful, Hayek thinks, unless there is a genuine reverence for grown institutions, customs, and habits: 'A successful free society will always in a large measure be a tradition-bound society.'[16] The reasoning here is familiar from Burke. Existing social arrangements are regarded as embodying the accumulated wisdom of many generations, and are therefore not lightly to be set aside or reconstructed. Those who created the institutions are not necessarily wiser than the present generation; nor may they have had the same knowledge. But their creations were not from nothing; they reflect the experiments of many generations and are therefore likely to embody more experience than is available to any individual or group of individuals in the present.[17]

Hayek notes that liberalism as a political and intellectual project has most often been associated with the tenets of constructivist rationalism, with its hostility to custom, precedent, and tradition. The evolutionary rationalism which he recommends has most often been the preserve of conservatives opposed to the ideas of the French Revolution and its programme of radical change. But Hayek is determined to remain a liberal. He does so by distinguishing between what he calls 'true individualism' and 'false individualism'. Intellectual history has been distorted, he thinks, by the tendency to equate the history of liberalism, and therefore the case for modern society, with the constructivist rationalism of the French tradition. The political doctrines associated with this tradition have tended to dominate, because they make such a strong appeal to human pride and ambition. Those hostile to this tradition have been cast as conservatives and reactionaries. But Hayek argues that this division is much too narrow. There is an alternative liberal tradition, entailing the true conception of individualism, which fully embraces modernity, and therefore is not reactionary in the sense of seeking to restore pre-modern institutions and conditions, but which rejects constructivist rationalism and supports an evolutionary and institutional understanding of the development of modern society, and is based on deep scepticism about the scope and powers of human reason and human action.

Hayek's standpoint divides liberals into sheep and goats, good liberals and bad liberals. The procedure is crude, but it is fundamental to his approach. What he is most anxious to ensure is that true individualism is not infected by constructivist rationalism. Where it has been, there is little to choose between liberalism and socialism for, after a while, the liberal tradition merges into socialism.

Hayek's criterion for differentiating between true liberals and false liberals is their attitude to knowledge and human reason, rather than any specific policy proposals. While in general he esteems the British tradition and denigrates both the French and the German traditions, he notes that both tendencies can surface anywhere. England produced two notable early constructivists in Bacon and Hobbes – Hayek particularly detests Bacon – and although through Mandeville, Hume, Smith, and Burke, Britain later proceeded to lay down the basic elements of true individualism, this tradition was later submerged by the spread of the rationalist utilitarianism of Bentham and the utilitarians. John Stuart Mill occupies for Hayek an ambiguous position. On the one hand, he rejected some of the crucial arguments of the utilitarians; on the other, he provided a set of arguments which allowed liberals to accept state intervention across a wide range of policy, thus paving the way for the New Liberals of the twentieth century. As Hayek puts it, John Stuart Mill was 'chiefly responsible for converting the intellectuals of the western world to socialism'.[18]

The intellectual dominance of Bentham and Mill in England in the nineteenth century, argues Hayek, obscured the real differences between the French and British schools. Bentham was much opposed to the French doctrine of natural rights; but from Hayek's standpoint, Benthamism shares with Cartesian rationalism a belief in human omniscience and complete rationality. The basic conflict for Hayek is between two theories of knowledge, two theories of liberty, and ultimately between two conceptions of democracy – liberal democracy and social or, more accurately, totalitarian democracy. He contrasts the French belief in the efficacy of government and organization and the benign use of public power in the public interest with the British belief that all interference is inherently despotic and must be limited to the minimum possible. On one side is a theory of politics and government which holds that it is the task of government to pursue an absolute collective purpose; on the other is a theory which values spontaneity and the absence of coercion and seeks wisdom in gradual evolution and learning through trial-and-error experiments. Hayek thinks it right to treat them as distinct, because they rest on quite different conceptions of how society works.

As a result, Hayek has mixed feelings about England. Not only did England produce the true principles of individualism; it came closer than any other society before or since to putting those principles into practice. At the same time, England is responsible for betraying and subverting its own liberal tradition. The utilitarians, like Bentham and Mill, and the New Liberals, such as Keynes and Beveridge, contributed to the rise of socialism and collectivism in the twentieth century and the concomitant betrayal of liberal principles.

Hayek's dogmatism is nowhere more powerfully displayed than in his attitude to rival intellectual traditions. It is never a question for him of there being two different perspectives on the same problem or two strands of the same tradition. He is as fierce as any nineteenth-century rationalist in claiming that his ideas are true and those of his opponents false. He agrees that both intellectual traditions belong to Western civilization, but this does not mean that they have equal legitimacy, since one is right and offers the foundations of 'a profound and essentially valid theory', while the other is 'simply and completely wrong'.[19]

His justification for such polemic was his feeling that the currents of constructivist rationalism had become so dominant in all branches of human knowledge that the tradition of evolutionary rationalism was in danger of being buried and forgotten and its crucial insights lost. Yet, as will be demonstrated, Hayek understood the importance of constructivist rationalism, and in one sense his whole project is an exercise in constructivist rationalism. It is because he appreciates the power of reason that he is so keen to keep it within what he regards as its proper limits.

Cosmos and Taxis

Perhaps the key concept which Hayek draws from what he sees as the tradition of 'true individualism', and the one for which he has become most widely known, is the concept of spontaneous order. In *Law, Legislation, and Liberty* Hayek defines order as follows:

> a state of affairs in which a multiplicity of elements of various kinds are so related to each other that we may learn from our acquaintance with some spatial or temporal part of the whole to form correct expectations concerning the rest, or at least expectations which have a good chance of proving correct.[20]

He distinguishes between two kinds of order: a made order and a grown order. A made order belongs to constructivist rationalism, and is closely related to authoritarian conceptions of order. Order in society is seen as resting upon a relationship of command and obedience. It signifies a hierarchy in which a supreme authority instructs individuals as to how they must behave.

Such an order is the order most often valued in conservative thought, in which rights and duties are clearly prescribed, and in which security and identity are created because authority is clearly defined and upheld. Organizations like large business corporations and the Roman Catholic Church are 'made orders' in this sense. But while Hayek does not dispute the need for such a concept of order with regard to organizations, he objects strongly to such a conception being applied to the whole of society.

He calls the two kinds of order 'taxis' and 'cosmos'. A taxis is a made order which flows from human will and intention. A cosmos is a spontaneous order which no one consciously creates. It is characteristic of Hayek that he believes that if authority is exercised, it will be authoritarian in form – top-down, centralized, and hierarchical. He has no conception of other, more democratic forms that authority and governance might take. Whenever he considers the problem, as in the case of economic democracy, he always dismisses it (see chapter 3). A taxis, he believes, should have a single will, a single source of authority, and should not be diluted or shared or compromised. His objection, it is worth repeating, is not to authoritarian organizations as such, but to the attempt to make the whole of society into a single authoritarian organization.[21]

This is an important argument for Hayek, which recurs at various times in his thought. Hayek quotes Marx's famous remark in *Capital* that apologists of the factory system have nothing more damning to urge against socialism than that it would turn the whole of society into one giant factory. Hayek is quite content to accept the challenge. He is an enthusiast for the factory system and for the imposition of discipline and precision on the work-force, while remaining utterly opposed to the attempt to organize the whole of society in a similar manner.

The reason is that, while the Great Society may contain many organizations within it, the secret of its success, in Hayek's view, is precisely that it has no single directing centre. The development of the society depends on no single will, but is the outcome of competition between many wills, the product of many experiments, many mistakes, many failures as well as many successes. There must be an order in society, but this order should be a cosmos rather than a taxis.

A spontaneous order in this sense comes about as the unintended consequence of all agents using the local knowledge at their disposal

to pursue their interests within a framework of general rules that
prescribe just conduct. No single agent will know the impact of
any particular action or the detailed outcomes of this order; nor is
it desirable that anyone should. But so long as everyone adheres to
the general rules that have evolved, expectations of others' behaviour will be such that all individual agents can make adequate
calculations to protect and advance their own interests as they see
them.

The most general kind of spontaneous order for Hayek is the
market order, which he describes as a catallaxy rather than an
economy.[22] The word 'economy', derived from the Greek word for
household, suggests planning and conscious control. In a catallaxy
no single person is responsible for planning the whole, because
knowledge is imperfect, fragmented, and local. There is nothing
perfect or miraculous about such an order. Throughout his writings Hayek is very careful not to attribute to the market order the
kind of qualities such as general equilibrium which is assumed
within the models of neoclassical economics. The market order is
riven by uncertainty and shortfall:

> The market order . . . will regularly secure only a certain probability
> that the expected relations will prevail, but it is . . . the only way in
> which so many activities depending on dispersed knowledge can
> be effectively integrated into a single order.[23]

The market order may be the best example of a cosmos, but it is
not the only one. Hayek recognizes that a spontaneous order as he
defines it is not confined to the macro-level of society. The contrast
he is making between two kinds of order is between two forms of
association. In one case the association is an organization directed
by the will of a single leader; in the second the association may act
as a spontaneous order. What is important in this case is that all
individuals observe the established rules of conduct without needing
to be commanded to obey them. The order is spontaneous because
it arises out of the individual wills of the participants, without any
of them needing to possess knowledge of the whole:

> The aim of the market order . . . is to cope with the inevitable ignor-
> ance of everybody of most of the particular facts which determine
> this order. By a process which men did not understand, their activ-
> ities have produced an order much more extensive and comprehen-
> sive than anything they could have comprehended, but on the
> functioning of which we have become utterly dependent.[24]

In this passage Hayek brings together his evolutionary account of the development of civilization, his anti-rationalist conception of how ignorance is a necessary component of order, and his warning that the discipline of living in the extended order of the Great Society cannot be discarded. The conception of a spontaneous order is one of the key concepts of Hayek's work. But what he fails to do is to demonstrate that spontaneous orders are always superior to made orders. There are many circumstances where it is reasonable to doubt that this is the case.[25]

Individualism and Socialism

One of the most important aspects of Hayek's work is his defence of capitalism as a moral order as well as a material order. He rejects the view that however successful capitalism has been in raising living standards, it lacks a secure moral foundation. In Hayek's view it lacks moral legitimacy only because the inappropriate and damaging moral instincts of socialism have been allowed to dominate public debate.

If the two chief virtues of socialism are altruism and solidarity, the two chief virtues of liberalism are freedom and responsibility. These moral rules have to be learnt by every generation, and they involve suppressing the deeper moral instincts that every individual inherits. Hayek believes that because of some (unspecified) mechanism of cultural transmission, everyone is born a socialist, so that, before individuals can become citizens of the Great Society, they have to learn through a personal struggle how to overcome their socialist selves.

Hayek had a fairly low opinion of human nature. He never believed in the doctrine of human perfectibility. In this he follows the Scottish school, which regarded human beings as lazy, improvident, and wasteful. Only if they were compelled by circumstances and regulated by institutions could human beings be made to behave in ways which would increase wealth, use resources economically, and adjust means to ends in a rational manner. Hayek and the Austrian school never favoured the notion of 'economic man', the perfectly rational, constantly maximizing agent of neoclassical economics. This was another invention of the constructivists: 'the homo economicus was explicitly introduced with much else that belongs to the rationalist rather than to the evolutionary tradition only by the younger Mill.'[26]

Moral behaviour in a market order required human beings to suppress their basic nature and instincts. The moral ethos of capitalism had therefore to be achieved afresh in every generation. At several points in his work Hayek describes this moral ethos. The moral market agent is 'the prudent man, the good husbandman and provider who looked after the future of his family and his business by building up capital, guided less by the desire to be able to consume much than by the wish to be regarded as successful by his fellows who pursued similar aims'.[27]

Hayek repeats many times that moral behaviour is conceivable only if there is a standard against which individuals can be measured. A moral order presupposes that some individuals will strive for excellence and that some will succeed better than others. Some will fail. The individuals who deserve the greatest praise from moralists are those who follow the moral rules appropriate to their society. In a capitalist society, to behave morally is often identified with behaving altruistically. But for Hayek, acting in accordance with self-interest within the rules of the market order deserves higher moral praise.

Hayek's position on morality is not altogether clear. On the one hand, he agrees with Hume that moral beliefs are deeply ingrained in every individual; on the other, he draws a distinction between moral instincts from the primitive past and the learned moral rules of the market order. How is an individual to decide how to act? How is it possible to distinguish between a moral instinct and a deeply ingrained belief? Why are some instincts from the primitive past, such as solidarity and altruism, inappropriate to the Great Society, while others, such as competition and self-interest, are essential to it? For all his anti-rationalist arguments, Hayek ultimately has to recommend the use of reason to determine the moral rules which individuals should follow. If he really believed in cultural selection, he should be confident that human beings will always in the end stumble on those moral rules which will enable them to prosper and survive. If they do not, they will lose out to other groups.

Hayek is not prepared to leave the Great Society to its own evolutionary logic, however. He believes that since there is only one true theory of liberty and only one true theory of how society works, this knowledge can be used to avoid the pitfalls and dangers created by constructivist doctrines. Hayek does not want to plan society in the sense of drawing up a detailed blueprint, but he does want to ensure that the general rules and institutions are the appropriate ones.

Freedom and Coercion

Critical comment on Hayek's moral theory has often centred on his distinction between freedom and coercion. It is important for Hayek's theory of liberty that there should be a very clear boundary between the two. He defines them as opposites. Freedom is 'that condition of man in which coercion of some by others is reduced as much as is possible in society'. Personal freedom is then defined as the 'state in which a man is not subject to coercion by the arbitrary will of another or others'.[28] Freedom thus becomes a relation of an individual to other individuals. Hayek naturally wishes to reject broader conceptions of freedom, which include political freedom and notions of autonomy. Full personal liberty, he insists, is still possible without what is conventionally understood as political liberty – defined as participation by citizens in the choice of their government, in the process of legislation, and in control of the administration. Hayek acknowledges that the notion of freedom has often been closely associated with political liberty in that sense. But he is uncompromising. 'To choose one's government', he writes, 'is not necessarily to secure freedom.'[29] Similarly, Hayek argues that positive conceptions of liberty also rest on a confusion. They identify liberty with power, the ability to do something. This leads quickly to the identification of liberty with wealth and to demands for the redistribution of wealth. Possession of power and wealth, however, does not guarantee freedom. Only the opportunity to avoid subjection to the arbitrary will of others can do that.

The essentials of liberty, for Hayek, are four:

> if he is subject only to the same laws as all his fellow citizens, if he is immune from arbitrary confinement and free to choose his work, and if he is able to own and acquire property, no other men or group of men can coerce him to do their bidding.[30]

Being subject to the same laws gives freedom from the arbitrary will of those in authority. The second condition gives freedom from arbitrary arrest. These are the classic negative conditions of liberty. Hayek's other two essentials, however, are rather more dubious. Freedom to choose one's work might be construed as a form of positive freedom, but what Hayek means is freedom from slavery or compulsion to work, rather than freedom to choose a particular kind of work. There is also a suspicion of positive freedom in Hayek's fourth condition, freedom to own and acquire property. In a society in which the opportunities to own and acquire property were limited not by the arbitrary decision of rulers but by laws which allowed only members of one minority group to hold property, would it be justifiable to advocate the redistribution of property to increase the total sum of liberty?

Hayek so distrusts political action that normally he would not sanction such a course. But he does seem to offer a positive, as well as a negative, conception of liberty, and does open up intriguing possibilities for political intervention to empower individuals and create the essentials of liberty. The example that Hayek himself gives, which has attracted considerable comment, is the desert spring.[31] If the only spring in an oasis is controlled by a monopolist who denies access to others, Hayek regards that as an act of coercion. The problem with the example, as many critics have pointed out, is that, on Hayek's own definition of coercion, this case hardly seems to qualify. The individual denied access because of the property rights of the spring-owner simply has to move somewhere else. To argue that he does not have to move implies that he has certain needs which override the property rights of the spring-owner. If Hayek concedes that there may be circumstances in which property rights can legitimately be overridden, the argument passes from principles to cases. Hayek is unable to find a principle which excludes all appeals to positive freedom, and therefore to conceptions of human autonomy and need.

Freedom is a key concept in Hayek's conception of morality. Coercion, he argues, is evil, because it eliminates the individual as 'a thinking valuing person' and makes him or her 'a bare tool in the achievements of the ends of another'. But Hayek is careful to draw back from the logic of his libertarianism. He still accepts a role for the state, as a taxis with specific functions to perform within the liberal cosmos. He concedes that coercion can be avoided altogether only by the threat of coercion. A state has to be formed which enjoys a monopoly of coercion, but use of its power is acceptable only if it is limited to instances where it is required to prevent coercion by private persons. Much of Hayek's writing is an attempt to specify how the power of the state might be limited.

The argument against socialism takes on a new twist in light of Hayek's dichotomy between freedom and coercion. Any attempt to implement a socialist programme must involve, according to Hayek, much higher levels of coercion. This is why the moral ethos of socialism in the Great Society is totalitarian. Socialism removes limits from the state, and sanctions far-reaching interventions in the lives of individuals. Since the attempt to recreate the altruistic, solidaristic primitive community is doomed to failure, the amount of coercion which has to be sanctioned tends to increase.

Socialism undermines morality in the Great Society, because it has an inadequate conception of the individualist basis of this civilization, and fails to understand the necessity for the sphere of the individual to be protected if this civilization is to continue to advance. Only if coercion is reduced to a minimum and the essentials of liberty are secured, will the conditions be created in which civilization can progress through cultural selection of the best rules and institutions.

Individuals must be free in the Great Society, and one of the conditions of that freedom is that they become responsible for their own lives, their own choices, and their own decisions. For Hayek, liberty and responsibility are inseparable. In the Great Society all able adults are responsible for their own welfare and that of their families. All individuals are capable of learning from experience and of guiding their actions by the knowledge they acquire.[32] All individuals in the Great Society pursue their own aims and are therefore self-interested, regardless of whether their objectives are judged egoistic or altruistic. Moral esteem depends on how others judge how individuals use their freedom. If there were no freedom, argues Hayek, there would be no moral esteem. One of the most important sources of moral esteem is the extent to which individuals accept their responsibilities. One test is employment: 'the necessity of finding a sphere of usefulness, an appropriate job, (for) ourselves is the hardest discipline that a free society imposes on us.'[33]

Hayek shares the classical liberal fear that, because the discipline is hard, many individuals may not embrace the moral doctrines and, still more important, the moral behaviour which the Great Society requires. The moral life, as he presents it, is not an easy path. For many individuals the path to independence and self-reliance involves asceticism and self-denial, a life of hard work and deferred gratification. Not all will succeed, and only the successful deserve moral approbation. In this way the moral ethic of the Great Society is similar to the Protestant Ethic which Weber used to explain the cultural distinctiveness of capitalism. Hayek, however, has no belief in an elect. Human beings are not predestined to be either damned or saved. All can learn the moral behaviour appropriate to the Great Society. But in practice the gulf remains. There is always a moral elite in capitalism, and the proof of their superior status, for Hayek as well as for Mises, is economic success. Entrepreneurs deserve higher moral esteem than other individuals because, by taking risks, they are the ones who move society forward, and provide benefits and higher living standards for everyone.

Hayek's criticism of socialism as a moral doctrine is that it creates dependency and discourages self-reliance, making it much harder for the values required by capitalism to triumph. The growth of dependency on the state, encouraged by state spending programmes of all kinds, robs individuals of the essential experiences in a market order which teach them to become moral beings. In *The Road to Serfdom* he writes of 'the utter difference between the whole moral atmosphere under collectivism and the essentially individualist Western civilisation'.[34]

By undermining individualism, socialism undermines morality and, eventually, all the achievements of Western civilization. It destroys the notion of personal responsibility, and corrupts both truth and reason. Hayek argues that socialism cannot tolerate dissent, improvisation, experiment, or competition – qualities that were so important in the rise of Western science. One of the chapters in *The Road to Serfdom* is entitled 'The End of Truth'. Socialism paves the way for totalitarian regimes which attempt to plan all activity and suppress dissent and independent thought.

Abstract and Concrete

One of Hayek's most interesting arguments is that modern civilization depends both intellectually and practically upon abstraction, and that this civilization is threatened by systems of thought that deny abstraction.

This idea is linked to the concept of spontaneous orders and to the limits of human reason which are such important themes in Hayek's work. Throughout his writings, Hayek treats socialism as a revolt against reason which puts at risk the achievements of Western civilization through ignorance of what has given rise to them. In *The Road to Serfdom* he writes: 'Man has come to hate, and to revolt against, the impersonal forces to which in the past he submitted even though they have often frustrated his individual efforts.'[35] These impersonal forces are created by the general rules which regulate the market order. Hayek detected a new unwillingness to submit to the workings of the market order or 'to any rule or necessity the rationale of which man does not understand'. This had serious consequences, since 'there are fields where this craving for intelligibility cannot be fully satisfied and where at the same time a refusal to submit to anything we cannot understand must lead to the destruction of our civilisation'. Civilization has been built not on transparent rational foundations, but on the evolution of rules and institutions the rationale for which no one has ever fully understood. Hayek's argument is that it is not necessary to understand them. In seeking to understand them, human beings are too ready to denounce submission to the impersonal forces to the market, without realizing that the alternative to submitting to these impersonal and seemingly irrational forces is submission to 'an equally uncontrollable and therefore arbitrary power of other men'.[36]

In subsequent writings Hayek builds this insight into one of the central pillars of his system. The great advance made by civilization was to develop a society whose members were bound together only by abstract rules of conduct and had no need to develop concrete common aims. Hayek uses the term 'abstract' here to mean general. Such rules do not refer to any particular circumstance, but cover a range of possible events and circumstances. To understand how this society works, it is not necessary or possible to know in detail the particular outcomes of all the exchanges that go on within it. It is only necessary to know the abstract general principles on which the order is based. Socialism attempts to bring back the concrete and the particular, and to make these the determinants of policy. But any attempt to do so means that all members of the society can no longer be treated equally. The consequence is that the state has begun to extend its coercive intervention beyond the minimum prescribed in a liberal order. It is compelled to resort more and more to force to implement its decisions, and to become more and more arbitrary and omnipotent. It is the return of mankind to tribal life. Socialism is a reassertion of the tribal ethics whose gradual weakening made an approach to the Great Society possible. What makes it so dangerous to Hayek is that modern socialism comes clothed not in its true colours as a reactionary anti-modernist doctrine, but as the rational fulfilment of Western liberalism.

Abstraction therefore resides in the general rules of the market order, but it is also at the heart of modern science and social science. Hayek's evolutionary rationalism recognizes abstractions as the indispensable means of the mind which enable it to deal with a reality it cannot fully comprehend. Hayek accepts the need to make reason as effective as possible, but he rejects the notion that conscious reason ought to determine every action.

One of his main targets here, perhaps surprisingly, is Hegel. Hayek condemns him as an ultra-rationalist, the origin of most modern irrationalism and totalitarianism. Yet he concedes that it was Hegel who most clearly saw the nature of modernity when he described liberalism as the view which clings to abstraction, over which the concrete always prevails and which always founders in the struggle against it. Hayek believes that only by clinging to abstraction can human beings understand and protect the civilization they have unwittingly created. It is a hard struggle: 'We are not yet mature enough to submit for any length of time to strict discipline of reason and allow our emotions constantly to break through its restraints.'[37]

Hayek goes further. The Great Society and the civilization it has made possible, he argues, is the product of man's growing capacity to communicate abstract thought. Reliance on the abstract is due not to human beings overestimating their reason, but to their appreciation of just how limited reason actually is. Whereas constructivist rationalism believes it can master all the particulars, evolutionary rationalism is content to understand the nature of modernity merely in abstract and general terms.

Hayek notes that many schools of philosophy are hostile to abstract reason, putting forward notions such as life and existence which elevate emotion, the particular, and the instinctive above reason. It is no surprise, he says, to find the adherents of such philosophies prominent in political movements based on race, nation, and class. Systems of thought like socialism, which abandon abstract reasoning, threaten the foundations of individual moral behaviour by trying to make society act morally. This, Hayek thinks, is an example of the intellectual error at the heart of socialism: 'Although we must endeavour to make society good in the sense that we shall like to live in it, we cannot make it good in the sense that it will behave morally.'[38]

Social Justice

From these distinctions Hayek develops a view of justice that is appropriate for the Great Society, and strongly attacks the concept of social justice which he regards as one of the main means by which collectivist agendas have been advanced. 'So long as the belief in "social justice" governs political action, the tendency to totalitarianism is present.'[39] Justice is inseparable from the establishment of the rule of law. Provided laws are properly formulated in terms of general, abstract rules, the outcomes will be just. 'All that is truly social is general and abstract in a Great Society.'[40]

The outcomes may also be very unequal. Hayek accepts that there may be a case for charitable giving, and even that it may be desirable for the state to provide help to some individuals and groups. What he completely opposes is that such assistance be recommended in order to realize social justice. The moral order of a free society is completely opposed to the notion of social justice:

> The cult of social justice tends to destroy genuine moral feelings. The demand that we should equally esteem all our fellow men is irreconcilable with the fact that our moral code rests on the approval or disapproval of the conduct of others ... the postulate that each capable adult is primarily responsible for his own and his dependants' welfare is incompatible with the idea that society or government owes each person an appropriate income.[41]

Hayek believes that in a market order there can be no such thing as social justice, because social justice implies that there is some superior criterion which can be applied to the outcomes of the market, a notion of just deserts or fairness, which justifies redistributing what the market has allocated. The notion of fairness belongs to pre-modern societies, however. Fairness implies that there should be a connection between individual merit (measured by effort and achievement) and reward. A market order breaks that link. It works as Mandeville described. Some of the least deserving individuals on conventional moral criteria receive the highest rewards, and some of the most deserving the least.

Hayek is not shocked by this. He argues that it cannot be otherwise. If we want the benefits of a market order, in terms of liberty and prosperity, then we have to accept many outcomes of which we disapprove. 'Freedom means that in some measure we entrust our fate to forces which we do not control.'[42] If we once start to tamper with the mechanism of allocation by substituting for the judgement of the market our own judgement of what market services are worth, then it will distort the market and lead to a misallocation of resources, and eventually to impoverishment and to the loss of liberty. There is in any case no way of measuring need objectively, or of making comparisons between individuals which would allow a rational redistribution to be made. Any redistribution will therefore be arbitrary, determined by the strength of prejudice, chance, and the power of special interests. As he put it:

> The whole history of the development of popular institutions is a history of continuous struggle to prevent particular groups from abusing the governmental apparatus for the benefit of the collective interest of these groups.[43]

The discourse of social justice is, for Hayek, the most deeply rooted and the most pernicious of all the doctrines associated with socialism and collectivism, because it commands such wide acceptance and because it appears to spring from such pure and noble motives. He cites the famous lines by Anatole France: 'The majestic equality of the law that forbids the rich as well as the poor to sleep under bridges, to beg in the streets and to steal bread.'[44] France is criticized for failing to understand what the function of law is in a modern society, which is to prescribe just rules of conduct, not to become involved in the outcomes of exchanges between individuals. 'To judge actions by rules not by particular results is the step which has made the Open Society possible.'[45] To accept France's argument, according to Hayek, would be to undermine the foundations of all impartial justice and to destroy the moral basis for a free society, because individuals will no longer be able to take full responsibility for their actions.

Hayek quotes Hume's view that there are three key rules of just conduct that have made the Great Society possible: stability of possession; its transference by consent, and the fulfilment of promises. He retitles them freedom of contract, inviolability of property, and the duty to compensate another for damage. So long as these are maintained, the outcomes of the market order will be just.[46]

Hayek's account of justice and social justice is entirely compatible with his anti-rationalist account of society and the market order. 'The complex structure of the modern Great Society would clearly not work if the remuneration of all the different activities were determined by the opinion which the majority holds of their value.'[47] Yet it provides no simple apologia for capitalism, since it acknowledges that a market order is amoral. If it is to work effectively, the link between merit and reward must be severed. This conception is subtle and counter-intuitive, and therefore difficult to communicate in a popular manner. But Hayek insists that it has to be done. In a market order justice must be procedural rather than substantive.

The market is a lottery, a game of chance, a catallaxy, in which no one can be sure of the outcomes or hope to control them.[48] 'Our only moral title to what the market gives us we have earned by submitting to those rules which make the formation of the market order possible.'[49] If there are casualties, they can be helped in some other way, but the basic principle must not be compromised.

In his theory of justice, Hayek's view of morality and the Great Society achieves its starkest expression. But the very elegance of his paradox about justice in modern society also makes it rather unreal. Comforting the dispossessed and the never possessed with the abstract beauty and justice of the market mechanism is unlikely to be persuasive or practical. Hayek bemoans the fact that the most popular justification for capitalism, put forward by Samuel Smiles and Horatio Alger, is that free enterprise rewards the deserving. 'It bodes ill for the future of the market order that this seems to have become the only defence of it which is understood by the general public.'[50] Hayek's view is bleak. He argues that there is a real dilemma over what to teach the young, since many of them who are unworthy will succeed, and many who are worthy will fail. Conventional morality has to be abandoned.

Yet, radical as Hayek's view appears, he is not prepared to travel all the way. He himself admits that there is a role for the state in providing a floor level of resources below which no individual should be allowed to fall. But once that concession has been made, the argument about social justice re-emerges. For all his polemics, Hayek cannot banish it. Social justice applied to a whole society is obviously a fantasy. But applied to particular areas and programmes, it has an important and indispensable role. Why should elected governments not choose to mitigate the impact of the market? As recent work by Len Doyal and Ian Gough has shown,[51] it is possible to develop objective measures of human need which can command broad agreement and can provide the basis for determining the desirable scope and scale of collective welfare provision. Michael Walzer has argued that there are areas of social life, such as health and education, where different criteria of allocation should apply.[52] In suggesting that any concession to allocation based upon substantive rather than procedural justice threatens liberty, Hayek makes a case which is implausible unless he is prepared to endorse a thoroughgoing libertarianism. Since he is not, and since he acknowledges an important role for the state, the ferocity of his warnings about the perils of succumbing to arguments about social justice, while salutary, do not ultimately convince.[53]

3

Markets

In a society which is to preserve freedom of choice of the consumer
and free choice of occupation central direction of all economic activity presents a task which cannot be rationally solved under the complex conditions of modern life.

Hayek (ed.), *Collectivist Economic Planning*

The second charge that Hayek makes against socialism focuses on
its economic claims. He argues that socialism impedes the production of wealth and may cause impoverishment. This was the critique on which Hayek embarked first, and it provided the first
critical application of his philosophical position. His understanding of the economic problem in modern societies, which he developed during his years in Vienna and London, is the pivot of his
social and political theory, and contributed some of his most
important insights.

This understanding was formed through his contact with the
Austrian school. With hindsight, it is easy to pick out the divergent
path that Austrian economics took from mainstream neoclassical
economics. In the 1920s and 1930s, however, when Hayek was
active as a professional economist, the differences were obscured,
and although different schools were recognized, it was commonly
assumed that all economists shared a common framework and belonged to a single research community.[1] The unity of this research
community was defined by the paradigm shift that had taken place
in the 1870s and 1880s – the marginalist revolution. At the heart of
this theoretical revolution was a new conception of value, which

received separate but convergent formulations from Jevons, Walras, and Menger.

The importance of the new economics was that it broke with some of the key assumptions and moved away from many of the problems associated with the earlier paradigm of classical political economy, as developed by Smith, Ricardo, and Mill, and utilized by Marx as the basis for his 'critique of political economy' in *Capital*. The most significant break was the abandonment of the labour theory of value. This theory was at the heart of classical political economy, and represented an attempt to find an objective measure of value, independent of price. Value was calculated according to the input of labour in the production of goods and services. The measure of labour input was time.

The new economics proposed an alternative theory of value which attributed value to the subjective assessments of utility made by each individual. These preferences, aggregated through the processes of market exchange, underlay the prices that were formed in the market. The consequence of this new theory in intellectual terms was to shift economics decisively from a multi-disciplinary study concerned with economic systems or, as Adam Smith put it, with the nature and causes of the wealth of nations, to a more specialized discipline dealing with a particular aspect of human behaviour. There had always been a tension in the writings of classical economists between understanding economic behaviour as relative to particular historical contexts and understanding it as a universal attribute of human action found in all societies in all historical periods.

Menger was one of the originators of this shift in the intellectual concerns of political economy, and his work and that of his pupils created the distinctive body of concepts and concerns which gave the Austrian school its identity. Its character became clear during the *Methodenstreit*, a fierce controversy among German-speaking intellectuals over the most appropriate method for studying society.[2] On one side were a group of historians and social scientists led by Gustav Schmoller, loosely called 'the Historical school' because they favoured historical and inductive methods of analysis. They included a wide range of political views from Marxists to conservative nationalists. On the other side were economists led by Carl Menger and his Austrian school. Other social scientists like Max Weber and Joseph Schumpeter occupied a more ambiguous position between the two camps, although on the whole they inclined towards Menger because of their belief in objective and

comparative modes of analysis. The split was particularly pronounced and fiercely fought in the German-speaking world, but in
Britain and the United States there were echoes of the controversy,
reflected in the increasing divorce between economics and economic history.[3]

The *Methodenstreit* assumed great importance for the Austrian
school, particularly because in the German-speaking world the
opponents of the Historical school tended to lose out in the academy. In the 1920s Mises complained that there were no economists
in Germany, by which he meant no Austrian school economists.
Members of the Austrian school saw themselves as beleaguered
both intellectually and politically, and looked beyond Austria and
Germany to those countries, particularly Britain, the United States,
and Scandinavia, where the new economics paradigm had put down
strong roots. These international contacts brought Lionel Robbins
to Vienna in the 1920s and Hayek to London, first to lecture, then
to a chair at the LSE. Many other members of the Austrian school,
including Schumpeter, Machlup, and Mises himself, were to leave
Austria and pursue their careers elsewhere, most often in the United
States.

Yet although Hayek had a strong affinity with Anglo-American
economics, there were some important differences between the two
schools, and they tended to grow rather than diminish. The tradition of the Austrian school has been kept alive particularly in the
United States, but has clearly separated from the mainstream.[4]
Hayek's own abandonment of his economic research programme
of the 1930s in part signalled his disillusionment with the way
economics was developing. His disagreement was partly political
and ideological, but primarily methodological. For example, he
strongly opposed the macro-economics of Keynes and the
Keynesians on political grounds, because he disagreed with their
policy priorities and policy prescriptions. But he also opposed
Keynesianism because he disagreed with the methodology of macro-
economics, believing that the aggregates that it constructed produced a misleading, inaccurate model of the economy.[5] In the 1970s
Hayek had much in common politically with monetarist economists
like Milton Friedman, with the result that he was often bracketed
with Friedman as an advocate of monetarism. But while Hayek
and Friedman shared many assumptions about the value of free
enterprise and markets, Hayek thought that the macro-economic
analysis underlying monetarism committed the same errors as
Keynesianism, and led to harmful policy prescriptions.

During the 1920s and 1930s Hayek still saw himself as part of the economic mainstream, contributing as a social scientist to the development of the dominant research paradigm in his discipline. But ultimately the differences between the methodological assumptions of the Austrian tradition and those of the neoclassical and Keynesian traditions tended to isolate Hayek as a professional economist. To have remained at the heart of the economics profession in the 1950s and 1960s, as he had been in the 1930s, he would have been obliged to modify his research programmes and his methods. He had become convinced, however, that a much more important task needed to be undertaken – a restatement of the basic principles of a liberal economic and social order.

Methodological Individualism

One reason for Hayek's inability to reconcile himself with neoclassical economics was the uncompromising position he took on methodological individualism. This method of analysis was a key component of the Austrian approach, and is responsible both for the hard analytical edge of Hayek's thought and for many of its blind spots. Methodological individualism makes two critical assumptions:

1   All actions are performed by individuals; therefore analysis of social reality must start from individuals, conceived as self-sufficient, fixed entities confronting the external world and responding to its opportunities and constraints by making choices and devising strategies.
2   A social collective has no existence and no reality beyond the actions of its individual members; therefore it is incorrect to argue as though collectives could have their own will and purposes. Collectives such as the government, the company, the union, the nation are all abstractions and have no reality beyond the individuals that compose them.[6]

Like realist theories in international relations, the strength of methodological individualism is that it cuts through to a level of reality which it regards as bedrock. From this standpoint, the success of the marginalist revolution in economics was due to the fact that for the first time it allowed economists to follow John Stuart Mill's injunction that to study the laws of society, it was necessary

to study the actions and passions of individual human beings. It
did this through its subjective theory of value. Instead of trying to
measure value objectively, it defined it as whatever was subjectively valued by individuals. What that was could be known only
through their actual behaviour and choices in a free market. Key
concepts such as wealth, scarcity, and cost were redefined in the
light of this definition. The cost of a particular good was not simply a sum of money, but expressed a relationship with all other
commodities. Cost for the Austrian school represents opportunities
forgone, alternative choices that are given up, the decision not to
spend the money in a different way. The system of relative prices
could thus be understood as reflecting the relative valuations placed
on different commodities by individuals. From this base comes the
notion of the sovereign consumer, just as from realism comes the
notion of the sovereign nation-state. Both are considered inviola-
ble, the basic building blocks of the system.

As an analytical strategy, methodological individualism has been
valuable for social science, because it is a debunking method. It
strips away the outer layers, and provides a constant reminder of
the need to disaggregate and to choose carefully the appropriate
level of analysis. Treating the government, for example, as a single
entity overlooks the different interests and organization of sectors
within it. Public choice theorists have urged that government should
always be disaggregated into 'politicians and bureaucrats', in order to demystify notions such as the public interest and national
policy.

But although it has a sharp cutting edge, methodological individualism is also extremely one-sided. It reduces everything to individual preferences and purposes, but refuses to examine the
institutional forces which mould individual preferences and purposes.[7] This makes it an extremely reductionist doctrine, because
its theory places the individual outside the social realm. Hayek is
at his least convincing here, and indeed, as was explained in the
last chapter, he smuggles back into his theory an evolutionary and
institutional view of how individuals have in fact come to be as
they are. But his original starting-point, as an economist in the
Austrian school, was that as far as economics was concerned, individual preferences and purposes must be accepted as given. Inves-
tigation of what shaped those preferences and purposes belongs
not to economics but to psychology. Hayek's own work on psychology never addressed this question. His interest was in phy-
siological explanations of psychic phenomena. What he never

explored is how preferences are formed and how they change. Yet this is a key question for any theory of institutions.[8]

The reason for Hayek's intransigence on this point goes to the heart of the *Methodenstreit*. The Historical school believed in applying the methods of natural science to the study of the past, in order to discover the general laws that governed historical progress. Hayek argued forcibly against this approach, because he believed that it misrepresented the distinctive character of human nature as opposed to physical nature, and that therefore it could not produce the kind of knowledge it sought. Instead, faced with the failure of its methods, it was bound to oscillate between an extreme positivism on the one hand and an extreme relativism and scepticism on the other:

> It was the essence of the standpoint of this school that the laws of economics could only be established by the application to the material of history of the methods of the natural sciences. And the nature of this material is such that any such attempt is bound to degenerate into mere record and description and a total scepticism concerning the existence of any laws at all.[9]

The leaders of the Historical school were Sombart and Schmoller, but for the Austrians the real intellectual forerunner of the school and the person they considered as their main intellectual adversary was Marx. Whereas Marx took much longer to become a major force within Anglo-American intellectual culture, his influence in Germany was already profound by the end of the nineteenth century. There were flourishing schools of Marxism and many Marxist groups and parties. The new mass social-democratic parties in Germany and Austria adopted Marxism as their official ideology, and framed their political programmes accordingly.

Marx was criticized by the Austrians for three main methodological errors, which Hayek summarized as follows:

1 An inability to see any of the permanent economic problems which are independent of the historical framework.
2 A denial of logic.
3 A refusal to investigate the future shape of socialist society.[10]

For the Austrians, Marxism purported to be a scientific doctrine, which investigated the economic laws that governed human history. But because its understanding of the nature of human society was defective, it produced results which were both unscientific and anti-rational. Only a method that starts from individuals and their subjective valuations can discover the common principles that underlie all human societies. Marx, instead, constantly used collective entities like social classes in his analyses. The Austrian school denied that such entities possess any reality.

Hayek and the whole Austrian school were entirely modernist in their conviction that there was only one right, scientific way to study society, and that this was the way of methodological individualism. Other methods such as those of Marxism were not just wrong; they threatened to subvert the whole Western rationalist tradition. Far from accepting Marxism's own evaluation of itself as the fulfilment of the Enlightenment tradition, the Austrians believed it to be a most pernicious doctrine of reaction which threatened the achievements of Western rationalism.

Mises expressed this point of view in most extreme form. He regarded the appeal of Marxism as entirely irrational and as encouraging 'dreams of bliss and revenge'. It was, he declared, 'the most radical of all reactions against the reign of scientific thought over life and action established by Rationalism'. The success of Marxism depended on its ability to 'dupe the masses', which was possible because of 'their ignorance and inability to follow difficult trains of thought'.[11] As a result, the world was faced with 'the inevitable decline of the civilisation which the nations of the West have taken thousands of years to build up. And so we must inevitably drift on to chaos and misery, the darkness of barbarism and annihilation.'[12]

This apocalyptic tone is a feature of Hayek's writing also, and has often been a barrier to a wider acceptance of his ideas, particularly in the Anglo-American academy, where Spenglerian pessimism has never been too well received. The language reflected the despair that Austrian liberals like Mises felt at the advancing tide of collectivism on both left and right which was sweeping the German-speaking world at the turn of the century, both in the academy and in politics. But it also expressed the firm conviction of Hayek and Mises that there were absolute criteria for rationality, which could not be questioned without threatening the project of modernity.[13]

The Impossibility of Socialism

It was the intellectual confrontation with Marxism which was responsible for the most famous intellectual contribution of the Austrian school – the attempt to demonstrate that socialism was impossible. The debate has been much misunderstood. Donald Lavoie has convincingly argued that the original article by Mises was an attack upon Marxism and its concealed utopianism with regard to future socialist society.[14] The challenge, in particular the claim that socialism was impossible, was taken up not by Marxist theorists, but by economists with Marxist and socialist political sympathies, who tried to show that the tools of modern economic analysis could be used to demonstrate that a socialist economy was entirely feasible. The nature of the debate was then further confused by Schumpeter, who reviewed the debate in *Capitalism, Socialism and Democracy*, and declared that the critics of Mises had won the argument, and that Mises' original contention had been refuted.[15]

Schumpeter suggested that there were two aspects to the debate: first, the claim that socialism was logically impossible, and second, that it was practically impossible. Mises had argued the former in an article published in 1920. Schumpeter countered that his case had already been refuted in work done by Enrico Barone, which had been published some years earlier. He suggested that Hayek and Robbins, who contributed to the debate in the 1930s, conceded the logical argument about socialism, and that they had substituted instead the claim that even if socialism were logically conceivable, it could not work in practice because of the complexity of the co-ordination tasks facing the public authorities. Schumpeter argued that Oscar Lange and Abba Lerner had shown conclusively that these claims were groundless.

Although he did not like socialism, Schumpeter regarded it as a viable economic system. He made it clear in *Capitalism, Socialism, and Democracy* that he expected capitalism to disappear and socialism to replace it. This view reflected the period in which the book was written, the late 1930s and early 1940s. Socialism appeared to be advancing throughout the world, while liberal capitalism was everywhere in retreat. A form of planned economy had been successfully established in Russia, and collectivist principles for economic planning and the provision of welfare were gaining ground throughout the Western democracies. With fascism defeated, and traditional forms of liberalism discredited, Schumpeter predicted that a new socialist civilization would come to replace the liberal civilization of the previous hundred years. From this perspective, the fears of Mises and Hayek represented an old-fashioned defence of the principles of a form of society which was fast disappearing.

Schumpeter's judgement on the outcome of the debate was widely accepted. But more recently, with the revival of older strands of liberal thought and the collapse of the economic and political systems of 'actually existing socialism', the debate has been reassessed. No one in the 1990s thinks of central planning any longer as the wave of the future. A typical contemporary judgement on the debate is provided by Janos Kornai in *The Socialist System*: 'Looking back after 50 years one can conclude that Hayek was right on every point in the debate. . . . The hope Lange held out was illusory.'[16]

The importance of the debate for understanding Hayek's thought is twofold. First, his involvement in the debate in the 1930s was one of the (few) early signs of his later intellectual trajectory, and showed that he was interested in a range of questions that went beyond the technical economic treatises on capital theory for which he was noted.[17] Second, his disagreement with his opponents in the debate turned less on differences in political views than on differences in method for analysing economic phenomena. The debate was thus an important turning-point in Hayek's eventual move away from economics towards social and political theory.

The calculation debate takes its name from the article published by Ludwig von Mises in 1920 entitled 'Economic Calculation in the Socialist Commonwealth'.[18] The context of its publication was important. The First World War had plunged Europe into turmoil: the old empires had collapsed; the Bolsheviks had seized power in Russia; and revolution was a possibility in many other parts of Europe. Socialist experiments in several countries seemed imminent. With the collapse of so many of the *ancien régimes* of Europe and the dislocation of the international liberal order of the world economy, much of the distinctive liberal nineteenth-century civilization seemed about to be swept away.

Liberals like Mises and Weber viewed the advance of socialism with foreboding. Independently, each developed a critique of the compatibility of the aspirations of socialism with the institutions of modernity. Hayek noted in his Introduction to *Collectivist Economic Planning* the convergence between the views of Weber and Mises. Weber, like Mises, he argued, had recognized the impossibility of rational calculation under socialism, and saw that the rational use and preservation of capital could be secured only in a system based on exchange and the use of money. Weber had also developed a parallel critique of the socialist aspiration to replace representative forms of state with direct democracy.

The main target of the Mises/Weber counter-attack on socialism was the claim that socialism represented a higher stage of human development beyond liberalism. They insisted that there was no scientific basis for such claims. The social and economic institutions of capitalism were not a stage on the way to anything else. They were the essence of modernity, and could not be transcended. Marx had scornfully remarked about classical liberal political economists that they had a very truncated view of history. For them there had been history, but there was no longer any. History was the period of long painful struggle during which human societies had gradually evolved the institutions of a liberal society. Once the stage of modernity had been reached, however, history, as Hegel said, had ended. There was no higher stage beyond it. Marx argued that the historical process had not stopped, and that further stages in historical development could be expected. It is this claim that Mises and Weber contested. They aligned themselves with the political economists in affirming that there is only one viable form of modernity.

Economic Calculation in the Socialist Commonwealth

The argument deployed by Mises in his 1920s article against socialism was a theoretical argument, derived from the particular Austrian understanding of the economic problem. The proposition which attracted most attention was the claim that there could be no rational economic calculation in a socialist economy: 'Without economic calculation there can be no economy. Hence in a socialist state wherein the pursuit of economic calculation is impossible, there can be, in our sense of the term no economy whatsoever.'[19] What Mises did not actually say was that socialism was impossible, although that is how he was interpreted by many of his critics. He was thought to be repeating the familiar anti-socialist argument that socialism was impractical, and that if a socialist economy were established, it would speedily collapse. Mises' original article appeared three years after the Bolshevik seizure of power in Russia, during the period of war communism, when an imminent collapse of the regime and the Bolshevik experiment looked extremely likely. But ten years later, the survival of some form of centrally planned economy in Russia seemed assured, and its apparent stability and freedom from cyclical fluctuations contrasted markedly with the global capitalist economy, which was afflicted by the Great Crash and the ensuing Depression. Experience seemed to have disproved Mises, and the theoretical responses of Oscar Lange, H. D.

Dickinson, Fred Taylor, Abba Lerner, and others set out to show theoretically how the original prognosis had been in error. Responding as a professional economist, Hayek attempted to defend the original position against these attacks.

Mises' argument was more subtle, however, than simply the claim that socialism would not work. He could hardly have been unaware of the existence of many historical examples of different forms of social system which lacked modern systems of economic calculation but which persisted for centuries. The issue for Mises was not whether such a social system could successfully reproduce itself, but whether a social system which had made the transition to modernity could dispense with the institutions of rational economic calculation. Some critics of Mises have been misled by his use of the word 'economy', supposing it to refer to a historically determinate economic system. But what Mises means by economy is a mode of rational calculation, a way in which individuals relate to goods, not the institutions and practices which define an economy.

For Mises, as for Hayek, there is a universal economic problem which all societies have to solve in some fashion if they are to survive – how to establish priority between a multiplicity of ends competing for a limited quantity of means. The nature and origins of economic value in this sense are the fundamental questions for economics. Hayek argues that the labour theory of value adopted by classical political economists and by Marx represented 'a search after some illusory substance of value rather than an analysis of the behaviour of the economic subject'.[20] Only when economists began to analyse the latter, were they able to uncover the basis of modern economic rationality, the significance or value attached by each individual to different goods. Individuals behaved differently towards goods because their valuations were different. Mises argued that the economy was a means for satisfying the needs that individuals have. Nothing has an intrinsic use-value. An objective use-value acquires an *economic* significance only if it has a subjective use-value for individuals. The value an individual places on a good creates the possibility for exchange.

The obvious difficulty with a subjective theory of value of this kind is how knowledge of the millions of individual preferences can be obtained. The answer given by the Austrians is that subjective preferences are expressed through monetary valuations. The independent valuations and calculations of a multitude of economic agents establish a set of prices for all goods being traded. The creation of a price system is at once the result of economic calculation and the condition for it. A system of prices and market exchange then makes possible the widening and deepening of the division of labour. Once a specialized division of labour has emerged, rational economic calculation requires money and exchange. In pre-modern societies economic calculation can be rational without markets and money, because there is no specialized division of labour. Calculations in kind are sufficient to establish priorities in production and consumption. But rational economic calculation in a modern society based on specialized division of labour cannot exist unless the subjective preferences of individual economic agents can be expressed in monetary terms. In a complex economy based on the division of labour, the production of capital goods becomes separated from the production of consumption goods. Mises argues that unless these capital goods are part of the price system, there is no way of assessing whether any particular activity in the work process is necessary or whether labour and other factors of production are being wasted.

Economy for Mises means husbanding scarce resources, combining and employing resources in the most effective way possible, in order to produce what individual consumers in aggregate want most. Direction of economic production in accordance with economic considerations requires that no obstacles be put in the way of the free determination of prices. The reason why he believes that rational economic calculation is not possible under socialism is because socialism would impose numerous obstacles. Hayek defines socialism as 'any case of collectivist control of productive resources, no matter in whose interest this control is used'.[21] The reason why collectivist control is so damaging is because monopoly of any productive resource distorts the price system and prevents 'true' prices, those representing the subjective preferences of consumers, from being established. The more that decisions of resource allocation are taken centrally, the more harmful the outcomes may be, and the more the pattern of economic activity may come to diverge from that which would best satisfy consumers. At the extreme, all production decisions become arbitrary, since there is no way of establishing what the demand is for any particular good.

Mises contrasts this with capitalism:

> Under capitalism the economic principle is observed in both consumption and production. . . . in this way arises the exactly graded system of prices which enables everyone to frame his demand on

economic lines. The scale of values is the outcome of the actions of every individual member of society. Everyone plays a twofold part in its establishment, first as a consumer, secondly as a producer.[22]

Capitalism is the most successful economic system known to history because decision-taking is decentralized. Planning and calculation take place, but at the level of the individual agent, not at the level of the whole economy. As a result, the system is more flexible and pluralist than any other. It is not driven from any single centre, but from many centres.

Mises also anticipated the argument of market socialism, which accepted that rational economic calculation in a society based on division of labour required markets and prices, but argued that this was entirely compatible with an economy in which all the means of production were collectively owned. Mises thought that this was an illusion, because rational calculation depended on the existence of private property in the ownership of capital goods as well as of consumer goods. As he put it, 'the market and its functions in regard to the formation of prices cannot be divorced from private property and the freedom of capitalists, landlords and entrepreneurs to dispose of their property as they see fit.'[23] The motive force of the whole process which gives rise to market prices for the factors of production is the ceaseless search on the part of capitalists and entrepreneurs to maximize their profits.

It can be seen that Mises' argument is an a priori one, which does not depend for its validity on any actual historical examples of socialist societies. It is a deduction from certain premises about human action, economic calculation, and the character of modernity. What he is most concerned to do is to controvert the argument of the socialists of his generation that a socialist society would inaugurate a higher rationality in the conduct of economic affairs by eliminating waste and poverty. He conceded that if people wanted socialism on other grounds, they were free to choose it.

> The knowledge of the fact that rational economic activity is impossible in a socialist commonwealth cannot, of course, be used as an argument either for or against socialism. Whoever is prepared himself to enter upon socialism on ethical grounds ... or whoever is guided by ascetic ideals in his desire for socialism, will not allow himself to be influenced in his endeavours by what we have said. Still less will those 'culture socialists' be deterred who ... expect from socialism primarily 'the dissolution of the most frightful of all barbarisms – capitalist rationality'. But he who expects a rational

economic system from socialism will be forced to re-examine his views.[24]

Market Socialism

Mises' main target was Marx and the Marxists. In that sense, his original article was a further episode in the long-running *Methodenstreit*. Marx's refusal to speculate about the form a socialist society would take struck Mises as a supreme evasion, and typical of historicism. Marx always refused to lay down blueprints in the manner of 'utopian' socialists like Owen and Fourier, on the grounds that principles of organization were intimately related to particular modes of historical organization, which were always worked out practically and could only be understood theoretically in retrospect. This impeccable Hegelianism did not impress Mises, because it refused to consider the question of how the universal problems of any human society would be addressed.

One consequence of this methodological gulf between the Austrian school and Marxism was that there was no Marxist response to Mises. His criticisms were regarded as irrelevant. Bukharin had already analysed the Austrian school and marginalism as a retreat from scientific analysis into ideology.[25] Marginalism was dismissed as the ideology of the *rentier* class, because it regarded all incomes, including 'unearned incomes', as equally productive and therefore legitimate, so long as they were generated through the market.

Mises' challenge was taken up by a different group of socialists, economists trained in the techniques and concepts of neoclassical economics who nevertheless retained socialist sympathies. It was obviously important for them, both professionally and politically, to refute Mises' confident claims that economic calculation was incompatible with a socialist organization of society. The key contributors to the debate were Oscar Lange, H. D. Dickinson, Fred Taylor, and later Abba Lerner.[26] They defined a socialist economy as one in which production had been socialized. All means of production had become public rather than private property.

The task of replying to Mises was made easier by work done earlier by two non-socialist economists: Vilfredo Pareto and his pupil, Enrico Barone. Barone had been intrigued by the purely intellectual question of whether rational calculation in the way that the marginalist revolution had defined it was possible in a socialist economy. The marginalist model assumed a decentralized market in which there were a multitude of competing agents and decision-making centres. A socialist economy was conceived as a limiting case – an economy in which all productive resources were owned and controlled by a public authority, a 'ministry of production', as Barone called it. Such an economy would have a single decision-making centre, and therefore would appear prima facie to lack an essential mechanism for determining prices and therefore rational co-ordination of economic activity. The competitive market in the neoclassical models of general equilibrium which Pareto helped to perfect relied on competition between a multitude of agents to establish a set of prices based on the lowest possible cost of producing different commodities. Only in this way could the fundamental economic problem in neoclassical economics – the problem of scarcity – be resolved. Competitive markets allow a set of prices to be established which enable all economic agents to make rational calculations about their priorities and trade-offs, leading to the maximization of consumers' satisfaction within the constraints imposed by available resources and technologies.

Barone, like Pareto, had no political sympathy for socialism, but demonstrated that in terms of subjective value theory a socialist economy was theoretically possible. He reasoned that, since the logic of economic behaviour was independent of the form of property ownership, a rational solution to the problem of scarcity could be achieved in a socialist economy, provided the ministry of production was willing to establish a set of prices for all commodities. He argued that production in a collectivist regime would not be organized any differently from production under capitalism, since the ministry of production would wish to ensure the highest possible level of output. To achieve this, it would be obliged to devise rules which reproduced the two fundamental conditions of regimes of free competition: a rule to ensure that the cost of production was always driven down to the minimum possible and a rule to make prices equal to the cost of production.

It was this theoretical demonstration of the feasibility of a socialist economy which Oscar Lange revived and developed to counter Mises. From within the neoclassical paradigm the key issue was whether the form of ownership of productive assets interfered with the rational allocation of resources among alternative uses. Lange argued that it would not do so if the public authority, which he preferred to call the 'central planning board', were able to establish a market process and a set of prices to guide economic activity. In the case of consumer goods, this appeared to pose few problems.

There was nothing to prevent a public authority establishing many autonomous enterprises which would compete with one another to satisfy consumer demand. All would be publicly owned, but would have operational autonomy. Income would be credited to individuals according to principles adopted by the central planning board.

Mises himself had conceded the point that a socialist economy could choose to create a market for consumer goods and for labour services, and could allow the logic of the market and consumer preferences to determine the pattern on production and consumption. The real difficulty arose over capital goods. If a socialist economy allowed a decentralized decision-making process to determine the production of consumer goods, it would still need to keep control over investment decisions if it were to be considered a socialist economy at all.[27] But if the central authority took all the decisions about production of capital goods, how would it ensure that these decisions were rational and reflected what enterprises in the consumer goods sector required? Mises thought that the absence of a market for capital goods and for factors of production apart from labour was the key weakness of socialism, and would make rational planning impossible.

Lange's solution was to propose a central board which would set prices for capital goods. Enterprises would then respond to these, and make their calculations accordingly. The central board would learn to adjust its prices through trial and error in the light of the performance of the economy and the identification of new strategic needs. In this way prices would perform the same function in a socialist economy as they did in a capitalist economy. All decision-makers would have to work within the parameters of the prices set by the central planning board. They would confront economic agents as an external reality in just the same way as they confront economic agents in a capitalist economy.

Lange argued, as Barone had done, that the logical problem of economic calculation under socialism was easily solved as long as an institution like the central planning board was prepared to perform the function of the market and set prices for producer goods. All other prices would then be set by the normal mechanisms of market exchange. It was the logical demonstration of this possibility by Barone, Lange, and Lerner which persuaded Joseph Schumpeter and later commentators such as Charles Lindblom that the critics of Mises had the best of the argument. There was no theoretical problem of rational economic calculation under socialism.

If socialism were to be opposed, it would have to be on other grounds.

Underlying this judgement was an assumption that, since markets were always imperfect in reality, a socialist economy might actually be able to come closer to the models of neoclassical economics which assumed general equilibrium between supply and demand, perfect competition, and consequently a set of prices flexible enough to clear markets with full employment of all factors of production. A central authority armed with the insights of neoclassical economics should be able to design a market system which would improve upon the unplanned market orders that had grown up under capitalism. Indeed, Lange argued that the price system in an unplanned capitalist economy involved at least as much trial and error as in a socialist economy, and was probably less efficient, because a central planning board would possess information about the whole economy which individual market agents lacked. It had more chance, therefore, of moving the economy closer to the equilibrium. He dismissed Robbins's argument that the central planning board would have to solve millions of equations in order to determine what prices should be, arguing that if such mathematical complexity were unnecessary for market agents in a capitalist economy, it would also be unnecessary for those planning a socialist economy. They would be able to operate by trial and error, guided by the objective of reducing surpluses and overcoming shortages. By this means, the practical problems of running a socialist economy would gradually be sorted out.

Critics of Mises were able to argue that he was mistaken, both theoretically and practically, about the possibility of a socialist economy. They turned the argument around, and even claimed that a socialist economy was necessary in order to approximate more closely a fully rational allocation of resources. What they conceded, however, was that markets, money, and commodity production were indispensable features of a modern economy. They did not envisage, as Marx had, the possibility of an economy without money and markets. Yet, as Lavoie has pointed out, it was the Marxist argument that there was an alternative way of organizing a modern industrial economy which Mises was seeking to discredit.

The Marxists did not take part in the socialist calculation debate, even though it was their position that Mises was challenging. The position would have been clarified had Hayek and Mises been prepared to concede that there were more ways than one to organize a market economy, and that even an economy in which all assets were publicly owned was compatible with a rational allocation of resources in the way in which this was understood by economists. But it was characteristic of them that they were never prepared to make this concession, because they refused to accept the neoclassical framework of analysis which the socialist economists employed in the debate.

The Uses of Knowledge

Hayek contributed to the calculation debate, first by editing *Collectivist Economic Planning*, in which he sought to rebut the arguments of Lange, and secondly by writing a reply to Joseph Schumpeter.[28] He was obliged to spell out why the Austrian school rejected the assumptions of neoclassical economics, and through this exercise, he developed what became his most enduring contribution to social science – his theory of knowledge.

Hayek's theory of knowledge develops two key Austrian insights: first, that knowledge is always imperfect in human societies, and second, that the cost of any economic activity is subjective. Instead of analysing societies as if perfect information were available, the Austrians start with the assumption that it is not. Hayek extended this insight by arguing that the character of knowledge in a market economy is dispersed, fragmented, and decentralized, and that it is because it has this character that markets are able to function as they do. Every agent has access to different knowledge about prices, production opportunities, availability of resources, and opportunities for buying and selling. What the market does is to bring all this decentralized knowledge together by co-ordinating the activities of the different agents, none of whom knows in detail every aspect of the whole of which they are part:

> The knowledge of the circumstances of which we must make use never exists in concentrated or integrated form but solely as the dispersed bits of incomplete and frequently contradictory knowledge which all the separate individuals possess.[29]

The second argument about the nature of economic cost reinforces this point. The Austrians define the cost of a commodity not in terms of inputs like labour time, which can in principle be measured objectively, but in terms of the alternative output which the same resources could be used to produce. Assessment of the value of this alternative output can only be made subjectively by each individual. It follows that the most important knowledge driving the economic system is individual, subjective, decentralized, and therefore inaccessible to any central authority.[30]

If the knowledge required for economic activity is necessarily subjective, dispersed, fragmentary, and distributed unevenly throughout society, a decentralized system of property and enterprise is required in order to provide effective economic co-ordination. Hayek argued that central planning, even of the kind proposed by Lange and the other market socialists, was fundamentally flawed, because it assumed that knowledge could somehow be collected by a central authority and employed to construct a more perfect market than the one which had evolved spontaneously.

The critique of the assumption of perfect knowledge lay at the heart of Hayek's difference with neoclassical economics. For Hayek, the market was not something that could be redesigned or refashioned by a central authority to yield higher levels of efficiency and consumer satisfaction. The market was a natural phenomenon that had evolved spontaneously. The task of central authority was limited to ensuring that the basic conditions of the market, such as protection of property and enforceability of contracts, together with a stable medium of exchange, were maintained, and that obstacles to the further development of the market, such as restrictions on the employment of certain types of labour or the sale of certain types of goods and services, were removed.

The attempt to centralize all knowledge, whether in theory or in practice, was for Hayek one of the clearest examples of constructivist thinking, the main source of intellectual error in the modern world. Hayek found that he could not answer the critics of Mises within the confines of the neoclassical paradigm of economics. Mainstream economics could be used to support socialist conclusions, because it had abandoned the insights of Adam Smith and the Scottish school about the market order as a natural system of liberty, the result of spontaneous evolution rather than rational design, whose beneficial results came about through the unintended consequences of social action rather than through intellectual foresight.

Pessimism about the capacity of human reason lies at the root of Hayek's theory of knowledge. The market is the instrument for mobilizing the knowledge that is dispersed in time and space throughout society. But there is no way that the knowledge can be utilized other than through the market process itself. Any attempt to collect the knowledge and centralize it in some central bureaucracy or panel of experts is doomed to failure. Hayek was careful never to claim that the market ensured efficiency in some optimum sense. It followed from his theory of knowledge that what that optimum might be could not be known. The market is an imperfect instrument, like all human institutions, because of uncertainty and ignorance. Hayek's point against rationalists and constructivists of all persuasions was not that the market was perfect, but that it was less imperfect than any available alternative, and certainly less imperfect than what would result from the attempt to centralize knowledge required by a socialist economy, even in the modified form proposed by Lange.

Kornai, in his comments on the debate in light of the experience of the socialist economies of Eastern Europe, argues that the real problem for socialism which Hayek identified was not whether a socialist economy could set equilibrium prices, but whether a socialist economy could provide the incentives required to allow dispersed information to be utilized in producing goods and services. Kornai argues that the market, competition, and private property are inextricably linked. Only capitalist institutions can ensure that market co-ordination will actually deliver an efficient economy. The problem of knowledge, or information, is therefore a problem also of incentives. Kornai concluded that socialist and capitalist systems contain incompatible elements, and that it has proved impossible to graft capitalist institutions like markets and competition on to socialist ones, as the reform programmes of the Communist states attempted to do. His bleak conclusion in *The Socialist System* is that there is no Third Way available between capitalism and socialism.[31]

The Theory of Competition

Hayek thought that central planning was doomed to frustration, because the knowledge necessary to make it work could never be collected. But he also argued that the attempt by a central authority to simulate a market would not be successful because it ignored one of the essential characteristics of the market, its functioning as a discovery process. By engaging in production and exchange, new needs and new ways of satisfying them are constantly discovered. The dynamism of the market economy for the Austrians is inseparable from the competition between individuals and enterprises to supply the goods and services for which there is effective demand on the market.

Lavoie terms this idea the 'concept of economic rivalry', and points out that in this respect Marx and Mises had a similar vision of the capitalist economy.[32] Both regarded rivalry between individuals and enterprises as an essential part of a market economy. Marx viewed competition between different parts of capital as the mechanism by which a climate of insecurity and continual change was created, obliging all enterprises to search constantly for new ways to cut their costs and increase their profits, or face being driven out of business. This pressure was the stimulus for the introduction of new products, the development of new technologies, and the global expansion of market relationships and commodity production into all spheres of human existence and all regions of the world. It had helped make capitalism easily the most productive mode of production known to human history.

Marx and Mises did not differ in their assessment of the importance of competition for capitalism, and there is much in Marx's account of the process of capital accumulation which parallels the Austrian account. But whereas Marx thought that the stage of capitalism was a transitional stage to a higher form of social organization which would combine the material achievements of capitalism with a new community and social solidarity, Mises, and later Hayek, argued that the market order was itself the highest form of development possible. If an attempt were made to suppress competition, it would result in suppressing the market and hence the basis on which the wealth of the modern world had been created.

The existence of competition is not optional, therefore, for the Austrians. Without the competition, effective co-ordination of all the economic activities in a complex modern economy cannot take place. All enterprises are therefore obliged to plan, making use of whatever knowledge is available to them in a bid to stay afloat in an uncertain and rapidly changing world. Many enterprises make mistakes and miscalculate, the co-ordination is never perfect, but there is no alternative. For the Austrians, Marx's apparent conviction that it was possible to combine a technologically advanced, globally interdependent, and highly productive economy with a conscious central plan was an illusion.

One of the strengths of the Austrian position, as Robin Blackburn has noted,[33] is its celebration of the positive side of decentralized decision-making which market capitalism made possible. By multiplying the number of decision-making centres, market economies enlarged spheres of freedom for more and more people, allowing them to create spheres of autonomy which were relatively free from control by traditional power centres. The widening of social and political participation which the spread of market relationships made possible allows the Austrians to argue that the issue is not whether there should or should not be planning in modern societies, but at what level planning should be attempted. Should individuals be given the freedom to plan for themselves within a market framework, or should all planning be done from above by a single central authority?

The Austrian argument was strongest against those strands of socialist thought which believed that a socialist economy could be realized by replacing co-ordination through markets with a central plan. It is weaker against the various formulations of market socialism. The prejudice against markets runs very deep in the socialist tradition, as does the concomitant belief that a socialist economy would mean the disappearance of commodities, money, and competition. Socialists have only gradually shaken themselves free from these notions, although some were more clear-sighted.[34]

Reflection on the experience of the semi-planned economies of the Communist bloc convinced most socialists that any feasible socialism would have to make use of markets to allocate resources. Maurice Dobb's comment in the 1930s that if consumer choice had to be sacrificed for the benefits of central planning, it was a price worth paying was no longer persuasive by the 1970s, when the scale of waste and inefficiency in the centrally planned economies became clear. Socialists have come to accept that some form of market co-ordination is indispensable.[35] The utopian aspects of socialist doctrine were perhaps unnaturally prolonged through the establishment and survival of the Soviet Union, the first workers' state, which appeared to show that there was an alternative to a capitalist market economy. But the decay and then collapse of the Soviet system has changed all that, and has finally forced all socialists to rethink the application of their values to modern society.

Although most socialists have become reconciled to the idea of markets as an indispensable mechanism in a modern economy, they are much less certain about competition and entrepreneurship. As a consequence, socialism can still appear as a doctrine which is concerned primarily with the corporate defence of interests against encroachment rather than with enunciating principles which could shape future social organization. Yet the scope for socialist renewal is considerable, once the pursuit of chimerical alternatives to capitalism is abandoned. Many of the Austrians' own concepts can contribute to the development of a new socialism.

As Robin Blackburn and Hilary Wainwright have noted, the Austrian doctrine of knowledge is double-edged. It can also be used to criticize concentrations of power in capitalist society which restrict the possibilities for wider participation and self-determination.[36]

One of the fundamental tensions in Hayek's thought is between his conception of the ideal liberal society and his defence of the realities of contemporary capitalist society as embodying that ideal. His theory of knowledge implies that the ideal society will be highly decentralized, and that as many individuals as possible should be directly involved in taking decisions about production. The ideal individual in the Great Society is the entrepreneur – individuals prepared to take calculated risks, make full use of the unique knowledge they possess, and take the opportunities that are open to them. Such individuals will acquire self-discipline by taking responsibility for themselves and their dependants, and will develop the essential moral traits that are needed to sustain the Great Society and help it to develop.

Such a society would be composed of independent, self-employed producers, who would own their means of production and exchange their products freely on the market. All members of the society would be equal before the law; there would be no differences of caste or class; and all would participate in the self-government of the community. This liberal vision of the good society has been an enduring aspect of the liberal imagination, but it has increasingly diverged from the reality of liberal societies, which have seen the growth of new forms of organization and hierarchy which have tended to make the great majority of individuals subordinate to higher authority. Some liberals responded to these developments by urging political action to dismantle concentrations of power, both political and economic, and to distribute power and property as widely as possible.

Hayek could have followed this course, but his Austrian faith in the invisible hand inclined him to accept as benign whatever evolved spontaneously. He therefore defends concentrations of market power and the existence of large-scale companies as legitimate agents of the market process. But if transnational companies the size of General Motors and IBM are to be accepted, what becomes of Hayek's insistence on the decentralized character of knowledge and the moral character of participation in the market?

Hayek never satisfactorily resolves this problem. On the one hand, he argues strongly that enterprise monopoly is a minor problem in the contemporary economy, and that anti-trust and anti-monopoly policies are unnecessary. The power of large companies will be constrained by competition. He also devotes some space in *The Constitution of Liberty* to arguing, first, that large companies do not pose the same dangers of monopoly power as trade unions, and second, that there is no coercion involved in the hierarchical relationships found in large bureaucratic organizations. Such organizations are characterized, he says, by voluntary agreement and co-operation.[37]

At the same time, Hayek is obviously deeply troubled by the rise of such bureaucratic organizations and by the tendency in modern society for most people to become employees, and therefore dependent on others for their livelihood. Hayek sees such dependency as undermining the moral basis for a market order. If individuals do not have to face the uncertainties of the market and take responsibility for themselves, they cannot learn the essential virtues that are needed to sustain a free market culture. They cannot become independent, sovereign individuals. They cannot be entrepreneurs. The consequence is that they are likely to demand both from their employers and from the state policies to protect their standard of living and provide security. Nothing in their life experience will give them an insight into the conditions necessary to preserve the institutions on which the Great Society rests. As will be explained in the next chapter, Hayek suggests that one reason why the advance of collectivism has been so irresistible and so hard to reverse is because in Western democracies the electorates are composed predominantly of employees rather than independent producers. Only a nation of entrepreneurs could have the experience necessary to keep the state strong, but limited, and the economy free.

Hayek was himself an employee throughout his life. He escaped the fate of his fellow employees through theoretical insight into the problems of modern society. But this route is only open to a few. The majority would form their political and social views in light of their direct experiences of work and the market. Hayek's pessimistic conclusion is that, so long as the majority of citizens are employees, the chances of breaking with collectivism are slim, because there is no reason why employees should appreciate the benefits of the market system. They will tend to be much more aware of its costs, and demand policies that protect them from it. Hayek is therefore caught between his approval of corporate capitalism and his awareness that the existence of large companies condemns most individuals to the status of employees. This status prevents them from ever understanding the basis of a free society.

The market order is undermined, because of the difficulty of educating the people whose prosperity depends on it. The moral ethos on which a market economy depends becomes harder to preserve, the more successful and developed capitalism becomes.

4

Politics

Democratic socialism, the great utopia of the last few generations, is not only unachievable, but . . . produces something so utterly different that few of those who now wish it would be prepared to accept the consequences.

Hayek, *The Road to Serfdom*

The third strand in Hayek's critique of socialism was his analysis of it as a political project. Sooner or later, he wrote, socialism leads to totalitarianism. It was the message of his most famous book, *The Road to Serfdom*, and he never departed from it. Yet his knowledge of politics and of political science was rudimentary. Having spent the first half of his life as a professional economist, he spent the second half writing about politics. But he always retained a strong aversion to politics and to political activity, even though he recognized it to be necessary to safeguard the kind of society he thought desirable.

A central purpose of his later work was to demonstrate that political co-ordination of societies through bureaucracies was inherently inferior to economic co-ordination through markets. He wished, accordingly, to minimize the role of politics and government as much as possible. But there remains the problem of how politics is to be kept to a minimum and what that minimum should be. Since Hayek is not an anarcho-capitalist, he accepts that the state must have a role, but his Austrian perspective makes him pessimistic that politics can ever be organized so as to preserve the features of the social order which he values.

The Road to Serfdom

Hayek dedicated *The Road to Serfdom* to the 'socialists of all parties'. Ostensibly the book is about Britain and the dangers of Britain losing its liberal traditions and slipping into totalitarianism. But the real subject of the book is Germany. It can be read as a series of reflections on the trends in German political and intellectual history since reunification of the country in the 1870s. Germany is taken as the paradigmatic modern country, and its history as a dreadful warning of how intellectual error can destroy the basis of Western civilization.

Hayek shared with Keynes the belief that ideas are more important than interests in determining political outcomes, and with Dicey the belief that the ideas which come to dominate public opinion are the ideas that shape legislation and the actions of governments, and therefore determine the scope and the extent of government in modern societies. Hayek had disagreements with Dicey about other matters, but he agreed with him about the role of ideas. There is a curious asymmetry in his thought between the determinism of his economics and the voluntarism of his politics. He had a very precise conception of the institutional form which economic co-ordination must assume in the modern world. The institutions he advocated imposed themselves on human societies as a structural imperative. They were the product of a natural process of social evolution, which could not be radically altered except at the risk of damaging prosperity and liberty. But in his analysis of politics, this civilization suddenly appears as a very fragile construction, which can be irretrievably damaged if its workings are not properly understood and if the wrong ideas gain ascendancy.

The basic premiss of *The Road to Serfdom* is that fascism and communism are closely related not only to one another, but also to socialism. 'Few are ready to recognise that the rise of Fascism and Nazism was not a reaction against the socialist trends of the preceding period, but a necessary outcome of those tendencies.'[1] The bitter conflicts between Communists, Fascists, and socialists were conflicts between different factions of a single movement. Hayek, in particular, contests the socialist claim that Nazism was an outgrowth of capitalism. Rather, Nazism belongs to the collectivist trend that is threatening liberal capitalist civilization.

Hayek never provides any evidence for these assertions. He is not interested in historical evidence about the Nazi regime and its relationship to German capital. He proceeds from first principles.

Capitalism belongs to the civilization based on liberal individualism, which socialism in all its forms attacks and undermines. Capitalism is therefore defined not as a historical mode of production,
but as a set of ideal principles of social organization, which for
Hayek underlies the civilization of modernity.

What happened in Germany, he argues, is that a trend of thought
became established which culminated in Nazism. Those who pro-
moted this trend of thought were often persons of high morals and
good intentions. The Germans did not fall into Nazism because of
something inherently evil in the German character, but because the
ground was prepared by the embrace of collectivist ideas:

> The problem is not why the Germans as such are vicious, which
> congenitally they are probably no more than other peoples, but to
> determine the circumstances which during the last seventy years
> have made possible the progressive growth and ultimate victory of
> a particular set of ideas, and why in the end this victory has brought
> the most vicious elements among them to the top.[2]

The contagion of socialist ideas had spread inexorably to Britain
and other countries. Hayek laments the fact that all the people
whose views influence developments are now in some sense socialists: 'Scarcely anyone doubts that we must continue to move
towards socialism, and most people are merely trying to deflect
this movement in the interest of a particular class or group.'[3] The
fate of Germany should be a warning to Britain, because Hayek
detects the same phase of intellectual development which culminated in Nazism in Germany as present in England: 'It is necessary
now to state the unpalatable truth that it is Germany whose fate
we are in some danger of repeating.'[4]

When it was first published, this point of view was neither popular nor credible. Churchill used the same argument when he suggested in a broadcast during the 1945 General Election campaign
that if the Labour Party were elected, it would introduce a Gestapo,[5]
a remark that boomeranged on Churchill, partly because of the
incredulity which greeted his suggestion that his colleagues in the
wartime coalition against Nazism might be about to introduce one
of the most loathsome features of the Nazi regime into Britain.
Although there is no evidence that Churchill ever read *The Road to
Serfdom*, he was certainly aware of it; it is likely that he received a
summary of Hayek's argument from one of his staff, and then used
it to try to score a party point. In other respects, he fitted exactly

Hayek's description of the socialists of all parties, fully committed in practice, had he been re-elected, to a major extension of state powers. Churchill's enthusiasm for the ideas put forward in *The Road to Serfdom* never extended beyond rhetoric. The Conservative election manifesto in 1950 proclaimed 'Set the People Free'. The Conservative Government elected in 1951 continued the dismantling of wartime restrictions which Labour had started, but it did little to undo the extension of state powers which the Labour Government had introduced.

In Hayek's eyes, the Conservatives in Britain were more responsible than the socialists for undermining the liberal order of the nineteenth century. He referred in particular to the 'inglorious years 1931 to 1939 when the country transformed its economic system beyond recognition'.[6] During this period, the Conservatives were continuously in office, and presided over the suspension of the gold standard, the ending of free trade with the introduction of imperial preference, and the proliferation of market-closing agreements in many industrial and service sectors. Hayek argued that the outlook of the government in Britain, irrespective of which party controlled it, had undergone a fundamental transformation. It was now preoccupied with managing the life of the people.

The title of *The Road to Serfdom* echoed Belloc's *The Servile State*. Hayek quotes Belloc approvingly: 'The effect of Socialist doctrine on Capitalist Society is to produce a third thing different from either of its two begetters – to wit the Servile State.'[7] Socialists, New Liberals, and progressive Conservatives were all people of good will, who imagined they were improving society and removing some of its defects. But their actions had unintended consequences, and, if not checked, would end in enslaving human societies. Two nineteenth-century liberals, Acton and Tocqueville, had both warned that socialism means slavery, but their warnings had been ignored.

Hayek's pessimism about the trends in modern society was very deep when he wrote *The Road to Serfdom* in 1944. The road to serfdom was not a recent development. It was the product of a deep conflict at the heart of Western civilization between two sets of ideas, one of which was increasingly paramount. Hayek saw it as wrong to draw a sharp dividing line between totalitarian countries and democratic countries. The democratic countries were infected with the same virus. Germany, Italy, and Russia were part of the same civilization, and their political regimes were products of a 'development of thought in which we have all shared'.[8]

Hayek contrasts the 'abandoned' road of nineteenth-century

liberalism with the collectivist road of twentieth-century socialism, fascism, liberalism, conservatism, and communism. Why was the liberal road abandoned? In contrast to Weber and Schumpeter and the classic sociological tradition, Hayek never accepted the argument that the reason for liberalism's failure was either the nature of liberalism itself or structural changes in modern industrial societies. His explanation is idealist and voluntarist: 'A change of ideas and the force of human will have made the world what it is now.'[9] But although ideas seem all-powerful in Hayek's account, this is not because human beings are in charge of their own destinies and can fashion the world as they please. The reason why human societies are embarked on a road to serfdom is not because that is a goal that has been consciously chosen, but because human beings are ignorant of the implications of the choices they make.

One of the central paradoxes of Hayek's work keeps re-emerging. His economic analysis demonstrated that there was only one form of economic organization which was appropriate to the modern world and would actually work, while his political analysis implied that there was no guarantee that human societies would choose the institutions which would preserve and strengthen the institutions that were the supreme achievement of Western civilization. On the contrary, he detected a perversity in modern society which meant that Western civilization was in danger of tearing up its own roots:

> We are rapidly abandoning not the views merely of Cobden and Bright, of Adam Smith and Hume, or even of Locke and Milton, but one of the salient characteristics of Western civilisation as it has grown from the foundations laid by Christianity and the Greeks and Romans.[10]

What was at risk in the twentieth century was not just eighteenth- and nineteenth-century liberalism, but the basic individualism inherited from Erasmus and Montaigne, Cicero and Tacitus, Pericles and Thucydides. Individualism, for Hayek, is the central idea of Western civilization, and is the opposite of socialism. He quotes the Nazi view that the National Socialist revolution was a 'counter-Renaissance', the decisive step in the destruction of the individualist civilization built up since the Renaissance. In Hayek's view, twentieth-century collectivism in its entirety is a 'counter-Renaissance', however much it may claim to be raising that civilization to a higher level. The explicit anti-rationalism and philistinism of Nazism show the true face of collectivism.

What does Hayek mean by individualism? In *The Road to Serfdom* he provides a conventional account. Individualism means recognition that the views and tastes of the individual are supreme in his or her own sphere, and that every person should be able to develop his or her individual gifts. The implications of this simple idea are profound, since it implies that no obstacles should be placed in the way of the individual entrepreneur or innovator. The triumph of liberal civilization, for Hayek, is measured by the extent to which these obstacles have been progressively removed. In most societies the views of the majority 'on what was right and proper' generally prevail and provide the pretext for interfering with individual liberty. The growth of individualism as a public doctrine, however, gradually established institutions which created a sphere of liberty in which social experimentation could proceed.

Hayek sees individualism as closely connected with commerce and science. In commercial and scientific activity, individual innovation requires a private realm which is free from invasion and control by external authority: 'Whenever the barriers to the free exercise of human ingenuity were removed, man became rapidly able to satisfy ever-widening ranges of desire.'[11] Liberalism became the political doctrine which reflected on the conditions under which individualism could advance. It had no inflexible rules such as *laissez-faire*. Instead, it was an enabling doctrine: 'In the ordering of our affairs we should make as much use as possible of the spontaneous forces of society and resort as little as possible to coercion.'[12]

In his later writings, particularly *Law, Legislation, and Liberty* and *Knowledge, Evolution, and Society*, Hayek became steadily more cautious and increasingly unwilling to sanction any intervention that might interfere with the pattern of spontaneous social evolution. But in *The Road to Serfdom* his constructivist liberal instincts were much more in evidence. He was not opposed to intervention as such: 'There is all the difference between deliberately creating a system within which competition will work as beneficially as possible, and passively accepting institutions as they are.'[13] It was because liberalism had been interpreted as accepting whatever emerged spontaneously as both natural and right that it had earned such enmity in the course of the nineteenth century. The doctrine of *laissez-faire* suggested that governments merely needed to sit back and do nothing in order for the economy to prosper. Hayek's view in *The Road to Serfdom* was that an active government was required, in order to ensure that the right institutions were created to release all the energies of individualism.

The difference between his conception of an active government, however, and that of the collectivists was that he wanted policies and institutions which would support the essential institutions of market exchange rather than replace them. Liberalism became the victim of its own success. The enormous advance which took place in the nineteenth century was due, in Hayek's view, to the acceptance of the principles of liberalism. But the increase in material wealth came to be ascribed primarily to technological progress, and, as a result, taken for granted. Its connection with the 'policy of freedom' was no longer understood.

The idea that the rise of modern industry was a guarantee of material abundance which was independent of the particular economic and political institutions which had accompanied it became a characteristic belief of the socialist era. The growth of centralized bureaucratic organization made possible alternative methods of production and distribution which did not rely on individual market exchange. Mass democracies and modern nation-states created a political process in which parties and pressure groups competed for the redistribution of resources, using the coercive machinery of the state. In such a climate understanding of how market society actually worked was lost, and with it, any sense of what was essential for preserving and reproducing it: 'With the decline of the understanding of the way in which the free system worked, our awareness of what depended on its existence also decreased.'[14]

Hayek saw this development as the great intellectual catastrophe of modern times. It had led to the abandonment of the individualist tradition, which had created Western civilization. If there were no longer any understanding of the role played by the spontaneous forces of individual initiative in creating wealth, prosperity, and innovation, then gradually more and more obstacles would appear to enterprise and initiative, individualism would be curbed, and societies would relapse into a condition of stagnation and servitude:

> We have in effect undertaken to dispense with the forces which produced unforeseen results and to replace the impersonal and anonymous mechanism of the market by collective and 'conscious' direction of all social forces to deliberately chosen goals.[15]

Hayek's work on the economics of socialism and the nature of knowledge in society had convinced him that any such attempt at conscious, collective direction was doomed to failure, and that it would have serious costs by damaging, and at worst destroying, the delicate institutional framework which permitted the flowering of individual talent and enterprise.

Hayek illustrates his argument by quoting – or rather misquoting – Karl Mannheim, another exile from the German-speaking world, whom he regarded as a typical representative of the modern intelligentsia who had been won over to the collectivist camp. Mannheim had written in *Man and Society in an Age of Reconstruction*: 'We have never had to set up and direct the entire system of nature as completely as we are forced to do today with society. . . . Mankind is tending more and more to regulate the whole of its social life.'[16] Hayek left out the qualifying phrase 'as completely', and ignored the context of Mannheim's argument. Mannheim was comparing the problems of regulating closed natural systems such as marshes with closed social systems such as factories.[17]

It is one of Hayek's greatest weaknesses as a social scientist that he never properly engaged with the arguments of modern sociology. He seems never to have read much of the sociological literature. References in his writings to sociology, even to Max Weber, are minimal. He never showed any interest in finding out what social science research could tell him about the workings of modern industrial society. His liberal doctrine was never based on what society was actually like, but on what it should be like. Mannheim, for example, was hardly advocating that the whole of society be regulated like a factory. He was instead pointing out that the way in which factories were organized made regulation inevitable.

Hayek often mistakes analysis for prescription. One of the conclusions that might be drawn from Mannheim's analysis is that the trend towards collectivism is not simply the result of ideas, but also arises from the way in which industrial societies are organized. Modern factories and organizations are highly collectivist institutions, and their internal co-ordination does not depend on individualist market exchange. Hayek acknowledges this, but never considers its implications for his theory. He deplores the fact that most individuals are forced to be employees, but at the same time sees no incompatibility between large-scale economic organizations and a liberal society. He continues to believe that individualism can be reconciled with a society in which most individuals have no scope for economic independence. If he had studied the sociological reasons for the growth of collectivism and the appeal of collectivist ideas, he might have concluded that to preserve the kind of individualist society he valued would require positive measures to restrict the size of organizations and promote an economy of small and medium-sized enterprises.

Hayek never develops such a line of argument, because his explanation for the advance of collectivism considers only the role of ideas. If the trend of ideas had not changed, collectivism would not have triumphed. The implication is that ideas are autonomous, and that political and social institutions are a matter of conscious choice. But this immediately conflicts with Hayek's other argument, that economic and social institutions cannot be chosen but evolve spontaneously.

The conflict here reflects a key tension in Hayek's thought, which he never satisfactorily resolved. Because he lacks an adequate analysis of politics, he moves uneasily between arguing that the only institutions capable of co-ordinating the Great Society are the product of spontaneous evolution, without the exercise of any rational foresight on the part of human beings, and at the same time arguing that human beings have to exercise rational foresight and make a positive choice between the individualist road and the collectivist road, otherwise they will unwittingly destroy what has evolved spontaneously. After centuries of blind evolution, human societies have reached a point where evolution can no longer be trusted to ensure progress. The free society has to be consciously endorsed if it is to survive.

What makes Hayek's position still more curious is that he acknowledges that the dark forces which threaten the Western individualist tradition are a central aspect of Western civilization, and have developed from the same roots. Hayek always regarded this split in the Western psyche not as a source of creative tension, but as a divide between truth and error, and ultimately good and evil. It also had a spatial location: England and Germany. In *The Road to Serfdom* he discusses how English ideas of individualism and liberty travelled east for two hundred years, and how since 1870 the process has been reversed. After that date, Germany became the new intellectual centre of Europe, and German collectivist ideas, represented by Hegel, Marx, List, Schmoller, Sombart, and Mannheim gained ascendancy and began travelling west.

Hayek goes so far as to suggest that in the twentieth century the advance of collectivism placed many countries outside Western civilization altogether. Western civilization came to be represented by those countries west of the Rhine. Liberalism and democracy, capitalism and individualism, free trade and internationalism, became confined to the citadel of Anglo-America, under siege from the dark forces of German historicism. The latter proclaimed English political ideals to be outmoded, and condemned free trade as a device to protect English interests. Hayek feared, however, that far from standing firm against the onslaught, the citadel was in danger of being surrendered from within.

Socialism and National Socialism

Crucial to Hayek's argument in *The Road to Serfdom* is the claim that socialism and national socialism belong together, and that national socialism is the natural destination of all socialist parties if they wish to remain socialist. What Hayek has to explain is why socialism developed such an intellectual appeal, and why collectivist arguments in general were able to take the moral high ground away from liberalism. By the end of the nineteenth century, he argues, liberals had been 'lured along' the socialist road, with the result that socialism was accepted by most liberals as the legitimate heir to the liberal tradition. Despite the warnings of nineteenth-century liberals such as Tocqueville that socialism was a serious threat to liberty and would lead to a new servitude, the socialist movement successfully enrolled under the banner of liberty and democracy. Socialist rhetoric promised a new freedom, and presented socialism as the fulfilment of the promises of liberalism. Socialists claimed that the universalism of the French Revolution with its promise of liberty, equality, and fraternity for all citizens could not be achieved within a liberal order, because it guaranteed only formal freedoms, not substantive ones. Only a socialist order could make these ideals reality.

Hayek argues that this was always an illusion. Any attempt to make the ideals of socialism a reality must end in fascism or Stalinism. His reasoning is as follows. There are only two ways of co-ordinating a modern industrial society: administration and markets. The first involves central direction, coercion, and the imposition of uniformity. Equality is achieved at the expense of liberty. The second method involves markets, individual exchange, and maximum liberty and variety. Hayek insists that there is no middle way between central direction and competition; they cannot be combined, because both are poor, inefficient tools if they are wielded only partially: 'the result will be worse than if either system had been consistently relied upon.'[18]

It is essential to Hayek's argument that there is no third way. It

allows him to identify socialism with central direction and liberalism with markets, and to argue that either socialists must go all the
way with central direction and suppress liberty, or they must abandon it and in effect become liberals. He never confronts the obvious objection that a combination of methods of co-ordination is not
only possible but necessary, and that no system anywhere, not
even in the Soviet Union or Hong Kong, has ever relied just on
central direction or just on markets.[19]

In order to establish his case, Hayek needed to be able to show
that there was no resting-place for socialists short of complete central direction of the economy and society. The utopia of democratic
socialism was built around the ideals of social justice, greater equality, and security. But to achieve those goals, socialists proposed to
abolish private ownership of the means of production and install
a planned economy. If they succeeded in doing so, they would
destroy the basis of prosperity: 'If we had to rely on conscious
central planning for the growth of our industrial system, it would
never have reached the degree of differentiation, complexity and
flexibility it has attained.'[20] Future progress depended on allowing
the division of labour to be extended through the spontaneous
processes of market exchange without imposing conscious control.

Hayek's argument depends on two assumptions: first, that there
is a necessary and not merely a contingent link between the growth
of civilization and 'a steady diminution of the sphere in which
individual actions are bound by fixed rules';[21] second, that there is
a domino effect. Once the state begins expanding and imposing
central direction in one sphere, it cannot stop until it has come to
dominate the whole society. There is no resting-point short of
totalitarianism.

The implication of the first assumption is that socialism is reactionary because it reverses the trend which is characteristic of
modernity. The implication of the second assumption is that socialists are prisoners of a logic they do not understand. Hayek does
not accuse them of bad faith: they want to achieve what they say
they want to achieve; but because they do not understand the nature
of modernity, they are doomed to disappointment.

Hayek recommends liberalism on two grounds: because of its
values and because it alone is adequate for understanding and
further developing the unique Western civilization that emerged in
the last few centuries. Hayek's statement of liberal values follows
Mill: individuals should be allowed, within defined limits, to follow their own values and preferences, rather than somebody else's.

While he concedes that individuals may come together in an association for common ends, the scope for agreeing common ends is strictly limited. The state is an association for common ends, but Hayek argues that these ends should be limited to a few basic functions. If the state goes beyond these, it will mean that some members of the state are imposing their ends on others.

It is by this route that Hayek comes to recommend a limited state. It is the only kind of regime that is compatible with maintaining an autonomous private sphere. Any encroachment of the state on the private sphere is viewed with suspicion. The more the state expands, the more the pressure grows for it to expand still further. Hayek states that already in 1928 the central and local authorities in Germany controlled more than half the national income (the same point that Milton Friedman was to make about Britain in the 1970s). Once the state was in such a position, it controlled indirectly the whole economy. It was comparatively easy, therefore, for Hitler to take full control, because the groundwork had already been laid.

Hayek returns to his basic theme again and again throughout *The Road to Serfdom*. Socialism and individualism represent two irreconcilable forms of social organization, the commercial and the military, the system of voluntary exchange and the system of command: 'We face here a real alternative and . . . there is no third possibility . . . either both the choice and the risk rest with the individual or he is relieved of both.'[22] Military organization achieves security, but only by drastically restricting liberty and imposing a hierarchical order. If the demand for security is acceded to by political authority, an erosion of freedom and of all activities involving risk will follow.

Hayek accurately identifies the demand for greater security as one of the most powerful sources of socialism's appeal. He does not, however, oppose it on traditional *laissez-faire* grounds. He accepts that the state has a role in ensuring reasonable security to all its citizens. But he fears that because collectivists do not understand how the market economy works, they will adopt policies to achieve security which will undermine the mechanisms and attitudes on which the market economy rests. The problem is where the line is to be drawn. Communities may be prepared to sacrifice considerable economic freedom for gains in economic security. At what point does the attempt to provide economic security turn citizens into serfs? Hayek provides no clear indication, but he never changed his mind that even moderate attempts to provide greater security were dangerous if the methods employed did not respect the character of the market order. If democratic socialism of the kind pursued in England after 1945 did not immediately lead to totalitarianism, the reason was that the socialists abandoned their convictions and pulled back.

A central part of Hayek's thesis was that a centrally planned system would inevitably lead to despotism. Liberal socialism was entirely theoretical; socialism in practice was everywhere totalitarian. The reason did not lie in the character of the individuals running the system. They might be well-intentioned. If a collectivist system was deemed necessary to achieve important ends, why should it not be run by 'decent people' for the good of the community as a whole? Hayek conceded that it would make a difference: 'If I had to live under a Fascist system, I have no doubt that I would rather live under one run by Englishmen than under one run by anybody else.'[23] But that would still not compensate for the gulf which separates a totalitarian from a liberal regime. The key difference, Hayek argued, lay in the moral atmosphere, the erosion of independence, self-reliance, and moral integrity, and, most important, the corruption of power: 'Just as the democratic statesman who sets out to plan economic life will soon be confronted with the alternative of either assuming dictatorial powers or abandoning his plans, so the totalitarian dictator would soon have to choose between disregard of ordinary morals and failure.'[24] Socialism can be put into practice only by methods of which (democratic) socialists disapprove. Once totalitarian methods are sanctioned for one purpose, they will be resorted to on other occasions. The end will justify the means.

Another casualty of socialism in practice will be its internationalism. Just as a centrally planned economy cannot be run democratically, so it cannot be organized on an international basis. The reason is that a redistribution of resources is difficult enough within a national community, but becomes impossible to organize on a global basis. The disparity between different societies and regions means that the size of the transfers that would be required makes them politically too difficult to implement. Socialism in theory is internationalist, but whenever there is an attempt to put its internationalism into practice, it becomes violently nationalist.

This is why Hayek believes that as long as internationalist democratic socialism seeks to implement its programme, it will always shed these attributes and become nationalist and totalitarian. It is in this sense that he treats Nazism as the highest stage of socialism.

The National Socialists he saw as just another faction of socialists, but a faction that could draw on an intellectual tradition which included Carlyle, Chamberlain, Comte, and Sorel, and was distinguished by its absence of illusions. National socialism, he argues, is not the ally of capitalism, but its opponent. It was not helped to power by the capitalist class, but succeeded where the capitalist class was weak. It was hostile to Marxism, but what it rejected was not the socialist elements within Marxism but the liberal elements – internationalism and democracy.

In chapter 12 of *The Road to Serfdom* Hayek traces the links between socialism and nationalism in Germany, through Fichte, Rodbertus, and Lassalle, and argues that authoritarian and nationalist elements in the German tradition were fused with socialism by intellectuals like Sombart. This process reached its climax in the First World War, which the (national) socialists of Germany saw as a clash between two incompatible cultures: the heroic culture of Germany and the commercial culture of England. They despised English liberalism for its commercial ideals and its dedication to material comfort and physical sport. In the German *Volksgemeinschaft*, Hayek argued, the individual has no rights, only duties, and one of those duties was to bear arms and if necessary die for the nation:

> War is to Sombart the consummation of the heroic view of life, and the war against England is the war against the opposite ideal, the commercial ideal of individual freedom and of English comfort, which in his eyes finds its most contemptible expression in the safety-razors found in the English trenches.[25]

Hayek quotes extensively from the theorists of national socialism to show the intellectual roots which fed Nazism in Germany. In particular, he picks out passages which identify liberalism as national socialism's main enemy. He dwells, for example, on Plenge, who defined organization as the essence of socialism, criticized Marx for betraying it through his attachment to the idea of freedom, and celebrated the First World War as marking the third great epoch of spiritual struggle in world history, the epoch of socialism and organization, the first two being the Reformation and the bourgeois revolution of liberty. The Germans are presented as the exemplary twentieth-century people. He quotes Spengler in similar vein. 'Old Prussian spirit' and 'socialist conviction' hated each other with the hatred of brothers, but were in reality one and the same. Spengler dismissed the German liberals, representatives of Western civilization in Germany, as 'the invisible English army which after the battle of Jena Napoleon left behind on German soil.'[26] Other national socialists like Mueller van den Bruck denounced liberalism as the archenemy, and called for a socialism adapted to German nature, undefiled by Western liberal ideas.

Hayek uses such examples to drive home his argument that socialism is not the fulfilment of Western civilization but the repudiation of it. What he draws attention to are the strong anti-rationalist, anti-Enlightenment, and mystical elements in the German tradition which fed Nazism. But he is unable to prove that German democratic socialism was inherently totalitarian, since it did not fuse with Nazism, but was crushed by it. His main charge against German social democracy was that in its few years in power during the Weimar Republic it helped prepare the way for Nazism by extending the role of the state, thereby creating the crisis which enabled the Nazis to seize power. But historically this ignores the fact that the Nazi seizure of power relied on support from the conservative parties in the Reichstag, who calculated that allowing Hitler to assume the chancellorship was the surest way of keeping the socialist parties out of power.

Hayek pays no attention to political analysis of the shifting balance of forces and rival coalitions in particular historical situations. He concentrates solely on the broad trend of ideas. The German Social Democrats were part of the tide of collectivist ideas which prepared the way for Hitler. What Hayek implies, although he does not put it this way, is that the German Social Democrats promised economic security, but failed to deliver it. Hitler delivered it by winning the support of key German industrial sectors for a huge expansion of state spending on arms and roads, after first destroying the independence of the labour movement. A political stalemate between capital and labour was resolved in a way that benefited capital and at the same time extended the scope and range of the state.

In some of his later writing Hayek drew a distinction between authoritarian regimes such as that in Pinochet's Chile and totalitarian regimes such as the Soviet Union. He preferred the former because, while such regimes destroyed political liberty, they did not interfere with economic liberty. Private property remained, and markets were not replaced by central direction. On these criteria, however, Hayek should have treated Nazi Germany as an authoritarian regime rather than a totalitarian one. The Nazi regime did not interfere with the basic property relations of the capitalist economy, and imposed wartime planning much later, for example, than Britain did.

Hayek's purpose in 1944 was not to draw distinctions between different kinds of authoritarian regimes, but to argue that all collectivist regimes were inherently authoritarian, and that if Britain experimented with social democracy, it would go down the same road as Germany. Chapter 13 of *The Road to Serfdom* is entitled 'The Totalitarians in our Midst', and is aimed fairly indiscriminately at the entire political class. He detected a strong similarity between the contemporary climate in England and that which preceded the rise of Nazism in Germany. The younger Conservatives such as Macmillan and Boothby were all socialists at heart. The views of Right and Left on economic policy had converged. Both were united in opposing the liberalism articulated by Morley, Sidgwick, Acton, and Dicey, which once had formed the basis of English politics.

Hayek reserves special venom for E. H. Carr. He regarded Carr as one of a number of intellectuals who were playing a role in England similar to the role which Sombart had played in Germany. Carr is criticized for putting forward a realist theory of international relations which asserts that morality must be subordinate to political calculation and expediency. Hayek quotes Carr as saying that 'we can no longer find much meaning in the distinction familiar to nineteenth-century thought between "society" and "state"'. Hayek states triumphantly, 'This is precisely the doctrine of Professor Carl Schmitt.'[27] What Hayek ignores, as in the case of the earlier quotation from Mannheim, is the context of Carr's remark. Carr was not expressing a view as to whether or not it was a good thing that society and state were no longer conceived as separate, but was arguing that they were no longer so in practice. Hayek regarded such realist analysis as treasonable. He believed it was the duty of intellectuals to take up moral positions and never to subordinate their values to existing practices and trends, however fashionable.

What Carr was describing was the revolution against the liberal ideas that had been dominant during the nineteenth century – liberal democracy, national self-determination, and *laissez-faire* economics. Hayek interpreted him to be saying that this was an inevitable development: 'We know the way the world is moving, we must bow to it or perish.' Carr draws on List, one of the early German protectionists, to develop his argument (widely held in the 1930s) that the future of the global political economy lay with regional blocs rather than with a liberal world trading order.[28]

The treason of British intellectuals like Carr in repudiating their liberal heritage was bad enough. But it was compounded by the political stance of the Labour movement:

> The fatal turning point in the modern development was when the great movement which can serve its original ends only by fighting all privilege, the Labour Movement, came under the influence of anti-competition doctrines and became itself entangled in the strife for privilege.[29]

When the Labour movement was still allied to the Liberal party there was some hope, but the emergence of a separate Labour party and the growing influence within the Liberal party of collectivist ideas turned the Labour movement into a strong advocate of collectivist solutions to social problems. In this way a great democratic movement ended up supporting a policy which must lead to the destruction of democracy.

What most concerned Hayek in this development was that in British democracy there was no party which was arguing a liberal case and defending the liberal institutional framework:

> That the advances of the past should be threatened by the traditionalist forces of the Right is a phenomenon of all ages which need not alarm us. But if the place of the opposition, in public discussion as well as in Parliament, should become lastingly the monopoly of a second reactionary party, there would indeed be no hope left.[30]

Democracy

Many of the dangers which the political project of socialism posed to the liberal order came about through democracy. Hayek was always ambivalent about democracy. His writings are littered with criticisms of the way in which democracy works, and he gives at best only qualified endorsement. The key to this attitude is his belief that democracy is a device which must be justified by its results. He refused to accord it the status of a first principle. As he put it in *The Constitution of Liberty*: 'Democracy . . . is not an ultimate or absolute value and must be judged by what it will achieve. It is probably the best method for achieving certain ends, but not an end in itself.'[31] The problem with democracy, in Hayek's view, was that it was too easily twisted to become the means for an assault upon liberty. He denies that elected majorities have any right to legislate as they please if this involves an encroachment on liberty. Democracy is tolerable only if it remains within strict bounds: '*If* democracy is taken to mean government by the unrestricted will of the majority, I am not a democrat, and even regard such government as pernicious and in the long run unworkable.'[32]

Hayek believed that under normal circumstances democracy was probably the best system for choosing governments, but he did not see it as sacrosanct. In circumstances where liberty is threatened, it may be appropriate to discard democracy. Indeed, democracy may sometimes be a greater threat to liberty than an authoritarian government, for a democracy may wield totalitarian powers, and an authoritarian government may act on liberal principles. Hayek has no doubt as to which of the latter is preferable.

The distinction between totalitarianism and authoritarianism is a critical one for his political thought. His ambivalence towards democracy arises because of the strong link between socialism and democracy and the phenomenon of what Talmon referred to as totalitarian democracy.[33] A democracy will tend towards totalitarianism unless its powers are constrained by an acceptance of liberal principles. Whereas liberalism is a doctrine about what the law ought to be, democracy is a doctrine about determining what the law will be. It has no content itself. It is merely a procedural device. Hayek goes further. Liberalism, he argues, 'accepts majority rule as a method of deciding but not as an authority for what the decision ought to be.'[34] This argument appears to suggest that liberals need not accept majority decisions as binding if they disagree with them. Democracy is acceptable to Hayek only if it produces liberal decisions. If it fails to produce liberal decisions, it endangers the market order, and makes an authoritarian regime the lesser evil.

Hayek's concept of democracy reveals again the narrow bounds within which he believes modern societies move. A procedural definition of democracy as a means of reaching decisions through majority voting might be combined with a pluralist view that whatever the majority decided should prevail. But Hayek is completely opposed to this, because he does not believe that there is a range of alternatives among which citizens of a democracy can choose. The nature of the Great Society limits the choice to one doctrine – liberalism, which alone has a correct view of the scope and purpose of government. The views that other doctrines take of the scope and purposes of government will unleash totalitarian tendencies that will undermine the market order, and thereby destroy both liberalism and democracy.

Many economic liberals, like Milton Friedman,[35] have argued that democracy requires capitalism, and Francis Fukuyama has claimed that the only viable democracy is liberal democracy. Liberalism and democracy are inseparable. Hayek, on the contrary, thinks that liberalism and democracy are too easily separated, and that the most usual form of democracy is socialist or totalitarian democracy. But he does agree that only liberal democracy, defined more narrowly than Fukuyama does, is viable. Totalitarian democracy soon empties democracy of any meaning, and although ritual elections may be held, there is no true majority decision-making. Democracy becomes a façade for absolute power.

Hayek acknowledges that there is a long tradition among both democrats and liberals that all decisions which require state action, particularly those which involve coercive rules, should be decided by majority vote. But he argues that there is a sharp divide between liberal and democratic thinkers about the scope of state action that should be determined by democratic decision-making:

> While the dogmatic democrat regards it as desirable that as many issues as possible be decided by majority vote, the liberal believes that there are definite limits to the range of questions which should be thus decided.[36]

At the root of this divide are two different views of popular sovereignty. The democratic tradition elevates popular sovereignty to the status of a principle which is at least as important as the liberal principle of freedom. As the expression of popular sovereignty, democracy is not just a procedural principle. Hayek argues that this makes majority rule unlimited and unlimitable. Democracy, which was originally advocated as a means to limit arbitrary power, then becomes the basis for a new arbitrary power. Any policy or new legislation can be justified as expressing the popular will, regardless of whether it infringes the rights of minorities or interferes with individual liberty. The doctrine of popular sovereignty encourages the majority to believe that it can do whatever it likes.

Hayek opposes the doctrine of popular sovereignty, because he is deeply suspicious of all political processes, and in particular of

any political action which claims a privileged position in the ordering of society. For Hayek the organization of society is already
given. It has evolved spontaneously. The institutions which define
the market order and guarantee liberty and progress are in existence. The job of politics is simply to preserve these institutions and
to protect the sphere of liberty from encroachment. Any ambitions
beyond this spell disaster.

Hayek also maintains that since democracy is only procedural,
no particular system of counting votes is intrinsically better than
any other. Proportional representation is not better than other systems because it is somehow more democratic. The only principle
that is important in determining the way in which a democracy is
organized is that the same impersonal rule apply to all. There is no
necessity, according to Hayek, to make universal adult suffrage
one of the criteria for democracy. It may be the best arrangement,
but many others are possible. Hayek states that a political system
that restricts the vote to persons over forty, income-earners, heads
of households, or literate persons is as much a democracy as one
which confers the vote on all adults at eighteen. He does not include a franchise determined by criteria of gender or race, although
he does not explicitly debar them either. His stipulation that the
same impersonal rule apply to all would appear to rule them out,
on the grounds that all persons should be treated alike. But if he
is prepared to treat persons differently according to their income,
age, property, and education, why not in terms of gender and
race? The political system he most admires, that of nineteenth-
century England, had a property franchise and a gender franchise.
The apartheid regime in South Africa in the 1950s and 1960s could
have been defended on Hayekian principles both as a democratic
regime, because the government was elected under simple plurality rules, and as a liberal regime which upheld private property and
protected the private sphere.

Hayek was aware of the argument put forward by liberals like
John Stuart Mill that democracy was not just a procedural method
for electing political leaders, but an institutional system which
encouraged the development of autonomous, public-spirited citizens through participation in public affairs. This argument focuses
on the culture of a democratic polity – the protection of rights,
freedom of speech, freedom of association – as the means whereby
a people learns to be self-governing.

In *The Constitution of Liberty* Hayek lists the arguments for democracy as follows:

1 It is the only method of peaceful change yet discovered.
2 It is an important safeguard of individual liberty, and is more
   likely than other systems to produce liberty.
3 It is the only effective method of educating the majority.[37]

But although he mentions the third argument, he does not dwell
on it. He does not value participation by individuals in politics in
the way that he values their participation in markets. The private
sphere always takes priority for Hayek. The public sphere is a taxis,
necessary but subordinate to what is really important, the cosmos
of the market. The conclusion is that it should be limited and restricted as much as possible. The public sphere is not a sphere in
which individuals should be encouraged to express themselves:

> The state, the embodiment of deliberately organised and consciously
> directed power, ought to be only a small part of the much richer
> organism which we call society. . . . the former ought to provide
> merely a framework within which free (and therefore not 'consciously
> directed') collaboration of men has the maximum of scope.[38]

Hayek contrasts the public sphere as the sphere of coercion and
conscious direction with the private sphere of freedom and spontaneity. It follows that the former should be as small as possible,
and should interfere as little as possible with the latter. But since
he is not prepared to advocate the abolition of the public sphere,
Hayek still needs a political theory to explain by what principles
this regrettable necessity should be organized, and how it can be
kept in check.

He devoted considerable sections of both *The Constitution of Liberty* and *Law, Legislation, and Liberty* to this question. He starts from
the premiss that the majority should not be allowed to do what it
likes. Minorities need protection. If a community were made up of
citizens who were all alike, held similar amounts of property, and
shared the same beliefs and values, then the differences and conflicts that arose would be over trivial matters, not fundamental
ones. In that case, Hayek argues, decisions made by a majority
vote would be easily accepted. But no actual society is like that:

> the current theory of democracy suffers from the fact that it is usu-
> ally developed with some ideal homogenous community in view
> and then applied to the very imperfect and often arbitrary units
> which the existing states constitute.[39]

It follows that in any complex modern state the scope of decisions resting on majority votes should be carefully circumscribed, if the authority of the state is not to be weakened. The pluralism of a Great Society means that it is impossible to unify it politically except through coercive means. There is not a sufficient consensus on beliefs and rules of conduct to make the substantive decisions of the state legitimate for all its citizens. The greater the scope of the state's powers, the more it will have to rely on coercion.

Hayek's pessimism about political processes led him to suppose that once the coercive powers of the state were increased, there would be no stopping-place short of totalitarianism and the extinction of liberty. There was always a strong tendency for democracy to degenerate into demagoguery, because right came to be how the majority defined it. To prevent this, the powers of 'temporary majorities' had to be limited by 'long-term principles': 'It is not from a mere act of will of the momentary majority but from a wider agreement on common principles that a majority decision derives its authority.'[40] The problem for Hayek is that the complexity of the Great Society which he so extols rules out not only the substantive kind of democracy which he abhors, but also the procedural democracy which he favours. If a liberal order depends on there being a general agreement on liberal principles among its citizens, its prospects are hazardous, especially since, as noted in the previous chapter, there is no way, as Hayek acknowledges, that the majority of citizens in a modern industrial economy can acquire the experience which will incline them to accept liberal principles. The implication, which is never far away in Hayek, is that authoritarian means may be necessary to impose a liberal order, if a consensus cannot be created to support it. Hayek was not an authoritarian, and stated many times that democracy was his preference. But it was never his fundamental commitment. It could be abandoned if necessary.

His writings are full of criticisms of the way in which actual democracies work. He thought that most things of value in the development of civilization were the work of minorities. Majorities often persecuted or ignored minorities, and there were no guarantees that democracy would give power to the wisest and the best informed. It was this consideration that led Hayek to endorse Mill's argument about free speech. Only if there was freedom of speech and discussion might it be possible for minority views to become majority views. Hayek accepted the notion of the market-place of ideas, although he noted gloomily that the worst was always likely to rise to the top: 'In the process by which opinion is formed, it is very probable that by the time any view becomes a majority view, it is no longer the best view.'[41] Hayek shares the pessimism of many twentieth-century intellectuals regarding mass society and the domination of the tastes and opinions of the majority. He worries constantly that there are too few individuals who are able to grasp how the liberal order works. Of those who have the ability, many have succumbed to the appeal of socialism and other totalitarian doctrines. He expected that because of their commitment to rational thought, most intellectuals would instinctively be socialists, and would favour planned solutions to social problems. He saw his role, and that of the Mont Pèlerin Society, as convincing these intellectuals that socialism was based on intellectual error. But he had no corresponding ideas regarding how to educate the masses. His thoughts therefore turn to disenfranchising them.[42]

The power of ideas is a recurring theme throughout Hayek's writings. In *The Constitution of Liberty* he states:

> The belief that in the long run it is ideas and therefore the men who give currency to new ideas that govern evolution, and the belief that the individual steps in that process should be governed by a set of coherent conceptions, have long formed a fundamental part of the liberal creed.[43]

This helps define his own role: 'If opinion is to advance, the theorist who offers guidance must not regard himself as bound by majority opinion.'[44] The reason is that decisions based on majority opinion will normally be mistaken. They do not have the higher superindividual wisdom which the products of spontaneous growth possess. What Hayek is claiming is that his minority opinion, although presumably no more a product of spontaneous growth than majority opinion, does possess that superior wisdom. No Leninist would claim more.

The dispute between the Austrians and the Marxists was fierce, because both sides believed that they were an intellectual and political vanguard, possessed of a method which offered special, exclusive insight into the nature of modern society. Both were scornful of majority opinion as a form of false consciousness, and each put forward its own idea of a guided democracy. For the Austrians, much the most detailed blueprint of their liberal democracy is provided by Hayek.

The Rule of Law

The centre-piece of this blueprint is Hayek's concept of the rule of law, to which he devotes considerable space in *The Constitution of Liberty* and *Law, Legislation, and Liberty*. Hayek makes a fundamental distinction between law and commands. The law is one of the key institutions of civilization, on a level with markets, language, and money. It was invented by no one, but emerged as a result of the evolution of the market order, in particular the passage from status to contract.

What Hayek means by law are the abstract general rules which govern the operation of the market order. These rules make possible not only the existence of a market order, but also liberty. Hayek argues that freedom under law depends on two features of a legal system:

1 The lawgiver does not know the particular cases to which his rules will apply.
2 The judge who applies them has no choice in drawing the conclusions that follow from the existing body of rules and the particular facts of the case.[45]

In such a legal system the administration of law will not be arbitrary, because the general rules will be applied to everybody. No one is outside the law, because the same rules apply to those who make the rules and apply them. Hayek believes that this safeguard ensures that law does not become coercive. The only instances he cites of general rules which are seriously restrictive of liberty are rules framed in accordance with religious doctrines.

Maintaining a rule of law in this particular sense of a set of rules which apply to everyone and cannot be waived because of particular individual circumstances is central to Hayek's conception of the public sphere and the proper functions of the state. The rule of law is constitutive of the market order, and emerged with it. No one engineered it. If human societies had been content to let the two continue to evolve side by side, all would have been well. Problems arose only once there were attempts to develop a different kind of law, a law based not on general rules but on specific commands.

Hayek attributes the totalitarian tendencies of the twentieth century to a decline in the rule of law. If the rule of law had been properly understood and observed, it would have been impossible for democracy to become such a threat to the market order. The unplanned co-ordination of diverse human activities which is the hallmark of a spontaneous order permits liberty, because it reduces coercion of one human being by another to a minimum. Being obliged to follow a general rule is not coercion, in Hayek's view, but the condition for being able to exercise free choice about life-styles, work, and consumption. The principle is seriously infringed once law is defined not as general rules but as specific commands aimed at particular circumstances. This reintroduces the idea of rule as obedience to someone else's will, and removes the impersonality of the rule of law.

Hayek believes that the definition of a law excludes the notion of a specific end, but he acknowledges that a conception of law as geared to specific ends has increasingly tended to drive out the notion of laws as general rules. The rule of law therefore becomes indistinguishable from the will of the government. Whatever the government chooses to put into legislation becomes law. Many of these 'laws' confer wide administrative powers on ministers and civil servants, which allow them to make decisions on specific cases without any reference to general rules.

Hayek's main charge against socialism as a political project was that it destroyed the rule of law, and made possible the rise of totalitarianism. His objection to democracy and the doctrines of popular sovereignty and nationalism was that they legitimated the return of absolutist, authoritarian government and the overthrow of the constraints on executive power which liberals had fought so hard to achieve. Democracy was compatible with liberty only if it preserved the rule of law. Socialism, as the supreme expression of rationalist constructivist thought, removed all constraints on state power, and accelerated the slide towards totalitarianism.

5

Conservatism

I'm becoming a Burkean Whig.
Hayek, *Hayek on Hayek*

Hayek's credentials as one of the century's leading anti-socialists are plain enough. No one would mistake him for a socialist, although Murray Rothbard has a good try. But anti-socialists come in different guises. Is Hayek best described as a liberal or as a conservative, or as some amalgam of the two? The new ascendancy of the doctrines of economic liberalism in Anglo-America in the 1970s and 1980s created some confusion for ideological labels. Proponents of the new liberalism were often forced to describe themselves as conservatives, in order not to be confused with supporters of collectivism and the extended state, which is what the term 'liberal' had come to signify. Many ways around this difficulty were sought, none of them very satisfactory. Terms such as 'liberal-conservative', 'conservative-liberal', and 'neo-liberal' were often adopted to describe the new groupings, but the new liberals themselves preferred either the term 'classical liberals' (which some other students of liberalism saw no reason to concede to them[1]) or 'libertarian'. The latter became particularly popular in the United States.

The term 'libertarian', however, carried some unwelcome associations. To conservatives it suggested an absence of authority and restraint and encouragement of the unbridled individualism to which they have always been strongly opposed. Nevertheless, libertarian arguments achieved increasing prominence within conservative politics. The convergence of conservative and libertarian positions from the late 1960s onwards in Britain and the United States was widely described as constituting a 'New Right', which spawned a considerable literature from both supporters and critics.[2]

The New Right had two distinctive features: first, it was a highly intellectual and ideological movement, and second, it combined elements of conservatism and liberalism. Some doubted that the New Right had any real coherence or unity as a movement, and argued that what united conservatives and libertarians was no more than expediency, a wish to form a common front against a common enemy – the doctrines of socialism and social democracy and the institutions of a collectivist polity. Others argued that with the apparent exhaustion of traditional conservatism and the collectivist turn of modern liberalism, a more permanent interlinking of the two traditions was taking place, a realignment not just of political forces but of political ideas.

The emergence of the New Right raised a number of questions. If conservatives were making common cause with libertarians against collectivism, what had become of the former opposition between conservatives and liberals, and of the collectivist strand within conservatism? Could conservatives be libertarians, without doing violence to the identity of both traditions?

Hayek is a key figure in this debate. He refused to accept the label 'libertarian', mistrusting the degree of constructivist rationalism he perceived in libertarian thinking. But he also refused to accept the label 'conservative', appending to the *Constitution of Liberty* a postscript entitled 'Why I am not a Conservative', in which he explained his reasons at some length.[3] He could find no satisfactory term to describe the views he held or the tradition he represented, 'Old Whig' being the closest.[4]

The question is not just one of labels. The emergence of the New Right as an intellectual phenomenon in the form of various think-tanks, journals, and publications and as a political phenomenon in the shape of the Thatcher Government in Britain and the Reagan presidency in the United States was a key ideological event in Anglo-America in the second half of the twentieth century. For many in the New Right, Hayek was the single most important intellectual influence on their thinking. In important ways Hayek provided bridges allowing conservatives and liberals to make common cause against socialism and collectivism. The man who declared that he was not a conservative and could not be a conservative in 1960 found himself feted fifteen years later by the new leaders of the British Conservative party as one of the most important inspirations for their new course.

How did Hayek come to occupy such a position of intellectual authority among conservatives? Was he in fact, despite his denials, a conservative after all? To determine Hayek's ideological location requires an examination of where he stands in relation to different strands of the New Right. This is best done by first considering Hayek's own 1960s statement of his position, and then analysing his relationship to three key components of the New Right: libertarian liberalism, cultural conservatism, and authoritarian individualism.

Hayek and Conservatism

Hayek's postscript to *The Constitution of Liberty*, 'Why I am not a Conservative', is a key text in the emergence of the New Right. It refused an easy identification of conservatism with liberalism, setting out instead the grounds on which the two ideologies differed and why conservatism offered no intellectual defence against collectivist arguments.

Hayek begins by admitting that many of the positions he defends throughout the book have often been described as conservative, although he himself has always been identified as a liberal. He wishes to clear up any confusion in his readers' minds. The confusion has arisen because the defenders of liberty and the true conservatives have been obliged to come together 'in common opposition to developments which threaten their different ideals equally'.[5]

This does not mean that the two have become one or will ever become so. Hayek perceives major differences between them. Conservatism, he concedes, is a legitimate, probably necessary, and certainly widespread attitude of opposition to radical change. But this does not make it acceptable to the liberal. There is a decisive objection to it:

> . . . by its very nature it cannot offer an alternative to the direction in which we are moving. It may succeed by its opposition to current tendencies in slowing down undesirable developments but, since it does not indicate another direction, it cannot prevent their continuance. It has, for this reason, invariably been the fate of conservatism

to be dragged along a path not of its own choosing. The tug of war between conservatives and progressives can only affect the speed, not the direction, of contemporary developments. But, though there is need for a 'brake on the vehicle of progress,' I personally cannot be content with simply helping to apply the brake. What the liberal must ask, first of all, is not how fast or how far we should move, but where we should move.[6]

Hayek then proceeds to list the points of major divergence between liberalism and conservatism. Of greatest importance are their different attitudes to change, to authority, and to knowledge. Liberalism, he argues, is never averse to change and never reactionary; nor does it ever attempt to preserve things as they are. Instead, liberals are always looking to see how institutions can be improved: 'What is most urgently needed in most parts of the world is a thorough sweeping away of the obstacles to free growth.'[7]

This is not an objective that conservatives can be expected to sympathize with. Yet Hayek is careful to register approval for conservative insights into how societies have developed and their appreciation of 'spontaneously grown institutions' such as language, law, morals, and conventions, which have similarities with the theories of Menger and the Austrian school about the origins and development of social institutions. Where conservatives are at fault is that they rarely convert their insights as to how social institutions have developed into positive support for new developments and spontaneous change. Instead, Hayek argues, 'conservatives are inclined to use the powers of government to prevent change or to limit its rate to whatever appeals to the more timid mind'.[8]

This fault is particularly serious with regard to market forces. Whereas the liberal is prepared to trust that the 'self-regulating forces of the market will somehow bring about the required adjustments to new conditions, although no-one can foretell how they will do this in a particular instance',[9] the conservative is always more inclined to want to make sure that change is controlled and orderly.

The second area in which Hayek detects a major gulf between conservative and liberal positions lies in their attitude to authority. Hayek complains of the complacency of conservatives towards the action of established authority. What matters for the conservative is that authority is not weakened, whereas for the liberal the essential thing is to ensure that its power is kept within bounds. This makes the conservative an unreliable ally in the preservation of liberty: 'The conservative does not object to coercion or arbitrary power so long as it is used for what he regards as the right purposes.'[10]

The liberal, according to Hayek, has different priorities. His aim is to build a peaceful society with a minimum of force. This requires commitment to a type of order in which, even on fundamental issues, others are allowed to pursue different ends. Hayek restates the classical liberal belief that moral and religious ideals are not proper objects of coercion. Conservatives and socialists, he argues, recognize no such limits on government action.

The importance which conservatives attach to authority is also present in another feature of conservatism which Hayek observes: a belief in the existence of a governing class of superior persons, whose inherited standards and values and social position ought to be protected so that they can play a major part in public affairs. Hayek does not deny that such superior people exist, but he argues that no one has the authority to decide who these superior people are. They should be allowed to emerge spontaneously from the processes of competition and market exchange.

The attitudes to change and authority are compounded by a third difference: the attitude towards knowledge. This is the key difference for Hayek. The problem with conservatives is that they base their politics on opportunism and expediency, rather than on principle. Conservatives have always distrusted abstract theories and general principles as a guide to politics. For Hayek, this is their greatest failing, since 'a commitment to principles presupposes an understanding of the general forces by which the efforts of society are coordinated'.[11]

Hayek believes that conservatives either lack such understanding or that their understanding of how societies are co-ordinated is defective. Most conservative insights into the problem of social order are in any case, he argues, derived from Whigs like Edmund Burke. In place of a rigorous set of principles derived from a clear conception of the nature of society, conservatives trust to intuition and judgement, and believe that order can be maintained so long as authority is attentive and rulers govern with regard to particular circumstances, not allowing themselves to be tied down by any rigid rule.

What Hayek objects to most in conservatism is its obscurantism. Conservatives are not inclined to follow an argument wherever it leads, and have frequently rejected new knowledge because they dislike some of the consequences that appear to flow from it. Hayek has in mind conservative resistance to the arguments of Charles Darwin on the origins of species. But the failing is most serious, Hayek believes, in the lack of understanding by conservatives of how the market economy works. Conservatives in the past have embraced the doctrines of nationalism and imperialism, and have rejected the liberal doctrines of free trade and international co-operation. This tendency of conservatives to prefer national to international solutions to problems is rooted in their attitude to knowledge and their failure to understand that the market mechanism knows no national boundaries. This failure establishes a bridge between conservatism and collectivism, since, as Hayek says, 'to think in terms of "our" industry or resource is only a short step away from demanding that these national assets be directed in the national interest'.[12]

Hayek's conclusion in his postscript, which first appeared in 1960, is that conservatives should be accepted as short-term allies in the fight against collectivism, but that they are likely to prove unreliable in the long run, because they have only a fragmentary understanding of how social order is created, and therefore no principles to guide their political action. Hayek notes that conservatives often oppose the excesses of collectivism for the wrong reasons. In the past, conservatives have often condemned democracy, but for Hayek this is a mistaken target. Democracy, he argues, should certainly be regarded as a means rather than an end. As a method of ensuring peaceful change and political education, democracy has many advantages over other arrangements. The problem with democracy is the problem with all political mechanisms – the problem of unlimited government. It is precisely this problem, Hayek argues, which liberals make central and which conservatives ignore. This is why he concludes his postscript with a ringing declaration of faith in Whiggery, 'the name for the only set of ideals that has consistently opposed all arbitrary power'.[13] Conservatives are selective in the arbitrary power they choose to oppose, because of their faith in authority and government so long as it is in the right hands.

The liberal task, as Hayek conceives it, is to revive the case for a market order and a limited government, which was advancing steadily up to the end of the nineteenth century, but was then buried under an avalanche of collectivist doctrines, institutions, and policies. As at the beginning of the nineteenth century, there is a pressing need to 'free the process of spontaneous growth from the obstacles and encumbrances that human folly has erected'.[14]

This requires hard thinking and the return of a politics informed by classical liberal principles. Conservatism does not match this requirement. Is there such a thing, Hayek wonders, as a conservative philosophy? 'It may be a useful practical maxim, but it does not give us any guiding principles to influence long-term developments.'[15]

Hayek's view of classical liberal principles, as noted in chapter 2, is a peculiar one, which depends heavily on his distinction between true and false individualism. Some commentators on his work have built on this distinction, and have argued that Hayek's tradition of true individualism is a tradition of 'Conservative Liberalism', which combines conservative insights and liberal ideas:

> Conservative liberalism is the recognition of the limits of individual reason combined with the acceptance of the extended society, and the consequent search for the theoretical understanding of the system of rules which enable us to overcome the limits of individual reason and enjoy the fruits of the extended society.[16]

Hannes Gissurarson divides the Western political tradition into individualists (Hobbes, Locke, and Mill) – Hayek's false individualists – and communitarians (Rousseau, Hegel, and Marx). This leaves a third tradition – Hayek's true individualists – which includes Hume, Smith, Constant, Burke, Tocqueville, Acton, Menger, and himself. According to Gissurarson, members of this last group are marked by a number of commitments which they hold in common: to spontaneous co-ordination, anti-pragmatism, traditionalism, evolutionism, and universalism.

All these positions can certainly be found in Hayek, although less certainly in some others in this tradition. What all these thinkers also share is a pronounced scepticism concerning human reason and the ability of human beings to control or plan societies. But this pessimism is combined, especially in Hayek, with a deep faith in the beneficial outcomes of the workings of the invisible hand.[17] Distrust of human reason does not extend to regarding human minds as incapable of discerning the institutional pattern which will bring prosperity and progress.

What underlies this standpoint is a conception of modernity which endorses and justifies the institutional structures associated with capitalism and modern industry, while rejecting the institutional structures of the state and democracy. The first are natural and spontaneous, the second artificial and contrived. But the problem remains, as noted earlier, that the first can be made secure only through the second. Spontaneous evolution does not of itself guarantee the preservation of the market order.

Libertarianism

The objection to calling Hayek a Conservative Liberal is that this stresses his conservatism rather than his 'liberalism'. Liberals wanting to distance themselves from collectivist forms of liberalism have taken to calling themselves libertarians. The term 'libertarianism' is now quite widely used to indicate a set of beliefs which were mainly, but not exclusively, associated with liberalism in the nineteenth century, and which used to be called 'individualism'. W. H. Greenleaf uses the term in preference to either liberalism or individualism to denote the opposite pole from collectivism in defining the boundaries of the British political tradition.[18] Greenleaf argues that it includes four crucial elements:

1 the importance of individuality,
2 the inalienable title of the individual to a free realm of self-regarding action,
3 opposition to the concentration of power,
4 the rule of law.

On such a broad definition, Hayek is certainly a libertarian, but then so are many of the liberals whom Hayek would characterize as false individualists. Greenleaf's definition would take in both arguments based on individual rights and pluralist arguments about the need for the diffusion of power. It would not restrict the term 'libertarian' to Hayek's true individualists or to those who placed a high priority on the institution of private property. Greenleaf's definition also permits the term 'libertarian' to be applied to conservatives and socialists, as well as liberals. On his conception, a national political tradition cuts across party-political organization. There is no simple dividing line of ideology and doctrine between political parties.

Hayek would not necessarily dispute this. Indeed, his dedication of *The Road to Serfdom* to 'the socialists of all parties' implies it. For Hayek, the key point was not the party label that people wore, but whether or not they had grasped the principles of a free society and the public policy commitments which flowed from them. But

Hayek could never be as even-handed as Greenleaf. Although Greenleaf states that his own sympathies are with the libertarian side of the tradition, rather than with the collectivist, he presents the tradition as a whole, implying that there is no monopoly of wisdom at either pole. For Hayek, by contrast, the two sides were not at all equivalent. One was the repository of truth, the other of error.

In contemporary political debate, libertarianism has acquired sharper and more precise meanings. Roger Scruton defines libertarianism as, first, 'the form of liberalism which believes in freeing people not merely from the constraints of traditional political institutions, but also from the inner constraints imposed by their mistaken attribution of power to ineffectual things'; and second, as 'a radical form of the theory of *laissez-faire*, which believes that economic activity must be actively liberated from the bondage of needless political constraints in order to achieve true prosperity'. Scruton sees the active libertarian as engaged in a process of liberation, prepared to 'wage war on all institutions through which man's vision of the world is narrowed'.[19] These institutions include religion, the family, and the customs of social, especially sexual, conformity.

Hayek was in no sense a libertarian in the first sense. He never advocated the lifting of all restraints on individual behaviour, or encouraged individuals to dispense with traditional codes of personal morality. He was sharply critical of the ethical ideas of G. E. Moore which had so much influence on Keynes. Hayek's view was a highly conventional one. The right moral code was the one which had grown up with the market economy, and any experimentation was dangerous. Hayek regarded libertarianism in this form as another example of the hubris of modern individuals who believed that they could make the world anew without regard for the complex rules and institutions which had evolved over centuries and had to be preserved if civilization were to survive and the human race prosper. The arguments by libertarians in the 1980s for scrapping state controls over immigration, drugs, and sexual behaviour find no echo or support in Hayek's writings. He did not favour setting the individual free in the sphere of personal morality.

The economy was a different matter, however. Here many would classify Hayek a libertarian, in Scruton's sense. Hayek was closely associated with the programme of economic liberalism which was advanced by the New Right in the 1970s and 1980s, much of which consisted in identifying the political and institutional constraints which were hindering the operation of the free market, and calling for their removal. But in other respects, there is a considerable gulf between Hayek and the libertarian doctrine as it has developed, particularly in the United States. This can be appreciated by considering the arguments of two leading libertarians, Murray Rothbard and Robert Nozick.

Rothbard puts the intellectual case for economic libertarianism, sometimes called 'anarcho-capitalism', in its most extreme and uncompromising form. His starting-point is that it is possible to conceive of a free market in which 'no invasion of property takes place . . . either because everyone voluntarily refrains from such aggression or because whatever method of forcible defence exists on the free market is sufficient to prevent any such aggression'.[20] The problem, he says, is that economists 'have almost invariably and paradoxically assumed that the market must be kept free by the use of invasive and unfree actions – in short by governmental institutions outside the market nexus.'[21]

He argues that since all government actions have to be funded from taxation, they involve a system of unilateral coercion. Attempts to make governments accountable or limit their powers are doomed to failure. The problem lies in the institution of government itself. Free market economists, he argues, who believe that the freedom of the market should be upheld and that property rights should not be invaded, also believe that a defence service cannot be provided by the market but only by government. Rothbard believes them to be caught in an insoluble contradiction, 'for they sanction and advocate massive invasion of property by the very agency (government) that is supposed to defend people against invasion'.[22]

Rothbard cuts through the whole debate about the role and limits of government by proposing to dispense with government altogether and to rely instead on the processes of market competition and free exchange. He intends there to be no exceptions. All existing government services, including defence and policing and the administration of justice, would be privatized. Individual citizens would decide whether or not to insure themselves with private protection agencies. Disputes between individuals or between their protection agencies would be settled by referring the matter to private arbitration agencies. There would be a strong incentive to do this, rather than resort to private coercion, because the latter would potentially incur much higher costs.

In this way the state would lose all its functions and all its monopoly powers, and would simply wither away. Existing state controls on land use, immigration, drugs, and pornography would disappear. So absolute is Rothbard's conception of individual rights, and so sensitive is he to the slightest infringement of these rights, that he rejects all arguments that liberal individualists have used to justify state action, such as public goods. For Rothbard there are no public goods.[23] Nothing can justify forcibly depriving the individual of any part of his income for some collective purpose.[24] The collective action problems to which philosophers and economists have devoted so much attention Rothbard curtly dismisses. If individuals will not pay for a service, that service should not be provided, regardless of whether individuals can be charged for their use of it. There may be free-riders, but the free-riders did not ask for their ride, so it is unreasonable to charge them.

To critics of his position Rothbard argues that he alone has a consistent and rigorous argument:

> How can the leftist be opposed to the violence of war and conscription while at the same time supporting the violence of taxation and government control? And how can the rightist trumpet his devotion to private property and free enterprise while at the same time favouring war, conscription, and the outlawing of non-invasive activities and practices that he deems immoral? And how can the rightist favour a free market while seeing nothing amiss in the vast subsidies, distortions, and unproductive inefficiencies involved in the military-industrial complex?[25]

Rothbard's logic is hard to fault if you accept his premises. But not many liberals do, and certainly not Hayek. Rothbard's statement of the extreme libertarian position draws attention to Hayek's recognition that there is a legitimate role for the state and for politics. But what is that role, and how is it to be defined? A libertarian answer was provided by Robert Nozick.

In *Anarchy, State, and Utopia* Robert Nozick gives an alternative account of libertarianism, which avoids the extreme position of abolishing the state altogether. He provides a rights-based argument for a minimal state.[26] Nozick, like Rothbard, seeks to construct his social theory from an account of individual rights and how they may be protected from infringement, but he rejects Rothbard's argument for abolishing the state altogether. Instead, he seeks to construct an argument for confining the state to the performance of minimal functions. These functions are the classic liberal functions of defence and the administration of justice. Nozick argues that handing the state a monopoly in these areas is legitimate, because market provision will not work. The disadvantages for the individual citizen of competing protection agencies outweigh, for Nozick, the disadvantages of giving the state coercive powers in this field. This is the price that must be paid for establishing free voluntary exchange relationships throughout the rest of the society.

Nozick believes that it is possible to show that in a condition of nature a single dominant protection agency, a state, which maintains a monopoly on all use of force except that used in immediate self-defence, will spontaneously arise. If such a state were to restrict its protection to those citizens prepared to subscribe for its services, it would be an ultra-minimal state. But Nozick argues that such a state, once it had secured a monopoly on the use of force, would be obliged to extend its protection to all citizens, since otherwise some persons' rights would be unprotected, and this would itself constitute a violation of rights. This would involve some redistribution of resources among citizens, and would make the state into what Nozick calls a 'minimal state'. But while Nozick believes it possible to justify the amount of coercion and redistribution which would be involved in setting up a minimal state, he does not believe that a more extended role for the state, such as to provide welfare, can be justified, since the coercive taxation required to support it involves an infringement of individual rights.

In some of his policy prescriptions, Hayek does not seem that far from Nozick. But the theoretical difference remains a wide one. Hayek is not willing to restrict his state in accordance with abstract principles of individual rights. What is important to Hayek is not individual rights as such, but the institutional framework of the market order. Preserving the institutions that will allow the Great Society to develop in the future is far more important than applying a rigid criterion for what is and is not illegitimate for the state to do. In this way a prudential concern enters Hayek's thought, which accepts that under certain circumstances the state may be right to provide a safety net. The problem, as libertarian critics of Hayek have been quick to note, is where the line is to be drawn. If it is left to politicians, there may be a steady encroachment of state functions and state activities, similar to the process which occurred in England at the end of the nineteenth century.

Rothbard and Nozick disagree on whether even a minimal state is legitimate, but share a common desire to found a libertarian politics on the idea of fixed, inalienable individual rights. They provide the principles against which all policy proposals and institutions can be tested. Hayek offers no such certainty. The ambiguities in his thought make him more congenial to conservatives than some of the more extreme libertarians. Yet Hayek remains firm that he is not a conservative, precisely because conservatives lack principles and clear criteria for determining what should and should not be done by the state.

Neo-Conservatism

Although Hayek is clearly not a libertarian in the style of either Rothbard or Nozick, and indeed has been rejected by many libertarians as insufficiently rigorous in his commitment to libertarian values, he has nevertheless been characterized by many conservatives as a libertarian liberal, and therefore as alien to conservative thought. Hayek is criticized by conservatives on two main grounds: that he puts liberty ahead of authority, and ideology ahead of statecraft.

The first criticism goes to the heart of Hayek's thought, and has been voiced by leading conservatives of the Anglo-American New Right, including Irving Kristol and Roger Scruton. For Kristol, the battle between capitalism and socialism was so important that it made an alliance between economic liberals and conservatives fruitful. But for conservatives, socialism is only one manifestation of a larger problem, which is liberalism itself and its doctrine of individualism and self-realization. Now that socialism has been defeated, the battle lines between conservatism and liberalism have once again become more sharply drawn, as they were in the nineteenth century.

The fatal flaw in the standpoint of economic liberalism, according to Kristol, is that it makes individual choice the corner-stone of its system.[27] It denies that there is any higher authority by which to determine how people should live their lives and what choices they should make. This argument was deployed to great effect against the socialist doctrine of central planning. Many economic liberals, including Hayek, wish to restrict the operation of this principle to the economic sphere. But for conservatives like Kristol, this is impossible. Once the genie of self-realization is out of the bottle, there are no secure grounds for resisting arguments to remove controls and regulations from individual behaviour in all spheres of social life.

One of the key assumptions of Austrian as well as neoclassical economics is that interpersonal comparisons of subjective valuations are impossible. Only the individual can know and estimate the value, and therefore the opportunity cost, of a good or a service. If this is true of economic knowledge, why is it not true of all knowledge? Only individuals can judge what is or is not in their interests and has value. As Kristol argues:

> If there is no superior authoritative information available about the good life or the true nature of human happiness, and if this information is implicit only in individual preferences, individuals have to be free to develop and express these preferences.[28]

Kristol observes that this principle is central to the way in which the discipline of economics understands the modern world. To think rationally in this world is to think economically, to make calculations about one's own interests based on knowledge about other people's preferences, as they are revealed through the choices they make in the market. Economics as a discipline not only describes how the mechanisms of choice and market exchange operate; it also endorses its normative basis, the autonomous individual.

Kristol acknowledges that these ideas are the keystones of modern secular liberal society, but contrasts them with pre-modern notions that objective, a priori knowledge of what constitutes happiness for other people is possible. The view that it is not defines happiness and satisfaction in terms of the production and consumption of commodities, and asserts that there is no higher wisdom about individual preferences on such matters than that of the individuals themselves. Liberal doctrine enshrines the sovereignty of the individual as its key organizing principle – in the polity, the economy, and the society.

Hayek agrees that individuals are sovereign, but argues that individuals can be allowed to make their own choices only within the general rules which underpin a free society. Individuals cannot be allowed to choose those general rules without endangering freedom and prosperity. The paradox at the heart of Hayek's thought emerges once again. Individuals are sovereign in the market order, and no one else can determine value. But individuals are not sovereign when it comes to determining the rules of that market order, particularly the moral and political rules. As far as general rules are concerned, by contrast with particular choices, Hayek shares Kristol's view that an intellectual elite knows better than the majority of individual citizens what form these rules should take. Left to itself, the market order will destroy itself, and by the very means, the sovereignty of the individual, which is the main source of its success.

For Kristol, the programme of the economic liberals contains a fatal flaw. It is impossible to separate the promotion of individualism in one sphere from that in other spheres. It will gradually come to infect them all. By celebrating the principle that, in matters of consumer choice, individuals have no higher authority to consult than their own preferences, economic liberals have no secure ground on which to argue against the extension of the principle to other spheres. They have no other way of defining the good life except in terms of the maximum possible amount of material satisfaction, as revealed through the behaviour of individuals in the market.

Conservatives like Kristol and Scruton object to economic liberalism, because ultimately it offers a purely secular account of bourgeois society, identifying the good with material prosperity and continuing technological progress. Its concentration on economic liberty blinds it to what is happening to the polity and the culture. Kristol identifies three key inadequacies of bourgeois society, as it is conceived by the economic liberals: it lacks a religious basis, a theory of political obligation, and a means of establishing rules of distributive justice.

Hayek has little to say about religion in his writings. He personally had no religious faith. He was not hostile to religion, and even recommended it as a useful support for the market order, because it inculcated a set of moral attitudes which were useful for market exchange. For Kristol, however, religion is much more than this. It is essential for containing human appetites. Setting individual wants free, as the modern consumer society does, has disturbing consequences:

> Liberal civilisation finds itself having spiritually expropriated the masses of its citizenry, whose demands for material compensation gradually become as infinite as the infinity they have lost.[29]

Kristol believes that the dreams of happiness which secular society promotes are a sham. The search for individual happiness, self-realization, and self-fulfilment place an increasing strain upon liberal society itself. The consolations of religion for failure and misfortune and the restraints it places upon individual desires are gradually eroded. 'I want it all and I want it now' becomes the new guiding principle. Many economic liberals like Hayek might prefer market agents to operate within a framework of traditional moral beliefs derived from religious faith and doctrine. But, as he points out, they have no grounds for objecting to the secularization of society.

Kristol's second criticism of bourgeois society is that it lacks a persuasive theory of political obligation. Its moral standpoint is utilitarian. Social and political arrangements are commended in so far as they advance the public good, defined as the greatest happiness of the greatest number. What such a theory cannot offer is a reason why individuals should sacrifice their lives for their country. The doctrine of nationalism, Kristol believes, with its emphasis upon national self-determination, popular sovereignty, and the equal rights and equal sacrifices demanded of all citizens, arose to fill the void. The search for a politics of identity becomes more, not less, pressing as bourgeois society advances.

Hayek recognized the importance of identity, but was strongly opposed to doctrines of nationalism, precisely because they were so closely linked with doctrines of popular sovereignty and mass democracy, and therefore with the trends towards unlimited government which he discerned as the greatest threat to the market order. But the erosion of older forms of identity and the rise of nationalism were brought about by the spread of markets and the rise of modern industry, which Hayek welcomed as aspects of necessary evolutionary progress. The appeal of unifying doctrines such as socialism and nationalism as part of new discourses of identity came from the very success of bourgeois society. From a conservative standpoint, the conception of political identity implicit in economic liberalism was always extremely thin.

Kristol's third criticism is that bourgeois society has always had great difficulty in establishing rules of distributive justice. One solution has been to suggest a direct link between personal merit and worldly success. There are so many exceptions and anomalies, however, that this kind of approach has generally been discredited. Hayek, as noted in chapter 2, chooses the alternative route, that of Mandeville and Hume, arguing that whatever is, is just, and that there is no connection between moral desert and what people receive. There is no such thing as social justice, and nothing fair about particular outcomes. The only arrangements that can be described as just are the general rules which govern market exchange. After that it is a lottery – of relative skill, luck, inheritance, education, timing, influence, privilege, and knowledge. However gross the inequalities which the market economy throws up, they can be justified so long as they do not infringe the general rules which govern the market order. In this way private vices can create public benefits.

Kristol does not dispute the power of this vision of modern market societies. He merely draws attention to the moral void at the heart of it, and to the political difficulty of winning support for such arrangements. Mandeville was not concerned with the legitimacy of the social order, only with describing how it in fact worked, and he took great delight in showing how what was considered morally reprehensible had beneficial consequences for the whole society. Hayek's admiration for Mandeville is such that he comes close to endorsing this position, although he stops short. He treats moral bads as accidental, rather than necessary, features of a market economy.

Mandeville's observation that without the vices of the rich there would be no employment for the poor is too blunt for modern liberals. Hayek prefers the sanitized version of the invisible hand found in Adam Smith, where virtue begets virtue, through the operation of the division of labour. By serving their own interests, individuals advance the interests of all. Self-interest is here quite compatible with moral uprightness. What Smith's doctrine showed was not only that moral uprightness was rewarded with personal and material success, but that it also contributed to the well-being of society. Mandeville advanced the more uncomfortable truth that viciousness can have unintended consequences from which everyone benefits, and that this is the true basis of the prosperity of modern society. Kristol argues that the doctrine of the invisible hand is very good at describing how modern societies work, but not at justifying the outcomes. Hayek calls socialism a reversion to the ethics of tribalism, but Kristol thinks that, with the erosion of traditional religion and morality, it is not surprising if doctrines which make an appeal to simple egalitarianism command wide support. Hayek believes that the question of whether a particular pattern of distribution is justifiable is strictly meaningless in the Great Society. But his refusal to use explicit moral arguments to justify the pattern of distribution he favours is a serious weakness in his theory.[30] It means that he simply asserts his preferred distributive principle without arguing for it.

For Kristol, Hayek's greatest failing as a thinker is his reluctance to interfere with the 'dynamics of self-realization' which modern bourgeois society has unleashed. He concentrates all his fire on socialism, without realizing that the real enemy of liberal society is nihilism, which attacks culture and morality in the name of individual fulfilment. Hayek clings to the view that to be free is to be good, while for Kristol that is only so if it is assumed that all the selves that are set free are Protestant bourgeois selves with a strong personal moral code which governs their behaviour. Increasingly, however, the link between morality and freedom has been broken, and the doctrine of self-realization has led to the creation of selves that are incompatible with the maintenance of a liberal market order, because they do not accept its disciplines or its constraints.

Kristol here reasserts one of the oldest conservative ideas: that human beings are not naturally good, and can much more easily be corrupted than perfected. Hayek is certainly no optimist about his fellow human beings. But he does have a residual optimism. For Hayek, the most important cause of human failing is intellectual error. So long as the institutions necessary for a free society are established and defended, there is no reason why freedom and virtue should not go hand in hand. His main misgivings about human nature, as explored in chapter 2, are not that human beings are innately wicked or sinful, but that the long experience of living in tribes has bequeathed to modern generations a collectivist consciousness which atavistic doctrines like socialism draw upon to resist the requirements of modernity. But although this consciousness is very strong, it can be overcome. It does not have to be accommodated. Hayek believes that a liberal society in which everyone enjoys liberty is possible. The dark forces of nihilism can be held at bay.

Limited Politics

The context of Kristol's critique of Hayek and economic liberalism was the reaction by neo-conservatives to disturbing developments in US society and politics in the 1960s and 1970s, notably the counter-culture and student rebellion of the 1960s and the Great Society programmes launched by Lyndon Johnson in 1964. For the neo-conservatives, the issues of extended government and welfare programmes were important, but they were not the main issue as they were for the economic liberals. Of greater significance for the neo-conservatives was the attack on culture, which they attributed to the secular liberal order itself. Hayek's concern with totalitarianism made him an ally for conservatives in their fight against the external ideological threat to America, Soviet communism, but made him blind or indifferent to the threat posed by the internal contradictions within the liberal order itself.

The neo-conservative critique of American liberalism is in some respects an old critique, which goes back to conservatives like Schumpeter, who observed that bourgeois capitalism was destroying its own foundations:

> capitalism creates a critical frame of mind which, after having destroyed the moral authority of so many institutions, in the end turns against its own; the bourgeois finds to his amazement that the rationalist attitude does not stop at the credentials of kings and popes but goes on to attack private property and the whole scheme of bourgeois values.[31]

Bourgeois capitalism, for Schumpeter, was a transient phenomenon, because its viability as a social and political order depended on moral codes and political structures which it had inherited from pre-modern pre-bourgeois cultures and was now rapidly eroding. Unlike the later neo-conservatives, however, Schumpeter did not imagine that there was some means to reverse the process. How could populations be reconverted to religion and taught once again to repress demands and appetites? Within the individualist culture required by capitalism, there was no way it could be achieved. Schumpeter concluded that the future lay with some kind of socialism, and took a perverse pleasure in spelling out why this had to be so.[32]

The reception of Hayek in England was very different. The dominant ideological tradition may have been liberal, but the dominant party of the state was the Conservative party. Hayek spent fifteen years in England, and came to know both its ideological traditions and its political practices very well. He despaired at the erosion of the British liberal tradition, and put the blame mainly upon the Conservatives. His strictures on conservatism in the postscript to *The Constitution of Liberty* were primarily aimed at English Conservatives, in particular their traditional practice of eschewing doctrine and being prepared to trim and make concessions depending on their judgement of what the situation demanded.

Hayek's characterization of conservatism would be shared by many Conservatives. What he sees as defects, however, they see as virtues. He rather neatly demonstrates the perils of ideology and all the things that English Conservatives wish to avoid. As a result, Hayek's *The Road to Serfdom* received a mixed reception among English Conservatives. Michael Oakeshott in particular was dismissive: 'a plan to resist all planning may be better than its opposite, but it belongs to the same style of politics.'[33] Maurice Cowling has confessed that when he first read *The Constitution of Liberty*, it left him cold.[34]

The distaste for Hayek among so many of the guardians of high Tory politics in England is a little hard to understand. The tradition which Hayek claimed to be reviving was that of Burke and Hume, precisely the tradition that Oakeshott himself acknowledged as the basis for an understanding of the state as a civil rather than an enterprise association, a state whose function was enabling rather than directive, attending to the general arrangements of the society within which individuals could make their own choices, rather than seeking to make their choices for them.

Hayek has a conception of social order which gives priority to those institutions such as the market, money, and the law which have emerged spontaneously, without conscious planning or rational design. The task of the statesman is to remove all obstacles to their further development. Yet Hayek never supports the application of an inflexible principle of *laissez-faire* in the manner of Herbert Spencer. He still leaves government with a surprising amount of discretion to determine which obstacles should be tackled and in what way, and sanctions a considerable scope for government action.

Several of Hayek's key concepts resemble those of Oakeshott. Oakeshott, for example, distinguishes between civil and enterprise association as two ways in which the state has been understood in the Western political tradition. Hayek uses the terms 'cosmos' for a spontaneous order resting on general rules and 'taxis' for a planned order directed towards particular ends, which he argues are equivalent to Oakeshott's terms 'nomocracy' and 'teleocracy'.[35] Oakeshott assails rationalism, while Hayek rejects constructivism. There remains, however, a crucial difference between them. For Oakeshott, enterprise and civil association are alternative ways of understanding the nature of the state as a binding association of individual citizens.[36] The state is a civil association, which imposes certain obligations on all its members. For Hayek, the state is a planned order, a taxis, which exists within the spontaneous order, the cosmos. It is the necessary sphere of coercion, which must be limited as much as possible to protect individual liberty. These

distinctions express the fundamental difference between a conservative and a liberal understanding of politics. This is explored further
in the final chapter.

Nevertheless, Hayek's endorsement of the English individualist
tradition, and specifically its evolutionary and anti-rationalist character as the essence of true individualism, was whole-hearted and
provided many bridges to English Conservatism. English Conservatives have continued to criticize him, however. He has been taken
as a symbol of the economic liberalism which many Conservatives
in the 1970s regarded as an alien import into the party. The fac-
tional fight which developed in the 1970s divided the economic
liberals and authoritarian individualists from the 'One Nation'
Conservatives who had been in the ascendancy throughout the
post-war period. One Nation Conservatives believed in the possibility of a middle way between *laissez-faire* and socialism. They
justified an extended state, without accepting the degree of state
control sought by socialists. Determining the limits of the state was
an activity for the practical politician. It could not be determined
by reference to a body of abstract principles, but only in accordance
with a judgement of what was appropriate in the circumstances.

The argument between One Nation Conservatives and Hayek
turned on this point. They accused him of proposing a body of
abstract principles to guide policy, while he pointed out that merely
to govern in accordance with circumstances gave no clear guidance as to which changes should be accepted and which should be
resisted at all costs. The Conservatives could happily accept any
particular increase in state powers and responsibilities so long as
it could be justified as preserving the stability of the state and
safeguarding its institutions.

But One Nation Conservatives regarded a pragmatic, flexible
approach to government as a virtue. It was much to be preferred
to government by abstract doctrine. As Disraeli had declared:

> In a progressive country change is constant; and the great question
> is not whether you should resist change which is inevitable, but
> whether that change should be carried out in deference to the man-
> ners, the customs, the laws, and the traditions of a people, or whether
> it should be carried out in deference to abstract principles, and
> arbitrary and general doctrines.[37]

What underlay the English Conservative faith in pragmatism
was the existence of a stable, self-perpetuating governing class which
could be trusted to govern wisely and well. These were the superior

persons whom Hayek did not trust, since, as Schumpeter observed, they were as happy to preside over industrial England as over agrarian England, protectionist England as free-trade England.[38] Concerned, above all, to preserve stability and continuity, they were willing to make concessions and accept a drift of policy towards collectivism.

The middle way and 'One Nation' became formulas through which Conservatives embraced the new collectivist order as a legitimate expression of the conservative tradition, and then proceeded to represent it as the authentic one. But the conservative tradition, like the socialist tradition, always had libertarian as well as collectivist strands. Although the drift of policy was towards collectivism in the twentieth century, the libertarian arguments within conservatism were never entirely silenced.

The revival of libertarian arguments in the 1970s did not occur outside a conservative tradition. It was not an aberration, nor did it represent the capture of conservatism by an alien doctrine. Many conservatives saw the new libertarian doctrines as signalling a return to true conservatism, the correction of an over-emphasis upon state powers and responsibilities which had grown up during the collectivist era. The rationalist individualist libertarianism of Rothbard or Nozick held little appeal except for a fringe; but the idea of limited politics commanded much wider support. Noel O'Sullivan has shown that among the conservative adherents of limited politics there are a range of different positions.[39] What they all share, though, is a belief that though politics must be limited in scope, it is also vital to the maintenance of the kind of society conservatives want. Reversing collectivism is not just a matter of emptying the world of politics.

The dividing line between conservatives and libertarians is the importance they assign to politics. The purpose of politics for conservatives is to maintain established power. This makes all conservatives, whether they incline to libertarian or collectivist arguments, advocates of a variant of the concept of a middle way between *laissez-faire* and socialism, because the middle way is not an abstract doctrine like *laissez-faire* or socialism, but a code of statecraft and political leadership.

This point has been put particularly strongly by Roger Scruton. 'Conservatism', he argues, 'recognises no purpose beyond that of government.' No citizen is possessed of a natural right which transcends his obligation to be ruled. Conservatives cannot therefore be advocates of the minimal state: 'What is objected to as totalitarianism is not the power of the state but power arbitrarily constituted and exercised.'[40]

Upholding the authority of the state is a much more important aim for conservatives than promoting freedom. Scruton argues that constraints on individual freedom should be judged not in terms of individual rights, but in terms of whether their removal will damage society. Laws which limit freedom embody the fundamental values of the society. Upholding custom, tradition, and common culture are the central tasks for conservatives.

Scruton notes that in England conservatism has sought expression through the activity of a particular party, 'a party dedicated to maintaining the structure and institutions of a society threatened by mercantile enthusiasm and social unrest'.[41] He is concerned that the English Conservative party has seemed ready to break with this tradition by joining in 'the competitive market of reform, endorsing the delegation of power, the code of economic internationalism, the free market economy which it once so strenuously opposed'.[42] This enthusiasm for reform, argues Scruton, has led to the adoption of measures which have threatened the continuity of the institutions that define English identity. Instead of protecting this identity, the Conservative party, under the influence of the new liberalism, 'has begun to see itself as the defender of individual freedom against the encroachments of the state, concerned to return to the people their natural right of choice, and to inject into every corporate body the healing principle of democracy'.[43]

For Scruton, there is nothing wrong with state intervention. Conservatives can accept economic theories like those of Keynes, which treat interference by the state in market processes as a social and economic necessity. He contrasts the political understanding of the conservative with the value-free science of economics paraded by Hayek and the economic liberals. Scruton ends up with his own version of the middle way. He rejects the idea that the choice lies between individualism and socialism. He rejects the claims of Nozick that all taxation beyond that necessary to fund the minimal state is inherently unjust. To concede such an argument, says Scruton, would be to abolish the conservative enterprise, because it would destroy the web of obligations by which citizens are bound to one another and to the state.

Nevertheless, Scruton reaches similar policy conclusions to the libertarians, on many issues, such as progressive taxation and public ownership. The difference is that his arguments are always political. The reason for opposing progressive taxation, for example, is that it destroys the bonds between the state and its more successful citizens. He derives his political principles not from the organization of the market, but from the organization of the state.

The problem for conservatives in a world of big government, the extended state, and collectivist institutions is how the conditions for the practice of limited politics can be restored without endangering the society that conservatives wish to preserve. This has led to very different assessments of the association between conservatism and libertarianism. For Conservatives as far apart in other respects as Roger Scruton and Ian Gilmour, the rise of libertarianism threatens to infect the Conservative party with doctrinal and ideological politics. The true purpose of conservatism, the governing of an existing society, is subordinated to the reshaping of that society in line with the requirements of free market doctrines.

Noel O'Sullivan has argued that conservatism went astray when it abandoned its concern for limited politics. The requirements for limited politics are a mixed or balanced constitution, the rule of law, an independent judiciary, a system of representative government, the institution of private property, and a foreign policy aimed at preserving national independence. He argues that both collectivist conservatism and the new libertarian conservatism are guilty of placing economic goals ahead of political goals. Instead of concerning itself with the constitutional requirements of limited politics, conservatism has sought to promote 'growth' or 'enterprise'.[44]

These criticisms appear to place Hayek outside the conservative tradition. He may have some conservative insights, into the nature of knowledge in society, for example, but he remains wedded to a view of society which puts goals such as economic freedom above goals determined through the activity of politics itself.

The most determined (although ultimately unsuccessful) effort to rescue Hayek was made by Shirley Letwin. She argued that there is a means of reconciling libertarianism and conservatism.[45] The dilemma between freedom and order is a false dilemma. So long as the order which conservatives seek is the order of a civil association, then order is not a constraint on freedom, but rather the condition for the exercise of it:

> The Conservative individualist wants something more than the absence of anarchy. Men who value their individuality as the essence of their humanity want not only to live together in peace and without fear of interference or intimidation. They want also to preserve

and make use of the resources made available by civilisation for
cultivating individuality and pursuing a variety of activities. The
kind of security that the Conservative individualist wants can only
be found in an order that rests on tradition and authority.[46]

Letwin claimed that Hayek's concept of freedom is not an abstract concept, but is similar to Oakeshott's concept of a civil association. Oakeshott, no less than Hayek, attempted to set bounds to
what politics could and could not attempt. Both were concerned
with seeking to make certain types of politics illegitimate. Even if
their basic understanding of politics was different, they could perhaps agree substantially on the social and political arrangements
they thought desirable.

The difficulty with the concept of civil association, or nomocratic
order, is that the precise bounds of this government remain vague.
To what extent should the state seek to widen opportunities and
ensure that all citizens have the means to cultivate their individuality? And how can the traditions and practice of a civil association
be restored once different styles of politics have gained ascendancy? As Letwin says:

> since what had been lost had never been explicitly recognised to
> exist, anyone who tries now to defend traditional British practices
> lacks a familiar language in which to do so. If he attempts to give
> coherent expression to his beliefs, he appears to be a utopian
> innovator.[47]

There was no shortage of 'utopian innovators' among the libertarians. The difficulty for conservatives in the 1970s was that, in
order to practise limited politics once more, what seemed required
for a time was a politics that was far from limited. If the order of
the civil association had been so corrupted by the evils which both
conservative and liberal strands in the New Right diagnosed, there
needed to be a period of struggle and reconstruction. The problem
for both Oakeshottian conservatism and Hayekian liberalism was
that such a project was a rationalist enterprise of the kind with which
radical politics has always been familiar, but which they had always
deplored.

J. H. Grainger has described the strength of the old constitutional state which Conservatives sought to defend: the 'unques-
tioned, safe, insular patria', which 'absorbed intelligentsia and
dissidence', 'dissolved all vain imaginings', and proved highly re-
sistant to 'presumptuous will', even of radical governments. In this

state the task of the Conservative party was simple. It was 'to put sand in the bearings of ideology, to salvage what it could from other wrecked enterprises, to correct, adjust, and moderate' – above all, to take over and keep the old constitutional state. This was the party that was the custodian of England, the embodiment of English civil society, a party 'innocent of ideology, avid only for office', a party 'never captured by a single branching idea'.[48]

What the English Conservatives stumbled upon in the 1970s was a new policy, a new doctrine, and a new ethic. As Grainger put it, they found themselves governing in the light of 'abstract principles and arbitrary general doctrines'. They were obliged to use the state to restore its authority, and to use it against enemies within and without. 'In dangerous times', wrote Grainger, 'the Conservative party is the appropriate party to sustain the country's institutions, to use the authority of the state.' But he believed that in the transition from freedom to the patria, Conservatives would 'recover maxims for public life more in keeping with their historical character than those lying behind liberal economics'.[49]

To restore limited politics, the Conservatives had to abandon limited politics. To challenge the 'Great Settlement of 1945–50', Conservatives had to become mould-breakers and iconoclasts. In this enterprise, the Conservatives were aided by the libertarians and economic liberals, who provided them with maps and plans for reconstructing every public and private institution. But these other groups proved dangerous allies. Libertarians and conservatives have different objectives. What some conservatives came to fear was that the attempt to set the economy free, as Hayek prescribed, required a progressive extension of the reach of government. In one of his essays, Oakeshott retells the story of the tower of Babel to illustrate the folly of conceiving of the state as an enterprise. The New Right utopia, for which Hayek was such an inspiration, has come to be regarded by many conservatives as a tower of Babel that will never be completed, but which is destroying English conservatism in the attempt to build it.[50]

6

A Constitution for Liberty

•

Although I profoundly believe in the basic principles of democracy as the only effective method which we have yet discovered of making peaceful change possible, and am therefore much alarmed by the evident growing disillusionment about it as a desirable *method* of government, much assisted by the increasing abuse of the word to indicate supposed *aims* of government – I am becoming more and more convinced that we are moving towards an impasse from which political leaders will offer to extricate us by desperate means.

Hayek, *Law, Legislation, and Liberty*

Hayek's relationship to Conservatives and conservatism was always ambivalent. Temperamentally, he was more a liberal than a conservative. He thought that ideas were more important than interests or circumstances in shaping events and determining outcomes, and that there were good and bad ideas. The crucial question in politics, therefore, was whether good ideas would prevail over bad ideas. The test of a good idea, for Hayek, was whether it was based on universally valid moral principles and on a scientific understanding of the nature of society.

This side of Hayek as preacher and proselytizer offended many Conservatives, and convinced them that he was not one of them. They saw him as a doctrinaire liberal of the old *laissez-faire* school whose iron certainties Keynes had successfully subverted. For these Conservatives, Hayek's message sounded like a message from a different time, with little relevance to contemporary problems. For a long while Hayek was noted but ignored. But this changed in the 1970s, when Hayek's doctrines came to be viewed by many traditional Conservatives as not just antiquated, but dangerous. In the crusading, revivalist atmosphere of the New Right in the 1970s and 1980s, other Conservatives found Hayek's moral certainty appealing, however, because it supplied a set of principles from which to criticize and refashion contemporary conservatism, tarnished from years of drift and retreat.

Hayek was not always a crusader for liberty. During the first half of his life, the controversies in which he engaged were primarily confined to the academy. He became involved in the argument over whether rational economic calculation was possible in a socialist economy, and also in that regarding the appropriate policy response to the Great Depression of the 1930s. But although singled out for attack by John Strachey in *The Nature of Capitalist Crisis*, Hayek was little known outside the circle of economic specialists. It was the unexpected success of *The Road to Serfdom* which propelled him into a more public role. In the second half of his career, Hayek became an active publicist for his brand of liberalism. This brought him a measure of public exposure and public notoriety, as well as some public honours. By the time of his death, he had become an ideological icon, a representative thinker of the twentieth century.

Hayek's willingness to adopt the role of ideologue came about because of his growing conviction that civilization was threatened by catastrophe, and that only a concerted effort by liberals would ensure that a free society survived. This theme is central to *The Road to Serfdom*, but it is present in many other lectures and articles which Hayek wrote during the war. The intensity of the struggle with Nazism was seen by many as a struggle between good and evil, between the forces of civilization and the forces of darkness. Hayek agreed with this characterization, but he also observed that the forces of civilization were themselves infected by the same doctrines which had led to Nazism. Seeing the battle as a battle between ideas, Hayek began to urge that the guardians of Western civilization bestir themselves before it was too late and purge their societies of the tendencies and false ideas which, if left unchecked, would lead to the same disasters as those in Germany and Russia.

Hayek's call to arms can be glimpsed in many of his writings at this time. He wanted, above all, to rally the intellectual defenders of the free society, recognizing that it could not be defended by economists alone. The insights of historians, lawyers, and philosophers were also needed. Hayek began discussing with a number of colleagues, including the economic historian Sir John Clapham, the possibility of forming a more active intellectual group to campaign for the idea of a free society when the battle against Nazism had been won. This idea had an antecedent in the meeting which took place in Paris in 1938 to discuss the crisis of liberalism in Europe. Le Colloque Walter Lippmann had been organized by Louis Rougier around the themes of Lippmann's book *The Good Society*, which had been published in 1937. Participants in the conference included Lippmann, Raymond Aron, Jacques Rueff, Wilhelm Ropke, Mises, and Hayek. Lippmann, Hayek, and Ropke were given the task respectively of founding American, British, and Swiss sections of the new organization.[1]

This plan quickly lapsed once war began, and no further meetings were held. But the meeting marked an important stage in Hayek's developing interest in the cause of liberalism. One of the conclusions of this meeting was that liberal fortunes had sunk so low that there was a pressing need for some new positive, popular statements of liberal philosophy. Both Hayek and Mises were to produce such statements in the next few years, but, surprisingly, it was Hayek who wrote the book that captured a wide readership. This catapulted him into new fame and notoriety.[2]

Many of the ideas expressed in *The Road to Serfdom* were common currency among the liberals who gathered for the Walter Lippmann Colloque, but Hayek gave them a special twist. Part of the novelty of his argument lay in his assertion that the victory against Nazism was not the end, but the beginning, of the struggle to reassert the principles of a free society. The conditions of the victory, particularly the alliance with the Soviet Union and the nature of the war economy, with its heavy reliance upon organization and planning, had reinforced the collectivist trends evident in all industrial societies by legitimating an extended role for the state. Hayek believed that these trends must be reversed if a free society was to survive. Nazism was merely one of the hydra heads of collectivism which had to be slain. The other heads were, if anything, more dangerous, because they were being presented as the affirmation of Western principles and values, rather than their negation.

A Liberal International

Hayek's desire to rally liberals to defend the free society against collectivism took practical shape in the organization of the Mont

Pèlerin Society, named after the hotel where the first meeting took place in 1947. Hayek had wanted to call it the Acton–Tocqueville Society, after the two nineteenth-century liberals he most admired. There was also a suggestion that the name of Jacob Burckhardt be added to the title as well. In the end, the simpler name of Mont Pèlerin was preferred.

The idea for a liberal international was explored by Hayek in a talk he gave to a meeting of the Political Society chaired by Sir John Clapham at King's College, Cambridge, on 28 February 1944, entitled 'Historians and the Future of Europe'. The paper starts from the premiss that unless Germany can be rescued for Western civilization after the war, the survival of that civilization in the whole of Europe may be at risk. In the task of re-education of the German people, historians would play a decisive part, just as they had played a decisive part in creating 'the veneration for the power state and the expansionist ideas which created modern Germany'.[3] Acton had remarked on 'the garrison of German historians' who had 'prepared the German supremacy together with their own and now hold Berlin like a fortress'.[4]

Hayek foresaw that during Germany's reconstruction there would be a struggle as to which ideas would triumph – new political myths or the truth. The outcome would depend on which school of historians 'will gain the ear of the people'. The most difficult problem, he thought, would be 'to recreate in Germany the belief in the existence of an objective truth, of the possibility of a history which is not written in the service of a particular interest'. But objective truth does not, for Hayek, imply neutrality or the suspension of judgement. On the contrary, he believed passionately that no historical teaching can be effective 'without passing implicit or explicit judgements and that its effects will depend very largely on the moral standards which it applies'.[5]

Hayek here displays a characteristic feature of all his writing. He believes both that scientific enquiry can be value-free and objective and at the same time that the social scientist armed with the insights stemming from his inquiries has a duty to be committed. Germany's misfortune, according to Hayek, was that its intellectuals were either partisans who imported their values and interests into their scientific work or disinterested scientists who adopted a stance of ethical neutrality in regard to practical questions and declared themselves unable to pronounce on whether one outcome was preferable to another. Hayek's position is clear:

I cannot see that the most perfect respect for truth is in any way incompatible with the application of very rigorous moral standards in our judgement of historical events ... the future historian must have the courage to say that Hitler was a bad man, or else the time he spends on 'explaining' him will only serve to the glorification of his misdeeds.[6]

A good dose of Whig history is what Hayek recommends for the Germans, and for the English too. Lord Acton is for Hayek the quintessential historian, because of the consistency with which he applies universal moral standards to all times and conditions. In his Cambridge paper, Hayek suggested that the best way to encourage the development of the right kind of historical studies in Germany would be to form an Acton Society, an international association of historians who accepted Acton's principles and historical methods. Hayek's reasons for choosing Acton reveal much about his own position:

There are many features united in the figure of Lord Acton that make him almost uniquely suitable as such a symbol. He was, of course, half German by education and more than half German in his training as a historian, and the Germans, for that reason, regard him almost as one of themselves. At the same time he unites, as perhaps no other recent figure, the great English liberal tradition with the best there is in the liberal tradition of the Continent – always using 'liberal' in its true and comprehensive sense, ... one to whom individual liberty is of supreme value and 'not a means to a higher political end'.[7]

Acton, Tocqueville, and Burckhardt are the three patron saints of Hayek's liberal international. What they share, according to Hayek, is an emphasis on power as the arch-evil, opposition to centralism, and a predilection for states which are both small and multinational. These three, he argues, would provide 'the kind of basic political ideals under whose inspiration history might give the future Europe the political re-education which it needs'.[8] The tradition they embody is the tradition of Edmund Burke, the political philosopher who, according to Acton, 'at his best was England at its best'.[9]

Acton's moral certainty chimes with Hayek's own. He quotes from the famous passage in one of Acton's letters about the nature of power and those who seek it:

Power tends to corrupt and absolute power corrupts absolutely. Great men are almost always bad men, even when they exercise influence and not authority: still more when you superadd the tendency or certainty of corruption by authority. There is no worse heresy than that the office sanctifies the holder of it.[10]

Hayek shared the same suspicion of political leaders and the activity of politics throughout his life. Although he was to became an intellectual guide for many political leaders, he himself placed few hopes in politics. By contrast, his faith in intellectuals and teachers was unbounded:

It is because, whether he wills it or not, the historian shapes the political ideals of the future, that he himself must be guided by the highest ideals and keep free from the political disputes of the day. The higher the ideals which guide him, and the more he can keep independent from political movements aiming at immediate goals, the more he may hope in the long run to make possible many things for which the world may not yet be ready.[11]

This vision, enunciated in 1944, reflects the role that Hayek had begun to see for himself. At the end of his Cambridge talk, he asked his audience for their reaction to his idea of setting up a society to forge contacts between representative liberals from different countries and different disciplines, and to do it under the name of Lord Acton. It seems that, at first, he thought of this initiative as a limited project, from which he would later return to his role as an academic economist. But once this enterprise got under way, it came to absorb him completely.

The Mont Pèlerin Society

Hayek delivered the opening address at the first Mont Pèlerin Conference in 1947. It is a defiant call to arms, remarkable for its certainty that liberalism, far from being vanquished in the battle of ideas, has the potential to rise again and reclaim its central position as the dominant public philosophy of Western civilization. But he warned that the task would not be easy:

If the ideals which I believe unite us . . . are to have any chance of revival, a great intellectual task must be performed. This task involves both purging traditional liberal theory of certain accidental accretions which have become attached to it in the course of time, and also facing up to some real problems which an over-simplified liberalism has shirked or which have become apparent only since it has turned into a somewhat stationary and rigid creed.[12]

The problem facing liberals, Hayek argued, was that they were few and were often isolated within their countries and their academic disciplines.[13] Ways must be found of linking these people and providing opportunities for them to share their experiences and different insights. Those who had experienced totalitarian regimes often had a sharper sense of the conditions and values of a free society. Many liberals in England and America were less ready to think deeply, and, as a result, were prepared to compromise, taking the 'accidental historical form of a liberal society which they have known as the ultimate standard'.[14]

Sharing the insights of different disciplines was equally important. Hayek encouraged historians and philosophers to participate in the redefinition of liberalism, to supplement the efforts of students of economics and politics. Being expert in one discipline was no longer enough. Liberalism required an interdisciplinary effort if it was to be relaunched. While the subject specialist might be able to recognize the beliefs which led to an acceptance of totalitarianism, ideas from other disciplines might be accepted uncritically.

The purpose of the Mont Pèlerin Society was therefore to combat the effects of academic specialization by encouraging an exchange between the representatives of many different disciplines. He singled out two key topics for the conference to focus on in its discussions. The first was the relation between free enterprise and a competitive order and the elements of a programme of a liberal economic policy. The second was the anti-liberal ideas of historical inevitability and historical relativism, the first denying any role to human agency and encouraging a mood of fatalism and despair, the second denying the relevance of any moral criterion except what was successful. Both these notions stemmed in Hayek's view from emphasizing 'material necessity as against the power of ideas to shape our future'.[15]

Hayek attributes many of the setbacks to the liberal cause to the ascendancy of the tradition of false liberalism, the tradition of liberal rationalism which was fed from Hegelianism and positivism. True liberalism, the liberalism of the Scottish Enlightenment and Acton, Tocqueville, and Humboldt, was overshadowed, but its recovery was the basis for reconstructing liberalism as the doctrine which is humble about the powers of human reason, and which 'regards with reverence those spontaneous social forces through which the individual creates things greater than he knows'.[16] In rejecting the intolerant rationalism of the liberal tradition, Hayek sees the prospect for a reconciliation between the forces of true liberalism and Christianity.

In order to make the Mont Pèlerin Society effective, Hayek proposed that its membership be closed, open only to those who already shared certain common convictions. The Society was to be a vanguard of intellectuals, charged with reviving true liberalism and popularizing it. This task of the Society – re-establishing liberalism as the public doctrine of Western civilization – also became the guiding principle of Hayek's life. As he put it in an essay on Leonard Read, the supreme need was to defend Western civilization against intellectual error.[17]

The intensity with which Hayek pursued this personal crusade alienated many liberals who might otherwise have been sympathetic. A famous incident occurred in 1955, at a world congress of intellectuals from Western democracies held in Milan on the theme of 'The Future of Freedom'. Amongst those attending were Hugh Gaitskell, Richard Crossman, Michael Polanyi, Colin Clark, Sidney Hook, Arthur Schlesinger, Raymond Aron, Bertrand de Jouvenel, and Hayek. According to Seymour Martin Lipset's account of the conference, despite the apparent differences in views represented, there was little disagreement. This was evidently too much for Hayek:

> On the last day of the week-long conference . . . Professor Hayek, in a closing speech, attacked the delegates for preparing to bury freedom instead of saving it. He alone was disturbed by the general temper. What bothered him was the general agreement among the delegates, regardless of political belief, that the traditional issues separating the left and right had declined to comparative insignificance. In effect all agreed that the increase in state control which had taken place in various countries would not result in a decline in democratic freedom. The socialists no longer advocated socialism; they were as concerned as the conservatives with the danger of an all-powerful state. The ideological issues dividing left and right had been reduced to a little more or a little less government ownership and economic planning. No-one seemed to believe that it really made much difference which political party controlled the domestic policies of individual nations. Hayek, honestly believing that state intervention is bad and inherently totalitarian, found himself in a small

minority of those who still took the cleavages within the democratic camp seriously.[18]

Hayek's differences with the majority at this conference were based on his conviction that they did not understand the basis of Western civilization and were not prepared to defend it vigorously enough against the challenges which it faced. Western intellectuals were too ready to make concessions to critics of the West and its ideals. Hayek was convinced that the liberal tradition had to be purged of its false doctrines and relaunched if it was to regain its authority and provide a new direction for public affairs. This position was often derided as seeking a return to *laissez-faire*. But Hayek's position was always much more complex than that. He was a strong critic of *laissez-faire*, which for him stemmed directly from the false rationalism of constructivist liberalism.

Hayek's position cannot be properly understood except in the context of his anti-rationalist, evolutionary social theory. He did not oppose a role for the state; on the contrary, he thought that the state performed certain necessary functions.[19] He was not in favour of the state being weak. To perform its functions effectively, the state needed to be strong. It had to police the market order, maintain the value of money, protect life and property, and enforce contracts and torts. Outside its legitimate sphere, the power of the state needed to be carefully controlled and monitored; but inside that sphere, its power should be unlimited. This sphere of legitimate state action was the guarantor of the set of rules which made a market order and therefore civilization itself possible. If all citizens were to enjoy personal freedom, the natural tendency of individuals to coerce, defraud, and oppress one another must be restrained by a superior coercive power, and that could be provided only by the state.

Libertarian critics have always been quick to note Hayek's ambivalence about the state, arguing that it stems from his unwillingness to base his case for personal freedom on rational choice arguments. Instead, contrary to his stress on methodological individualism for the analysis of social phenomena, Hayek believes that what is most important for personal freedom is the institutional framework which guarantees the market order.[20] This institutional order is not the product of rational choice, because human beings cannot know enough to will it rationally. It has evolved out of the experience and choices and experiments of many generations. The problem, for Hayek, is how to preserve this unique structure on which civilization depends for future generations. He is as suspicious of rational choice arguments as he is of collectivist arguments. Both are constructivist, because both defer to the sovereign power of reason of the present generation of individuals.

The implication of this view is that Hayek must place his trust in an elite which is wise enough to govern in such a way that the basic essentials of the market order are preserved. Hayek's dilemma is that he does not believe that there is any reason why such an elite, even if it exists, should be entrusted with government. In any case, such an elite is always likely to be outbid by those who promise either liberation from existing constraints or the use of collective power to raise everyone to a higher standard of living.

Hayek's problem is a familiar one. He had no doubt what the essentials of Western civilization were and what kind of policy was needed to safeguard the future. But the operations of the political system, particularly the operation of mass democracy, had created a style of government that was inimical to it. To reverse this trend might require a return to political authoritarianism, which in extreme cases of collectivist penetration, as in Chile in 1973, or collectivist threat, as in Spain in 1936, Hayek thought justifiable. The only alternative was a radical restructuring of democracy itself.

Hayek was already aware of the need for such a restructuring of democracy in *The Road to Serfdom* and *The Constitution of Liberty*, but he does not address the problem in any detail. In *The Road to Serfdom* he argues that the chief problem with democracy as a doctrine about how government should be organized is that it encourages the unfounded belief that, so long as the source of power is the will of the majority, that power cannot be arbitrary. For Hayek the reverse is the case. 'It is not the source but the limitation of power which prevents it from being arbitrary.'[21]

Law and Government

In *The Constitution of Liberty* he develops this theme, by exploring the history of constitutional thinking and the various attempts made to constrain the powers of the state. Gradually there emerged a conception of the state which separated law from government. The distinction between a government of laws and a government of office-holders depended on a prior distinction between law as a set of commands and law as general rules. Only when the latter became the dominant form of law was there a possibility of establishing a rule of law in Hayek's sense.[22]

The path towards the creation of a public realm in which the offices of state were separate from the office-holders and in which the personal will and commands of the rulers were less important than the enforcement of a system of general rules was slow and tortuous. The elimination of arbitrary elements from systems of government and their replacement by rules which were known to everybody and applied to everybody, so that individuals could make plans with some certainty, was resisted by established power.

Hayek argues that the process of overcoming that resistance started with the Greeks. It was they who first formulated the principle of the rule of law in the concept of isonomy – governance in accordance with known rules which were applied equally to all. He cites Aristotle's dictum that 'it is more proper that the law should govern than any of the citizens'.[23]

This emphasis on law as a set of stable rules beyond the power of individual rulers to alter was also a feature of Roman thinking on law in the late republic and early empire, seen in writers such as Cicero, Livy, and Tacitus. The key conception contributed by Roman law was the idea that legislation should protect the freedom of the individual, and should therefore be based on a set of general rules. Hayek cites Cicero's opinion that the judge is merely the mouth through which the law speaks and his doctrine that we obey the law in order to be free. Hayek ascribes the prosperity and power of Rome at this period, despite the substitution of autocracy for republican government, to adherence to these doctrines, which permitted almost complete economic freedom. He then characteristically, but with little historical sense, blames the decline of Rome on 'state socialism'. Whereas Gibbon saw Christianity as the bacillus that destroyed Rome, Hayek saw the curtailment of economic freedom as the fundamental cause. It was not the spread of Christianity, but the abandonment of free market economics and the rule of law, which was decisive: 'From the second century AD state socialism advanced rapidly,'[24] culminating in the regime of Constantine, which introduced price controls and other interventionist measures. In the later codification of these ideas by Justinian, the idea that legislation should protect the freedom of the individual was lost.

Hayek's treatment of Imperial Rome, although cursory and historically dubious, is part of his political argument against socialism. Rome fell because its leaders failed to understand that they should not meddle with the market order. Exactly the same problem, Hayek implies, confronts Western industrial civilization in the twentieth century, on an even grander scale. Hayek's strong faith in evolutionary processes is always counterbalanced by his sense of how fragile they are. Intellectual error can cause political leaders to embrace policies which threaten everything that human civilization has achieved. No one constructed this civilization through an act of will or intellect, Hayek insists, yet acts of will and intellect are now required if it is to be preserved.

The collapse of the Roman Empire entailed the collapse of the classical conception of law and the conception of individual liberty which it expressed. In Hayek's view, the conception of individual liberty did not return until the seventeenth century, in England. The medieval period he saw as having no general conception of individual liberty. There were liberties, but these took the form of 'privi-leges' – literally, exceptions to the law which were granted to estates, corporations, and particular persons. Nevertheless, Hayek notes that the Middle Ages did have a deep-rooted conception that law pre-dated the state. The state could not make or create law. Law already existed, and had to be discovered and interpreted. It arose out of customs and practices inherited from the past. The job of governing bodies was not to make or promulgate new law but to find out what the law actually was. Only gradually did the idea of parliaments as law-making rather than law-finding bodies emerge.

The key change came in England. The civil war between Crown and Parliament arose over specific grievances, but the intensity of the struggle raised general questions about the conduct of government and the relationship between state and people. Hayek saw the civil war through the eyes of nineteenth-century Whig historians, particularly Macaulay and Acton, for whom it was a critical episode in the development of liberty. The abolition of the prerogative courts such as the Star Chamber was regarded by Maitland, for example, as critical in the development of a conception of the rule of law. The Star Chamber, on this view, had become a court composed of politicians enforcing a policy rather than judges administering the law. Hayek saw mass democracy in the twentieth century as having permitted the return of Star Chambers in most areas of public policy. The subversion of the rule of law has been the result.

The Star Chamber became the symbol for English liberals of arbitrary action by an executive power which was not prepared to be constrained by pre-existing law. The definition of what was arbitrary came to hinge not on the source of the authority making the decision, but on whether the decisions could be said to conform to the general principles of law that already existed. As a result of the struggles with the Stuart kings Charles I, Charles II, and James II, a mixed constitution emerged, in which the different elements were so balanced that arbitrary action was minimized and the framework of general rules that permitted the development of civil society and a large degree of personal freedom, particularly for property-owners, was assured.

England plays a key role in Hayek's account of the story of liberty. He gives decisive importance to the civil war in the seventeenth century, endorsing the traditional liberal view of its significance. In another of his rather improbable historical analogies, Hayek states that the dispute over economic issues between King and Parliament was very similar to the policy debate of 1960. Then, as in 1960, the economy was threatened by industrial monopolies which owed their existence to protective legislation. What is important about this characterization, however, is that it shows Hayek arguing that conscious acts of policy making, even involving civil rebellion, are necessary to establish the rule of law which the full flowering of the market order requires.

The triumph of liberalism in England is represented by Hayek as the result of both political and intellectual struggle. It was not the result of an evolutionary process. The specific doctrines on which it was based were frequently challenged within England itself, by rationalists like Bacon and Hobbes. Hayek cites Hobbes disapprovingly for treating the doctrine of government by law instead of by individuals as another error of Aristotelian politics. Hobbes advanced the view that law flowed inescapably from power. The society was constituted by a political act which guaranteed the security of all individuals by centralizing the means of coercion and the right to make rules in the hands of a sovereign.

Hayek's antipathy to Hobbes is marked throughout his writings. He sees Hobbes as an arch-rationalist, whose belief in the power of self-determining reason is the source of the intellectual errors which led to constructivism, the Enlightenment, and ultimately to socialism. The link may seem a little tenuous, but Hayek had no doubts. It reflects his fundamental belief that there are two traditions in liberalism: one emphasizing the power of human beings to shape the world rationally in accordance with plans they devise themselves, the other emphasizing the ignorance of human beings and the need for extreme caution in altering the pattern of economic and social institutions which have evolved. Hobbes's fault in

Hayek's eyes stems from the fact that the power vested in the sovereign to ensure civil peace is in practice unlimited. There is sharp disagreement here with Oakeshott. For Oakeshott, it was precisely Hobbes's unrivalled grasp of the necessary relationship between authority and liberty which made him the pre-eminent English political philosopher.[25]

As far as official public doctrine in England was concerned, Locke proved more influential than Hobbes. A civil society and a polity evolved in which the limits on government and the need to maintain a balanced constitution were rated more highly than the absolute power of the state. This outcome reflected the result of the civil war, and created for two hundred years, until the advent of democracy, a political system which in Hayek's eyes came as close to perfection as is possible. Liberty flourished in England, however, not just because the balance between the Crown and the two Houses of Parliament ensured the independence of the judiciary and an important range of individual rights which could be defended against the executive, but also because the legal system was based on common law, a set of general rules governing conduct and economic practice which had evolved over a very long period and were treated by the courts as authoritative.

This tradition, as a public doctrine, received further reflection and refinement in the eighteenth century from Hume, Blackstone, Burke, and Paley. Hayek, like Montesquieu and other observers at the time, considered the English eighteenth-century constitution to be much superior to the forms of government which had been established in the rest of Europe. But he noted that there was no further development of the English constitution after the eighteenth century, and that this was a serious drawback. The advance of French ideas of political liberty, particularly when they were advocated by rationalist liberals like Bentham, led to the neglect of the native tradition of individual liberty. The doctrine of unlimited parliamentary sovereignty, which Hayek thought tolerable when power was balanced between Crown, Lords, and Commons, became inappropriate and even dangerous when the powers of the Crown and the Lords were drastically reduced, and the Commons, elected by universal franchise, came to dominate. The English *ancien régime* had held at bay the doctrines of constructivist rationalism popular elsewhere in Europe. But once the franchise was extended, aspects of the doctrine of popular sovereignty, such as electoral mandates and policy programmes, became established in all parties. The doctrine of parliamentary sovereignty became a valuable

weapon in the hands of the executive, because it imposed no checks
and limits on what the executive could do. An executive composed
of Hayekian liberals might use its unlimited power to defend the
liberal order, but the same doctrine could be employed to justify
all kinds of interventionist actions.[26]

In this climate the doctrines which had sustained English liberty
for so long, such as unlimited parliamentary sovereignty, became
liabilities. Torn from the context of a balanced constitution, the doctrine of unlimited parliamentary sovereignty in the hands of a
democratically elected government claiming to represent the popular will soon became the basis for legitimating a vast extension of
government powers. With no codified constitution and no right of
the courts to overrule Parliament except on technicalities that 'Parliament cannot have meant this', the British system was shown to
be extremely vulnerable to socialist and collectivist penetration.[27]

The United States Constitution

The alternative for Hayek lay in the constitutional traditions of
the United States and Germany. He treats the eighteenth-century
US Constitution and the nineteenth-century German *Rechtsstaat* as
two examples of liberal constitutional experiments which sought
to prevent government in the modern state from becoming unlimited. The US Constitution was consciously designed as a constitution of liberty, intended to protect the individual against all arbitrary
coercion.

After England, Hayek thought that the United States of America
was the most important source of ideas underlying the creation of
the conception of a rule of law required by the market order. Again,
it required a major conflict to produce constitutional innovation
and a clarification of the principles involved in limiting state power.
The conflict was precipitated by British Government imposition of
taxes on the American colonies, which were seen by many in the
colonies as arbitrary and therefore illegitimate. The eventual defeat
of the British gave the colonies their independence, and produced
one of the political foundation documents of the modern era – the
US Constitution.

Hayek is in some difficulty over the US Constitution, since it
appears at first glance to be a product of rationalist constructivist
liberalism, and owes little to evolutionary development. It sets out
first principles, and reconstructs the political system in accordance
with them. One of the key architects of the Constitution, Thomas

Jefferson, is regarded by Hayek as one of the high priests of the tradition of false individualism (he sympathized with the French Revolution), along with Rousseau, Bentham, and Godwin.

Hayek argues, however, that French rationalism was only one influence upon the founding fathers. They were saved from French rationalist excesses by a pragmatic concern with procedures. Hayek claims that this made the US Constitution a product of accident rather than design. The argument is expedient, but unconvincing. It saves him having to designate the US Constitution as stemming from false liberalism, but it would be difficult to point to any historical example of an attempt to implement a constructivist design, including those of Soviet communism or the Swedish welfare state, which was not substantially modified by accident and circumstance.

Hayek also believes that the impulses which gave rise to the US Constitution were important because they led to a new understanding of constitutions and constitutionalism. The formula that all power derives from the people might seem a prime example of the fatal conceit, the hubris of human reason. But Hayek is more charitable. He prefers to interpret it as referring not to the principle of popular sovereignty exercised through election of representatives, but to 'the fact that the people, organised as a constitution-making body, had the exclusive right to determine the powers of the representative legislature'.[28] The Constitution was the means of protecting the people from all arbitrary action by government.

Hayek is therefore able to interpret the US Constitution not as a piece of social engineering, but as a clarification and an extension of the English tradition of liberty. A constitutional system of the US type might not be able to place absolute limits on popular sovereignty, but it could ensure consideration of long-term objectives and the subordination of immediate objectives to them. Citizens agree to be governed by the party which wins a majority at an election, because they know that this party will govern within the limits set down by the Constitution.

The US experiment was recognized by liberals in the nineteenth century as an important means for safeguarding liberty. What struck them in particular was that it formalized the requirements for a balance of power both between the various arms of government at the centre and also between the central and local levels of government. The target was the curbing of absolute royal power, but the same principles were found to be useful in devising restraints for the new mass democracies which extensions of the suffrage began to create. The name which liberals gave to these principles was 'federalism'. Hayek quotes Acton's endorsement: 'Of all checks on democracy federalism has been the most efficacious and the most congenial.'[29]

The British with their unitary state had always resisted federalism, but the Americans embraced it as a constitutional principle which helped place firm limits on the powers of the central executive. Dividing central power was the best way of keeping it in check. Federal government, for Hayek, was one of the best ways of ensuring limited government. Hayek was a strong supporter of federalism, because federalism made limited government more likely by dividing sovereign power.[30] A political system in which there was conflict among the executive, the legislature, and the judiciary would be more likely to keep government limited to its basic functions. But he also came to recognize that in the absence of a strong public philosophy endorsing economic liberalism, this would not necessarily be the outcome.

On Hayek's account, constitutionalism is about legitimacy. He objects to Hobbes's account of sovereignty because it is based on individuals making rational calculations about their interests and neglects the sphere of non-rational beliefs and institutions. Constitutionalism is a device which recognizes that individuals will obey the state not because they are coerced to do so or because they perceive it as in their interest, but because they regard the state as legitimate.[31] The basis of that legitimacy in a constitutional system is the existence of a system of rules which cannot easily be changed, and whose change requires a different procedure from the one which elects the government. It is for this reason that Hayek regards the US Constitution as a true constitution of liberty, because its basic purpose was to protect the individual from arbitrary government, rather than to extend the powers of arbitrary government over the individual.

For Hayek, the Anglo-American tradition made the principal contribution to the idea of limited government. The triumph of political absolutism in Europe buried the traditions in most other parts of Europe for more than two hundred years. The revolutionary movement at the end of the eighteenth century made the reclamation of liberty and the re-establishment of the rule of law top priorities. But in Hayek's view, the French Revolution was an unmitigated disaster, not only because it ended in terror and dictatorship, but also because it bequeathed a set of ideas about society and political organization which became the basis for many of the ideologies of the modern era, at times submerging or corrupting the Anglo-American tradition, which Hayek continued to regard as the true tradition of liberty.

The French Revolution made the doctrine of popular sovereignty the basis of political legitimacy. All citizens were equal in the sense of having equal rights and entitlements and opportunities. Society had to be reconstructed to make the possession of these rights a reality. The Revolution established a political tradition in which entitlements and rights were given priority, while doing little to disturb the power of the administrative authorities, which were given new spheres to organize and control.

The challenge to the power of the strong bureaucracies established under absolutism came not from the French Revolution but from Germany, through the idea of the *Rechtsstaat* which arose as a response to criticism of the traditions of absolutist government which had dominated so many European states in the early modern period. Hayek traces the development of the German conception of the rule of law through Kant and Humboldt. Kant's categorical imperative in ethics, that a person should act 'only on that maxim whereby thou canst at the same time will that it should become universal law', was for Hayek the basic idea underlying his conception of the rule of law.[32] To this Humboldt added the argument in *The Sphere and Duty of Government* that the enforcement of the law was the only legitimate function of the state. Following the Napoleonic wars, there was a concerted attempt to apply these ideas to the design of a constitution which would limit the formal powers of government and make all administrative acts subject to judicial review by the courts.

Hayek notes that these attempts to create a *Rechtsstaat* were short-lived and mostly abandoned after 1870. But he uses the concept to illustrate his general thesis that doctrines can change and that there is nothing permanent or irreversible about the triumph of either liberal or anti-liberal ideas. From one standpoint *The Road to Serfdom* is an account of how anti-liberal ideas triumphed over liberal ideas in Germany. The general argument of that book is reiterated in *The Constitution of Liberty*. Hayek singles out Germany as the source of the modern theories, especially historicism and legal positivism, which have undermined the rule of law. Doctrines of historicism have produced a climate of moral relativism, which makes all knowledge relative to its context, and justifies projects for remaking institutions.

Legal positivism challenges the argument of the natural law school that there are objective rules which should be beyond interference by legislators. Legal positivists defined law as the commands of a particular human will, and denied that the state could be bound by law. Every state that issued authoritative commands was entitled to be called a *Rechtsstaat*. Hayek cites the comment of the Soviet jurist E. V. Pashukanis that all law is transformed into administration.[33]

The German liberal movement had used the introduction of Napoleonic legal codes into Prussia to argue that there should be formal constitutional limitation of the power of the state, backed up by specific curbs on administrative activity which would be enforceable through the courts. Hayek specifically commended the idea of administrative courts as an important innovation, and criticized Dicey and other Anglo-American lawyers for being blind to the importance of finding new ways to bring the bureaucracies of the extended state under the rule of law. Dicey simply condemned the existence of separate administrative courts as being the denial of the rule of law, and failed to see that new institutions were necessary to deal with the new powers that state agencies were acquiring.

Following the achievements in England, the United States, and Germany in refining the meaning of limited government in institutional terms, the period after 1880 saw the rise of different ideas, which put the whole tradition of the rule of law at risk. The shift away from the idea of the rule of law in Hayek's sense was particularly marked in Germany, with moves on both left and right to state socialism; but similar trends were present in Britain and in the United States. The central challenge was to the idea that law and policy could be kept apart. Hayek argued that it was a fatal error to claim, as did Karl Schmitt and many others, that whatever the representatives of the people willed had the force of law. The immediate preferences of a temporary majority were no basis on which to change the institutions on which survival and reproduction of the civilization depended. Hayek viewed the law rather like a genetic code which must not be tampered with. Its complexity and value could be recognized, but it could not be fully understood. It represented the stored-up wisdom accumulated over many generations as to how best to regulate a market order.

Hayek's belief that even the most moderate forms of state intervention risked plunging Western civilization into a new dark age of serfdom which would see the extinction of personal liberty was based not on the motives of those who advocated social democratic programmes, but on their methods. Because their policies disregarded the importance of the rule of law, no limits were placed upon how far state intervention might go, and there was no way of measuring the damage that might be done before it was too late.

A Constitution of Liberty

Hayek's response to these problems was to indulge in some new constitutional thinking of his own. The full results are laid out in *Law, Legislation, and Liberty*, but the germ of the idea is already present in *The Constitution of Liberty*.[34] He noted there that the word 'law' was being used in two quite separate ways: to refer to the specific commands used to direct the apparatus of government to achieve concrete ends, and to refer to the general rules governing the behaviour of citizens. He wondered whether

> it might not be desirable to prevent the two types of decision from being confused by entrusting the task of laying down general rules and the task of issuing orders to the administration to distinct representative bodies and by subjecting their decisions to independent judicial review so that neither will overstep its bounds.[35]

He was led to this conclusion by the inadequacy he discerned in the tradition of liberal constitutional thinking for dealing with the new forms of intervention associated with the modern state. Limited politics cannot be regained simply by going back to the nineteenth-century ideal. There must be a development of constitutional thinking to deal with the new situation, as well as new institutions.

In *Law, Legislation, and Liberty* Hayek reaffirms his commitment to democracy as the only effective method yet discovered of making peaceful political change possible, but also restates his deep misgivings about the way in which democracy is organized. The 'deeply entrenched defects' of the contemporary form of democratic government create a bias towards totalitarianism, because such government constantly encourages interference with the delicate relationships of the market order on which individual freedom and economic progress rest.

Hayek believed strongly in the necessity for a constitution of liberty to safeguard individual freedom, but it must be a constitution of a new type. Limiting the coercive power of the state by traditional constitutional devices he judged a failure. Governments everywhere had obtained, by constitutional means, powers which it had been intended to deny them. The reason lay in the incompatibility between the idea of constitutionalism – that the powers of government should be exercised within strict limits – and the idea of modern democracy – that the will of the majority on any particular issue should always prevail. The supremacy of this second doctrine in the modern era has made constitutionalism at times seem an anachronism, an impediment to the efficient working of government in carrying through programmes approved by the electorate.

Hayek remains firmly committed to the goals of the liberal constitutionalists, but argues that new institutions are now needed if these goals are to be achieved. Liberal constitutionalism has lost ground because three of its central beliefs no longer command support. These three propositions are that justice should be defined independently of personal interest, that legislation should not be used to achieve particular results for specific persons or groups, and that the functions of directing the government and articulating the rules of just conduct should not be entrusted to the same representative assembly.

Hayek wishes to preserve democracy as a method of choosing governments while emptying it of any substantive content and, in particular, disengaging it from the doctrine of popular sovereignty. If democracy is a method and not an ideal, it can be assessed entirely in terms of its results. In *The Constitution of Liberty* Hayek attacks the notion that there is some perfect form of democracy. As discussed previously, he argues that proportional representation is not better just because it seems more democratic, and that universal suffrage is not an indispensable requirement for democracy. All that is necessary is that the same impersonal rule applies to all. Any form of suffrage, provided it does not violate this rule, is therefore as democratic as any other. A restricted franchise is as democratic as an unrestricted franchise. So long as anyone who comes within the relevant category is not denied a vote, such a voting system is no less democratic than universal suffrage.[36]

This idea is developed at length in *Law, Legislation, and Liberty*[37] in the form of a blueprint for a new form of democratic polity which would not have the structural defects of the old. Hayek's model is firmly within the liberal constitutionalist tradition, but unlike some other New Right constitutional reformers,[38] Hayek is less interested in stipulating specific items that a model constitution should contain, such as a requirement that the budget be always kept in balance, as in identifying the institutional mechanisms which can oblige governments to act only in particular ways. He focuses on re-creating the separation between the two functions of a representative assembly – considering questions concerning the general rules governing interactions between individuals and considering questions arising from the conduct of government business.

His main proposal is that these two functions should be discharged by two quite separate assemblies. The idea of separate assemblies or chambers with different functions, elected in different ways, is not a new one. Hayek notes that it developed in England once it was acknowledged that the House of Commons had precedence in the consideration of money bills, while the House of Lords retained responsibility for the rules of common law. If the House of Lords had asserted an exclusive right to alter by statute the rules of just conduct, then the system might have developed along the lines Hayek proposed. But the distinction between the two houses based on function was overshadowed by a distinction based on social class, which became sharper as the franchise was extended during the nineteenth century. The constitutional battle which resulted ended in the stripping from the House of Lords of most of its powers in the name of the doctrine of popular sovereignty.

Hayek sees the distinction between the two functions as crucial to a successful constitution. His model constitution therefore includes a legislative assembly and a government assembly. The role of the legislative assembly is to represent the opinion of the people regarding what sorts of government actions are just and what are not, while the government assembly is guided by the will of the people on the particular measures to be taken within the framework of rules laid down by the legislative assembly. Party divisions are entirely appropriate for the government assembly, and indeed the best way of carrying out the business. But they are inappropriate for the legislative assembly. This view echoes that of many of the authors of the US Constitution.

The government assembly would be similar to the lower house in many parliamentary systems, and would be elected by all the citizens, voting for particular party representatives. The voting system Hayek recommends is simple plurality, rather than any form of proportional representation. He argues that the need to elect a strong, effective government outweighs the demand for fairness in the distribution of votes. All citizens above a certain age would vote, with one important qualification: all those employed by the state or dependent on the state for income support, including pensioners, would be ineligible. Depending on how this rule were interpreted, the number of those entitled to vote in countries with large public sectors and transfer payments could be substantially reduced. Hayek's purpose in proposing it was to minimize the number of voters who would have a personal stake in the expansion of state-funded programmes. As a state-funded university professor, he would presumably have been disenfranchised by his own constitution.

The legislative assembly would not be concerned with appointing the government and scrutinizing and approving its actions. Instead, it would be concerned with what Hayek regarded as the proper sphere of legislation: formulating general rules which would prescribe which actions were right and which wrong, and establish rules of just conduct. Such general rules would conform to the principle that they be framed so as to be applicable in an unknown number of future instances. The basic clause of such a constitution would be that in normal times individuals 'could be restrained from doing what they wished, or coerced to do particular things, only in accordance with the recognised rules of just conduct designed to define and protect the individual domain of each'.[39] Only the legislative assembly could amend these rules; the government and the governmental assembly would be obliged to work within them. Hayek states explicitly that this basic clause would not define the functions of government or the services which governments could offer, but only the means by which they could offer them.

Members of the legislative assembly would be elected in a very different manner from those of the government assembly. They would all be aged forty-five at election, and would serve for fifteen years. They would not be eligible for re-election, and to minimize the pressures on them, they would not be required to find employment in the private sector once they ceased to be members of the assembly. They would be elected by all those aged forty-five. Thus each age cohort on reaching forty-five would elect a number of individuals to serve in the legislative assembly, with one-fifteenth of the assembly being replaced each year. Hayek's justification for this curious electoral process is that the assembly would represent 'that part of the population which had already gained experience, had had an opportunity to make their reputation, but who would still be in their best years'.[40] Those who had been members of the government assembly or who had worked for party organizations would be ineligible. It should be noted here that new members of the British House of Lords are recruited on almost the opposite principle.

Much remains unclear from Hayek's blueprint, in particular the business that would come before the legislative assembly and how the relationships between the government and the two assemblies would be handled. Would the legislative assembly have enough to do? Once elected, with security of tenure for fifteen years, its members might go to sleep, and it might become entirely inactive. Hayek acknowledged the danger, but thought nevertheless that with a few minimal safeguards such an assembly would work effectively and would be concerned not only with criminal and commercial law but also with the principles of taxation and regulations on health, safety, competition, and corporations.

He proposes the establishment of a constitutional court, which would arbitrate on conflicts and pronounce on which assembly had competence in relation to a particular issue. Whether this would be enough is questionable. For the system to work, the elected government and the government assembly would have to be prepared to work within whatever constraints were imposed by the laws passed by the legislative assembly.

Hayek's assumption is that the legislative assembly would be a highly conservative body conscious of its responsibility to maintain the market order and the institutions which he regards as essential for the preservation and further development of civilization. But his constitutional model is in itself neutral. It is consistent with a number of alternative societies. If opinion were collectivist and this were reflected in the legislative assembly, there would be nothing to stop the passing of legislation framed as general rules but with a collectivist content. What Hayek's constitution would rule out would be command socialism – the issuing of direct commands by central authorities – and pork-barrel socialism – the domination of the policy-making process by special interests. But forms of socialism which were cast in the form of general rules would not fall foul of his principle.

In the end, Hayek falls back on his belief that liberal ideas will triumph because they are superior to collectivist ideas. But his model constitution intriguingly opens up the possibility of there being a range of societies which would meet Hayek's criterion of safeguarding individual freedom and limiting the coercive powers of the state. Since Hayek believes that the state must retain some coercive powers, the question of the scope of these powers is left indeterminate. It is a practical question to be decided case by case. Hayek assumes that the legislators in his ideal constitution will embrace a liberal political philosophy. But he offers no reasons why they should.

7

The Economic Consequences
of Keynes

Another colleague had also prepared a paper arguing that the 'middle way' was the pragmatic path for the Conservative party to take, avoiding the extremes of Left and Right. Before he had finished speaking to his paper, the new Party Leader reached into her briefcase and took out a book. It was Friedrich von Hayek's *The Constitution of Liberty*. Interrupting our pragmatist, she held the book up for all of us to see. 'This,' she said sternly, 'is what we believe,' and banged Hayek down on the table.

Ranelagh, *Thatcher's People*

Hayek devoted his life to exposing the intellectual errors of socialism. But many of those he was anxious to reach and convince were not socialists, but liberals and conservatives. The intellectual opponent who provided the most searching challenge to Hayek's worldview was not on the Left, but a fellow liberal – John Maynard Keynes. Hayek's work can be read at one level as a long debate with Keynes and the Keynesians over the political means and policies which would best safeguard a liberal society. Much of Hayek's political effort after 1945 was devoted to trying to reverse the influence of Keynes on economic and social policy.

Hayek and Keynes

The debate began in the 1930s, in part stimulated by theoretical disagreements, in part by policy disagreements over how governments should react to the Great Crash of 1929 and the ensuing

Depression. An intellectual opposition developed between the LSE and Cambridge, with Hayek and Robbins at the LSE developing a theory of money and the business cycle which challenged that of Keynes, and led to very different policy prescriptions for dealing with the slump. Hayek wrote a very critical review of Keynes's *Treatise of Money* in *Economica*, in particular challenging Keynes's assertion that there was no automatic mechanism in the economic system to keep the rate of saving and the rate of investing equal.[1] Keynes reacted angrily to the criticism. In his published reply in *Economica*, he attacked Hayek's own recently published book, *Prices and Production*, as 'one of the most frightful muddles I have ever read . . . It is an extraordinary example of how, starting with a mistake, a remorseless logician can end up in Bedlam.'[2] In notes written on his copy of Hayek's review of his own book, Keynes expressed his bitterness: 'Hayek has not read my book with that measure of "goodwill" which an author is entitled to expect of a reader. Until he can do so he will not see what I mean or whether I am right. He evidently has a passion which leads him to pick on me, but I am left wondering what that passion is.'[3]

The passion which led Hayek to attack Keynes was only in part theoretical disagreement with Keynes's new-fangled monetary theory. At its root was Hayek's perception that Keynes was denying what for him was essential – the idea that the market economy was capable unaided of adjusting to structural shifts in demand. Hayek suspected that Keynes and the Cambridge school were seeking theoretical justification for expanding the role of government and abandoning traditional policies of non-intervention.

Hostilities between the two camps continued with a savaging of *Prices and Production* by Piero Sraffa in the *Economic Journal*.[4] The fierceness of the exchanges did not persist through the 1930s, however. Although the intellectual gulf between them was as wide as ever, Robbins and Hayek were surprisingly silent when Keynes published the *General Theory* in 1936. Cambridge appeared to have won a complete victory in the intellectual battle, especially since several of the best younger economists at the LSE, including John Hicks, Nicholas Kaldor, Evan Durbin, and Abba Lerner all accepted the new Keynesian paradigm.

Hayek never gave a satisfactory explanation of why he did not write a rejoinder to the *General Theory*. Much later, reflecting on Keynes and the Keynesian revolution, Hayek gave as a reason the fact that, following his exchange with Keynes over the *Treatise*, he had entered into correspondence with Keynes, a correspondence which ended when Keynes announced that he had changed his mind, and no longer believed many of the things he had written in the *Treatise*. Hayek claims that it was the thought that he might change his mind again, and very quickly, that stopped him from entering a detailed critique of the *General Theory*. This is highly implausible, and as Robert Skidelsky has shown, Hayek was in any case wrong about Keynes's attitude to the earlier *Treatise*. Keynes never said that he had changed his mind.[5]

More plausible is the second reason Hayek gives for not contesting the claims of the *General Theory* as a professional economist. He disagreed fundamentally with the macro-economic approach which Keynes adopted. Methodologically, Hayek regarded the attempt to study the economy through aggregates as misguided. The only proper method was to start from the micro-foundations of the economy, the preferences, intentions, calculations, and choices of individual agents. This methodological objection made him unsympathetic to the problems which Keynes was seeking to solve, and disinclined to become involved in detailed technical debate, given that he did not accept the premises from which Keynes was starting.

Hayek's failure to respond, however, meant that he ceded the intellectual ground to the new Keynesian school, which captured the younger generation of economists and proclaimed a revolution in economic thought and economic policy. Hayek's own research programme was marginalized by the rise of the new macroeconomics, and this may well have been a contributory factor to his abandonment of economics for political philosophy.

Although he did not confront the arguments of the *General Theory* directly, Hayek was to spend the rest of his life confronting the set of theoretical assumptions and policy prescriptions which underlay them. Hayek never wavered in his belief that the economic consequence of Keynesianism was inflation, and that as a policy it was unsustainable. It required ever greater injections of spending in order to maintain high levels of activity, which created ever faster inflation, and made the eventual cost of adjustment ever more painful.

Hayek was fascinated by Keynes, like most people who came into contact with him.[6] The personal impression Keynes made was 'unforgettable'. Hayek remembered in particular 'the magnetism of the brilliant conversationalist with his wide range of interests and his bewitching voice'.[7] But he also made it very clear that, 'although indisputably a great man', Keynes was great despite, rather than because of, his economics. Hayek could find very little to praise in Keynes's contribution to the discipline. His best work, he thought, was to be found in some of the unsystematic insights contained in the second volume of the *Treatise*. The rest of Keynes's work was based on a series of intellectual errors which, in Hayek's view, vitiated the results entirely. He went further, arguing that one of Keynes's problems was that he knew very little economics. He was a dilettante who had learnt most of the economics he knew from Marshall, and had never bothered to become acquainted with the theorists of other leading schools, such as Wicksell and Böhm-Bawerk. Trusting as he did to intuition, and confident in the correctness of his own judgement, Keynes was never a scholar, and was often impatient with the methods of scholarship. He produced a dazzling display, but in the end his influence on economics and on economic policy was almost wholly malign. Hayek believed that in the future, when Keynesianism had run its course,

> the 'Keynesian Revolution' will appear as an episode during which erroneous conceptions of the appropriate scientific method led to the temporary obliteration of many important insights which we had already achieved and which we shall then have painfully to regain.[8]

Hayek remained relatively silent on Keynes during the period of Keynes's greatest eminence, the 1940s, 1950s, and 1960s. But with the ending of the long boom of the post-war years and the acceleration of inflation at the end of the 1960s, his deep mistrust, even detestation, of Keynes came to the fore. He made clear that it was Keynes whom he blamed for this inflation. Keynes, he argued, was the greatest contemporary illustration of his own maxim about the power of ideas which appears at the end of the *General Theory*. Keynes had written:

> If the ideas are correct . . . it would be a mistake, I predict, to dispute their potency over a period of time. . . . the ideas of economists and political philosophers, both when they are right and when they are wrong, are more powerful than is commonly understood. Indeed the world is ruled by little else. Practical men, who believe themselves to be quite exempt from any intellectual influences, are usually the slaves of some defunct economist. Madmen in authority, who hear voices in the air, are distilling their frenzy from some academic scribbler of a few years back. I am sure that the power of vested interests is vastly exaggerated compared with the gradual

encroachment of ideas . . . Soon or late, it is ideas, not vested interests, which are dangerous for good or evil.[9]

Hayek believed that it was the hold which Keynes's theories had
over economists, policy-makers, and politicians which explained
the post-war inflation. He told readers of the *Daily Telegraph* in
1974 that

> the responsibility for current world-wide inflation, I am sorry to say,
> rests wholly and squarely with the economists, or at least with that
> great majority of my fellow economists who have embraced the
> teachings of Lord Keynes. What we are experiencing are simply the
> economic consequences of Lord Keynes. It was on the advice and
> even urging of his pupils that governments everywhere have fi-
> nanced increasing parts of their expenditure by creating money on
> a scale which every reputable economist before Keynes would have
> predicted would cause precisely the sort of inflation we have got.
> They did this in the erroneous belief that this was both a necessary
> and a lastingly effective method of securing full employment.[10]

Hayek absolved Keynes from direct responsibility. Keynes, he
was sure, would have been among the first to lead the fight against
inflation. Indeed, Hayek claimed that Keynes had told him as much,
shortly before he died:

> I had asked him whether he was not getting alarmed by the use to
> which some of his disciples were putting his theories. His reply was
> that these theories had been greatly needed in the 1930s; but if these
> theories should ever become harmful, I could be assured that he
> would quickly bring about a change in public opinion.[11]

Hayek's complaint against Keynes was not that he himself had
advocated inflation, but that in seeking short-term remedies for the
economic problems of the 1930s, he had given a new credibility to
a number of older, false doctrines about money. In calling his theory
a general theory, he elevated what were intuitive, not fully developed, ideas for dealing with a practical problem into the status of
a general theoretical paradigm, which misled a whole generation
of economists and policy-makers. Hayek compared Keynes to John
Law, the eighteenth-century financier. Both were inflationists who
could not free themselves from the 'false popular belief' that, as
Law expressed it, 'this addition to the money will employ the people
that are now idle, and those not employed to more advantage, so

the product will be increased and manufacture advanced'.[12] In *Choice in Currency* Hayek wrote that Keynes and his followers gave the sanction of scientific authority to the age-old superstition that by increasing the aggregate of money expenditure, it is possible to ensure lasting prosperity and full employment.[13]

Hayek's exasperation with Keynes was due to the damage he had done to liberal public philosophy and the economics which underlay it. Hicks had proposed that just as the second quarter of the century was the age of Hitler, so the third quarter, between 1950 and 1975, should be known as the age of Keynes. Hayek commented, only partly in jest, 'I do not feel that the harm Keynes did is really so great as to justify *that* description'.[14]

In the 1970s it became fashionable to demonize Keynes as the author of all the misfortunes which had befallen the Western capitalist economy. Hayek played an important role in this process. As a veteran of the battles of the early 1930s, he could speak as one who had denounced the Keynesian heresy when it first appeared, predicted what its consequences would be if it were applied, and was still around forty years later to declare that those predictions had been borne out by events. The vindication was less dramatic than the vindication of the Mises–Hayek analysis of the command economy by the collapse of communism at the end of the 1980s, but it was nevertheless considerable.

Yet the complete opposition between his world-view and that of Keynes that is suggested by some of Hayek's wilder utterances at the end of his life is too facile. Although there were some key differences, there were also some important similarities. They shared many basic values. Keynes read *The Road to Serfdom* on his way to the USA in 1944, and wrote a letter to Hayek in which he praised the book highly:

> In my opinion it is a grand book. We all have the greatest reason to be grateful to you for saying so well what needs so much to be said. You will not expect me to accept quite all the economic dicta in it. But morally and philosophically I find myself in agreement with virtually the whole of it; and not only in agreement with it, but in a deeply moved agreement.[15]

Twenty years earlier, Keynes had given a short talk to a Liberal Summer School, entitled 'Am I a Liberal?', which is instructive to compare with Hayek's 1960 postscript 'Why I am not a Conservative'. Keynes spends much time explaining why socialism of any variety holds no attraction for him, but also turns on conservatism: 'It leads nowhere, it satisfies no ideal, it conforms to no intellectual standard, it is not even safe, or calculated to preserve from spoilers that degree of civilisation which we have already attained.'[16] What Keynes demanded, as Hayek was later to do, was 'an attitude, a philosophy, a direction'.[17]

There are other similarities as well. If anything, Hayek had a stronger commitment to democracy than did Keynes. Many commentators have noted Keynes's technocratic bias and his deep distrust of mass participation in politics. One of the main reasons that kept him from closer involvement with the Labour party was his conviction that the way the party was organized meant that the intellectual elements would never exercise adequate control. 'Too much will be decided by those who do not know at all what they are talking about.'[18] Keynes placed great confidence in the intellectual elite. He described his fundamental position as follows:

> I believe that in the future, more than ever, questions about the economic framework of society will be far and away the most important of political issues. I believe that the right solution will involve intellectual and scientific elements which must be above the heads of the vast mass of more or less illiterate voters.[19]

The problem, as Keynes saw it, anticipating aspects of Schumpeter's later analysis, was that in a democracy all parties had to win support from this mass of ignorant voters, and could gain office only if they could win their confidence either by promising to promote their interests or by gratifying their passions. This created the constant danger that the right policy would be sacrificed to the policy which won votes. But Keynes thought that the danger was greatest in those parties which were most democratic in their internal organization. He praised the Conservatives because 'the inner ring of the party can almost dictate the details and the technique of policy'.[20] This offered the possibility for the party to separate its pursuit of votes from its conduct of government.

Hayek and Keynes shared both prejudices and silences. An example of the first is that both believed that government should be entrusted to an elite – although Keynes's elite was considerably narrower than Hayek's. An example of the second is that neither had anything significant to say about the states and economies outside the prosperous metropolitan cores of the global political economy.

One of the main grounds on which Hayek criticized Keynes was his immoralism. He returned many times to the passage in *My Early Beliefs* in which Keynes set out the principles on which he and his friends had acted in their youth:

> We entirely repudiated a personal liability on us to obey general rules. We claimed the right to judge every individual case on its merits, and the wisdom, experience, and self-control to do so successfully. This was a very important part of our faith, violently and aggressively held, and for the outer world it was our most obvious and dangerous characteristic. We repudiated entirely customary morals, conventions, and traditional wisdom. We were that is to say in the strict sense of the term, immoralists . . . we recognized no moral obligation, no inner sanction, to conform or obey. Before heaven we claimed to be our own judge in our own case.[21]

For Hayek, these comments of Keynes were not idiosyncratic but representative of a generation of intellectuals which sought to free itself from the constraints of traditional morals.[22] Hayek thought this one of the most damaging delusions of the twentieth century, and saw it as closely related to the disease of constructivism, because it meant putting faith in human reason above inherited rules and traditions. Hayek noted that Keynes often referred to 'conventional wisdom' disparagingly (although Hayekians did the same when the conventional wisdom was Keynesian). He also criticized Keynes's belief that it was possible to use rational judgement as a basis for action rather than submit to traditional abstract rules. The most shocking remark that Keynes ever made, as far as Hayek was concerned, was his disparagement of the long run: 'this long run is a misleading guide to current affairs. In the long run we are all dead.'[23] Hayek interprets Keynes to be saying that 'since in the long run we are all dead it does not matter what long-term damage we do; it is the present moment alone, the short run – consisting of public opinion, demands, votes, and all the stuff and bribes of demagoguery – which counts'.[24] As an interpretation of Keynes, this is preposterous, particularly given Keynes's views on mass democracy and the need to keep government in the hands of a small educated elite. But for Hayek the remark represented a view of policy and government that was incompatible with the maintenance of the Great Society: 'The slogan that "in the long run we are all dead" is also a characteristic manifestation of an unwillingness to recognise that morals are concerned with effects in the long run – effects beyond our possible perception – and of a tendency to spurn the learnt discipline of the long view.'[25]

The disagreement between Hayek and Keynes is more complex than Hayek presents it, however. As so often, Hayek caricatures the position he is attacking. Keynes was far from having a naïve view of the powers of individual reason. In some of his writings he is as sceptical as Hayek about the possibilities of human knowledge. His scepticism about taking the long view was precisely that so little could be known about it. Far from being a constructivist, Keynes was significantly influenced by Edmund Burke:

> Burke ever held and held rightly, that it can seldom be right . . . to sacrifice a present benefit for a doubtful advantage in the future . . . It is not wise to look too far ahead; our powers of prediction are slight, our command over results infinitesimal. It is therefore the happiness of our own contemporaries that is our main concern; we should be very chary of sacrificing large numbers of people for the sake of a contingent end, however advantageous that may appear . . . We can never know enough to make the chance worth taking.[26]

Hayek seeks to consign Keynes to the camp of false liberals and constructivists. In fact, Keynes's position is much closer to Hayek's own. Both prize the English political tradition of liberalism. For Hayek, however, it is an inheritance which is in danger of being lost because of intellectual error; whereas for Keynes, it is a living reality which is in danger from ossified forms of thought and stupidity, and can be preserved only through creative political action. This is the meaning of the lines in his letter to Hayek following the publication of *The Road to Serfdom*: 'Dangerous acts can be safely done in a community which thinks and feels rightly, which would be the way to hell if they were executed by those who think and feel wrongly.'[27]

The Middle Way

The real disagreement between Keynes and Hayek was identified by Keynes in that same letter, the question of knowing where to draw the line between intervention and non-intervention. Keynes's criticism of Hayek was that he accepted that the logical extreme of no intervention at all was not possible, but gave no guidance in *The Road to Serfdom* as to where the line should be drawn. This was the same criticism made later by the libertarians. But unlike them, Keynes thought that it was a matter of practical judgement, not principle. He acknowledged that Hayek would draw the line differently than he would, but criticized him for underestimating the practicability of a middle course. He also argued that since Hayek accepted that a line had to be drawn, it was disingenuous of him to imply that 'so soon as one moves an inch in the planned direction you are necessarily launched on the slippery path which will lead you in due course over the precipice'.[28]

From Keynes's perspective, the problem of preserving a liberal capitalist order was not one of principle but of means. He thought the crisis of the inter-war period so serious that capitalism and the individualist culture which he so much prized would disappear if steps were not taken to prevent this. He thought it was an emergency which justified desperate measures. Hayek entirely disagreed. If there was an emergency, it was because the intellectuals were deserting the true principles of liberalism.

Keynes proposed his middle way as a means of harmonizing individualism and socialism. In 'The End of Laissez-Faire' he argued that the doctrines of the nineteenth century, in particular the idea that private and social interest necessarily coincided in a system based on free markets and private property, had been discredited.[29] In the face of the dislocations of the international economy, the high, persistent levels of unemployment, the questioning of the legitimacy of the distribution of income and wealth, and the problems of poverty and welfare, Keynes suggested that what was needed was to define afresh what Bentham called the agenda and the non-agenda for government. Drawing the line meant identifying those areas where government should be involved and those where it should not. The real need for government intervention, Keynes argued, was not to do those things which could be done by private individuals, but to do those things which were not being done at all.

Keynes thought that institutional changes in modern capitalism, particularly the rise of organized producer groups and the divorce between ownership and management, and the growing responsibilities of the state for welfare and prosperity were irreversible. He ascribed them to a process of social evolution, whereas Hayek regarded them as the products of malign ideas. Hayek repeatedly accused Keynes of bending his principles to accommodate what he believed was politically acceptable. This had always been the classic dilemma within ruling groups seeking to avert revolution – whether to make concessions in order to continue to govern, or to govern in such a way as to make concessions. Keynes's practical judgement was that the art of politics required acceptance of certain realities if policies were to be found which would command broad-based consent.

Viewed in this light, the argument between Hayek and Keynes is less a matter of fundamental principles, than one of practical judgement. It was present from the very beginning in their dispute over the best means to cope with the world slump and depression which overwhelmed the capitalist world after 1929. Hayek's Austrian theory of the business cycle traced the cause of periodic slumps and booms to the functioning of the credit system.[30] If money were kept strictly neutral, then changes in consumer demand would be matched by changes in production. The balance between consumption and investment, present and future goods in Austrian terminology, would be maintained through changes in the rate of interest. But the issuing of credit through the banking system meant that there was a tendency for the rate of interest to reflect changes in monetary conditions rather than changes in consumer preferences. This sent the wrong signals to producers, and created a mismatch between consumer preferences and the structure of production. In order to bring the two back into alignment, a reduction in the money supply and a change in the structure of costs through price reductions were unavoidable.

Hayek's theory therefore suggested that the crucial requirement for restoring profitability and recreating the conditions for economic expansion was to reduce costs by bringing down prices. He and Robbins were completely opposed to an expansionary monetary policy aimed at raising activity and employment without first restructuring production. In Hayek's view such attempts were misguided, because further increases in credit, whether introduced directly through the banking system or indirectly through government spending, did nothing to raise savings, but only further distorted the structure of production. The consequence was inflation, which would become endemic in the system. In each new cycle, ever greater monetary expansion would be required to keep activity high, so the prospect was that inflation would steadily accelerate from one cycle to the next, making the eventual deflation much more drastic than would have been needed at the beginning.[31]

A temporary reduction in unemployment might be achieved, but at the expense of long-term problems. Hayek thought there was no short-cut to achieving sound money. Adjustments in relative prices would frequently be painful, resulting in bankruptcies and unemployment, but they were essential to re-create the conditions for stable, non-inflationary growth. They were the price that had to be paid for a credit economy. The essential problem, in Hayek's view, was one of over-investment by producers, which lax credit policies encouraged. Producers were investing more than consumers were willing to save. The result was a collapse of profits and a slump, followed by a reorganization of production so as to bring it back into line with consumers' preferences regarding present and future goods. The slump was nature's cure, a purgative which eliminated those investments which were not financed by genuine savings. If such investments were preserved by an expansionary monetary policy, this meant that the government was pursuing a policy of forced savings in order to protect the present structure of the economy. The correct cure was to create conditions for more real savings, which would then finance more investment and lift the economy out of the slump.

Keynes was not impressed by Hayek's arguments as set out in *Prices and Production*, Hayek's LSE lectures. Keynes agreed that the causes of the slump were monetary, but he diagnosed it as crisis of under-investment not over-investment. The problem was not too little saving, but too much. A way had to be found to stimulate economic activity by increasing aggregate demand, and to release idle savings which were not being used productively because the marginal efficiency of capital was too low. Hayek's cure would mean a further deflation of demand being imposed on an already depressed economy. Keynes doubted the economic wisdom of such a step, and still more the political wisdom. Reducing prices meant bankruptcies, higher unemployment, and wage cuts. He also thought that the institutional structure of the modern capitalist economy made it unlikely that nature's cure could be made to work. A long period of stagnation was more likely, because of the difficulty of getting prices to fall far enough or fast enough to make the necessary adjustment. It was much easier to accept the economy as it was and use the powers of government to adjust the financial aggregates.[32]

Hayek always regarded this attitude as defeatist. Keynes, he thought, was not prepared to advocate the policy that was intellectually right, because he judged it politically impossible to implement. Hayek believed that it was necessary to make such policies politically possible by changing where necessary the institutions and the behaviour which impeded the functioning of the market order. Keynes called the left socialists the 'party of catastrophe', because they believed nothing could be done to prevent capitalism from self-destructing. Hayek belonged to his own party of catastrophe in the 1930s. As Skidelsky notes, he agreed with Keynes that a capitalist economy based on credit was violently unstable, but thought that nothing could be done about it. Matters must be allowed to take their course, because for the state to intervene would compromise the market order, and prevent solutions emerging from the initiatives and responses of individuals.

This gulf was expressed in policy terms in an exchange of letters in *The Times* in October 1932, at the depth of the slump in Britain. Keynes and a group of Cambridge economists argued that a policy which restricted consumption increased unemployment. Keynes had earlier expressed this in his populist manner in his slogan 'whenever you save five shillings you put a man out of work for a day'. Hayek, Robbins, and two other LSE professors replied, restating the case for balancing the budget as the first priority of policy.

In his *Autobiography* Lionel Robbins admitted that he had been wrong in his policy prescriptions in the 1930s and in the book he wrote on the causes of the Depression.[33] But Hayek never conceded that he was mistaken in his analysis, although he did come to accept that deflation was not, and never had been, a practicable option in restoring the market.[34] The great success with which Keynesian policy was associated in the next forty years left him unmoved. As soon as it faltered, he claimed that it vindicated his analysis in the 1930s.

The political argument in the 1930s was between those who believed, like Hayek and Robbins, that the disciplines of bankruptcy and unemployment must be allowed to work and were essential elements of a market economy, and those like Keynes who thought that the political and economic costs of stabilization were too high and unnecessary. Other means existed for restoring profitability without resorting to drastic cuts in prices and wages. The collapse of the gold standard in 1931 allowed governments to begin experimenting with expansionist policies which increased domestic activity and employment through the simple expedient of allowing prices to rise.

Most of these policies, whether the New Deal in the United States, the Nazi recovery programme in Germany, or the protectionist policy in Britain, owed little to new economic theory, but in his *General Theory* Keynes produced a theoretical rationalization for such policies which helped to create a new policy orthodoxy. The *General Theory* was published in 1936, and quickly transformed debate in the economics profession. The Keynesian revolution shifted the paradigm of theoretical debate, and the Second World War and its policy aftermath completed the process.

In the 1930s the policy debate between Hayek and Keynes was

given a great deal of attention by John Strachey. In a series of books, most notably *The Coming Struggle for Power* and *The Nature of Capitalist Crisis*,[35] he used the two explanations of the crisis in the debate – under-investment and over-investment – as examples of the dilemma facing capitalist governments. Belonging as he did at that time to the party of catastrophe on the left, Strachey naturally found Hayek's arguments more congenial, because they laid bare what for him was the essential nature of capitalism. Restoration of profitability could not be achieved by half-measures. It required a comprehensive assault on the wages and working conditions of the working class. But, like Keynes, Strachey questioned whether such a drastic capitalist stabilization policy could be effected politically. He praised the 'much higher intellectual level' and theoretical insights of what he called the 'Hayek–Robbins ultra-deflationary school', but criticized the school's lack of political realism:

> Just as the insight into the nature of capitalism of the 'deflationary' school is greatest, so the remedies which their analysis forces them to propose are the least practicable, the most hopeless of application. Their very theoretical realism drives them to propose the most hopelessly unrealistic practical politics. They have grasped the true conditions for the continued existence of capitalism. But they find it hard to pretend, even to themselves, that these conditions can ever be reestablished.[36]

Strachey saw Hayek as one of the leaders of the 'market restorers', while Keynes was at the head of the 'national planners'. The market-restorers or free-traders identified the problems from which capitalism was suffering as being due to interference with free exchange. Strachey quotes Arthur Salter lamenting the loss of the perfect economic mechanism of the nineteenth-century global liberal economic order. 'The economic and financial structure under which we have grown up was indeed at the moment of its greatest perfection, more like one of the marvellously intricate structures built by the instincts of beavers or ants than the deliberately designed and rational works of man.'[37] To recreate that structure under which demand and supply adjusted spontaneously, without the need for anyone estimating the one or planning the other, and bring back business confidence required at least four major reforms:

1   the re-establishment of world free trade by the ending of tariff barriers and 'administrative' protectionism;

2   the restoration of competition through the break-up of mono-
    polies, cartels, and market-closing agreements;
3   the re-creation of labour market flexibility by reversing the tend-
    ency to the establishment of collective social services and to state
    and trade union protection of wage rates;
4   the restoration of international monetary stability through a
    return to the gold standard.[38]

Keynes's diagnosis was very different. The remedies proposed by
the market-restorers would only deepen the Depression, because
they would further depress output and profitability, and therefore
investment, and would unleash ever more desperate social and
political struggles. The way forward was to use the powers of
the state to help the economy recover: 'The right remedy for the
trade cycle is not to be found in abolishing booms and thus keeping
us permanently in a semi-slump, but in abolishing slumps and thus
keeping us permanently in a quasi-boom.'[39]

Inflation and Social Democracy

The market-restorers had few successes in the 1930s. The national
planners were in the ascendancy. National protectionism became
predominant in all the leading capitalist states, and economic liberalism everywhere was on the retreat. The world split into currency
blocs and military blocs, and the competition for resources and
territory intensified.

National protectionism, however, could not re-create world economic prosperity. In that sense neither the market-restorers nor the
national planners won in the 1930s. It needed a world war and the
reconstruction of political and economic arrangements which that
made possible and the emergence of a new, modified liberal economic order under US leadership to recreate the conditions for an
expanding international capitalist economy. The successful establishment of those conditions retrospectively came to be seen, however, as a triumph for the national planners and a defeat for the
market-restorers. The causes of the Great Depression and the break-
down of the old liberal economic order were ascribed to a lack of
planning. Keynesianism as a doctrine of public policy after 1945
justified the extension of public responsibility for the maintenance
of full employment, economic growth, and social security, while
leaving intact the basic legal relationships of a capitalist economy,
private property and contract.

As the Keynesian avalanche gathered pace, Hayek lost interest in economics, and quickly became a marginal, forgotten figure within the profession. He told his wife when Keynes died that he was probably now the best-known economist living. But in retrospect he acknowledged that within ten days it was probably no longer true.[40] His attack on Keynesianism and on the welfare state was to be conducted through his writings on political philosophy and social theory, rather than through economics. In recent years there has been some revival of interest in Hayek's economics, particularly in his conception of markets as discovery processes and in his ideas as to how the decisions and actions of agents are co-ordinated and how knowledge is distributed. Some bridges have been built with mainstream literature in rational expectations theory, game theory, and New Keynesianism.[41] But the attack on Keynesianism as an economic doctrine was spearheaded by the monetarist school, not the Austrian school.

Hayek's influence was felt in other ways. He was the inspiration for many of the ideas that fed the ideological critique of Keynesianism and social democracy in the 1970s. He became a magnet for the mushrooming think-tanks and groups on the New Right which were seeking explanations as to why capitalism after two decades of unprecedented success seemed to be falling apart. By explaining inflation and recession in terms of the growth in the scope and scale of the state, Hayek provided the basis for a far-reaching critique not just of the conduct of economic policy, but of the institutional organization of the post-war state.

Think-tanks

The think-tank in England with which he was most closely associated was the Institute of Economic Affairs, founded in 1957 by Anthony Fisher, Arthur Seldon, and Ralph Harris.[42] The IEA was committed to fundamental thinking, and to not being limited by what was 'politically practicable'. As Harris put it: 'It was one of Arthur Seldon's most seminal principles that IEA authors must pursue their analysis fearlessly and indicate conclusions for policy without regard to what may be thought, in the short run, to be politically impossible.'[43]

Hayek supplied the IEA's need for fundamental thinking about the principles of a liberal order which could furnish criteria for judging the objectives and outcomes of policy. The institute published numerous pamphlets by him. Particularly significant were *A Tiger by the Tail: The Keynesian Legacy of Inflation*, edited by Sudha Shenoy and published in 1972, which consisted of selections from his writings on inflation going back to the 1930s; *Full Employment at Any Price?*, published in 1975, which includes the text of his Nobel Prize Lecture; and *Choice in Currency: A Way to Stop Inflation*, published in 1976, his move towards the idea of free banking.

The IEA helped acquaint a new readership with Hayek's work, seeing its potential for rethinking post-war policy. His influence was given a further boost when Keith Joseph and Margaret Thatcher established the Centre for Policy Studies in 1974 to provide an alternative source of policy advice. Alfred Sherman, its first director, was a leading proselytizer for Hayek's ideas, and through him Hayekian ideas were introduced to Joseph, Thatcher, and other leading Conservatives. Hayek's status increased still further in Britain when Thatcher became leader of the Conservative party in 1975. He was quickly recognized as the intellectual authority behind the change of direction which was being charted, and became a target for attack by those Conservatives, like Ian Gilmour, who wished to resist any move of the party in that direction.[44]

Although Hayek met Thatcher and other leading Conservatives, his main influence was through the dissemination of his ideas and approach to the analysis of economic and political problems by the think-tanks and the new intellectuals of the Conservative party. All the leading think-tanks and many of the most prominent New Right intellectuals and writers acknowledged their debt to him. In the United States his influence was less than in Britain, partly because of the strength of other forms of liberalism, but it was considerable none the less. The libertarian movement, as well as the neo-conservatives, regarded him as one of the fundamental sources of their ideas.

As an economist before 1945, Hayek was mainly preoccupied with theoretical rather than policy questions. In his political and philosophical investigations after 1945, he was again primarily concerned with general theoretical issues. His work was mainly directed towards the legislative assembly rather than the government assembly of his ideal constitution. He was more interested in re-creating the intellectual case for a liberal public philosophy than engaging in policy analysis and debate. As noted above, Keynes had gently chided him with not setting out in *The Road to Serfdom* where the line should be drawn between state action and private action. In *The Constitution of Liberty*, however, he devotes a long section to setting out the policy implications of his liberal outlook. Hayek's approach to policy was always governed by his understanding of the institutions and processes that are required for a market order. He seeks to remove obstacles to the working of those institutions and to ensure that government policies are constructed in such a way that they facilitate the workings of the market order rather than undermine it.

One of Hayek's central concerns was with money and the conditions for monetary stability. The absence of sound money did more than anything else to distort the working of the economy and to make individuals prepared to support interventionist policies and organizations which promised security but reduced liberty. The liberal order faced erosion from two sides: from politicians proposing collectivist programmes to win votes and special interest groups putting pressure on governments for favours and subsidies. Hayek's diagnosis of the problems of the Keynesian political economy started, therefore, with money. But he always argued that restoring sound money was not just a technical question; the political conditions for it had to be created, and that meant tackling the trade union monopoly and the extended state. Only if limited government and a liberal public philosophy could be restored, would it be possible for governments to return to policies of sound money. The key task was thus to reduce the role of government by reducing its responsibilities and the expectations which citizens had of it.

Monetary Policy

In the 1970s monetarism became the cutting edge of the New Right critique of Keynesian economic management. It was often assumed at that time that Hayek and Friedman were the two leading monetarists. But Hayek never accepted monetarism. He was in profound disagreement with the monetarist analysis, seeing it as another version of macro-economics which, in seeking to use aggregates, made a fundamental methodological error. But although he disagreed with monetarists like Milton Friedman as economists, he sympathized strongly with them politically. He saw them as much closer to the truth than the Keynesians, because they were returning to a version of the quantity theory of money, which, though itself flawed, had the right objective – the achievement of sound money.

Hayek never believed in the elaborate monetary targets which some monetarists proposed.[45] He was against any attempt to fine-tune economic aggregates, whether these were the demand aggregates of the Keynesians or the financial aggregates of the monetarists. His goal in policy was always to seek to create the right institutional framework. Then the free play of experimentation and choice would search out the best possible outcomes. Sound money was not a matter of deliberate policy, but of the right institutions. In the 1920s and 1930s Hayek was a strong supporter of the gold standard (although an opponent of Britain's return to gold in 1925 at pre-war parity). Like many other economists and bankers, he viewed the collapse of the gold standard in 1931 as a disaster, chiefly because it freed governments from external restraints and allowed them to pursue domestic policies of monetary expansion which were inflationary.

The chance to reconstruct the world economic order after the Second World War along true liberal lines was, in Hayek's view, missed. The Bretton Woods monetary system, although based on a modified gold standard system – the gold exchange standard – he interpreted as a victory for the inflationary policy of Keynes, establishing a permissive international monetary environment in which credit was made easily available and there was no pressure on deficit countries to eliminate their deficits. This allowed inflationary pressures generated by countries with lax domestic policies to be transmitted throughout the system. The strains created by the accumulation of surpluses and deficits and the acceleration of inflation finally brought about the collapse of the Bretton Woods system in 1971–2. This discredited national Keynesianism, and ushered in a period of vigorous debate about economic management, in which monetarist and free market programmes which accepted the constraints of the international market quickly became dominant in several countries and within key international institutions.

Some commentators, such as William Rees-Mogg, editor of *The Times* during the 1970s, argued strongly for the return of the gold standard.[46] Despite his earlier criticism of Keynes in the 1930s for being defeatist about the possibility of returning to the gold standard, Hayek did not support this call, arguing that it was politically impossible to restore a functioning gold standard. Instead, he sought a new institutional device for achieving sound money. He proposed ending the monopoly which governments had long enjoyed over the issue of legal currency in their territory. If all internationally traded currencies were available, individuals could choose which currency to use for transactions and which for saving and investments. In this way, good money would drive out bad, because individuals would choose to hold only those currencies which were so managed that they retained their value. Currencies tied to lax monetary policies would be punished because no one would want to hold them.

In his writings on choice in currency and the denationalization of money,[47] Hayek contributed to the revival of interest in the idea of free banking and the dismantling of the monopoly enjoyed by central banks. In line with his evolutionary ideas, which by this time were dominant in his thinking, he argued that any government monopoly was harmful to free evolutionary development and should therefore be abandoned if possible. The government monopoly of money was preventing experiments with new and more successful arrangements. Many specialists on banking thought the proposal utopian, because they did not believe that governments would ever consent to give up their monopoly over a function which was so close to defining what government and national communities were,[48] as well as so important in funding core state activities, not least war.

Other proposals canvassed for international monetary reform focused on the creation of some form of international money, either at regional level, as in the EMU proposals in the European Union, or at the global level, in the revival of Keynes's ideas for a new currency which would not be under the control of any single state. Hayek regarded both proposals as too statist. His proposal was typical of his thought. It questioned the role of government, and suggested an institutional mechanism which would allow individual consumers to protect themselves from the harmful effects of monetary decisions made by governments. It was a principle which delighted the liberal wing of the New Right, and could have been extended, had Hayek been inclined, to other previously sacrosanct areas of state monopoly, such as policing and defence. But here he remained cautious.

Trade Unions

The most serious danger posed to the survival of the market order by Keynesian political economy was the encouragement it gave to the spread of special interests. The gravest threat of all came from the trade unions. In *The Constitution of Liberty* Hayek declared that 'the whole basis of our free society is gravely threatened by the powers arrogated by the unions'.[49] From being unfairly discriminated against in the nineteenth century, trade unions had achieved a position in which they had become uniquely *privileged* institutions, in the sense that they were no longer subject to the general rule of law, and were able to use coercion in ways not available to any other organization outside the state.

Since Hayek was opposed to the notion of abstract, inalienable rights, he denied that trade unions had any special claim to be treated differently under the law, or that the right to strike is a principle that justifies protecting trade unions against claims for damages. Trade unions acquired their powers by operating in ways which Hayek argues 'would not be tolerated for any other purpose, and which are opposed to the protection of the individual's private sphere'.[50] In 1980 he wrote to *The Times* urging the Thatcher Government to repeal the 1906 Trade Disputes Act, which he regarded as one of the key moments in the transformation of England from one of the most liberal societies to one of the least.

So negative is Hayek's assessment of unions that he declares himself in favour of their complete disappearance. But he is not prepared to recommend outlawing them: 'in a free society much that is undesirable has to be tolerated if it cannot be prevented without discriminatory legislation.'[51] What has to be done is to bring them back within the rule of law:

> As is true of all problems of economic policy, the problem of labour unions cannot be satisfactorily solved by ad hoc decisions or particular questions but only by the consistent application of a principle that is uniformly adhered to in all fields.[52]

Unions offend Hayek because, although they began as voluntary associations, they have developed into coercive organizations which restrict the freedom of their own members, and which are employed to persuade governments of the merits either of general collectivist schemes or of measures that will provide particular benefits for their members. He finds it difficult to think of any positive function that trade unions perform. In *The Constitution of Liberty* the only role he can imagine for them, after they have been stripped of their coercive powers, is that they might assist with the process of wage determination in large organizations: 'in any hierarchical organisation it is important that the differentials between the remuneration for the different jobs and the rules of promotion are felt to be just by the majority.'[53] Hayek does not explain why a principle which is quite unacceptable if applied to society as a whole should be acceptable when applied within hierarchical organizations. It would have been more consistent for him to have advocated the dismantling of hierarchical organizations. But so long as these are business enterprises, they are legitimate in his view, in a way which trade unions are not.

One of the distinguishing features of Hayek's analysis of inflation in the 1970s was his appreciation of the institutional and political factors involved. Where Milton Friedman ascribed inflation to bad theory, Hayek showed the institutions which had grown up under the regime of Keynesian political economy to be responsible. He agreed with Friedman that inflation was ultimately a monetary phenomenon, but argued that it could not be explained just as the result of the mistaken ideas of the monetary authorities. The pressures on the monetary authorities to expand the money supply had also to be understood. Hayek agreed that the proposition that unions caused inflation by bidding for higher wages was incorrect as a general proposition, but he thought it was true under the conditions created by Keynesian political economy:

> Since it has become the generally accepted doctrine that it is the duty of the monetary authorities to provide enough credit to secure full employment, whatever the wage level, and this duty has in fact been imposed upon the monetary authorities by statute, the power of the trade unions to push up money wages cannot but lead to continuous progressive inflation.[54]

Hayek blamed inflation on the interaction between governments committed to maintaining full employment and trade unions acting to increase wages. Without the disciplines of bankruptcy and unemployment, there was nothing to hold union wage pressure in check. It could only be accommodated through increasing the money supply.

Hayek's analysis of Keynesian political economy has similarities with that of Michael Kalecki in his article 'Political Aspects of Full Employment', published in 1944, although their political conclusions are diametrically opposed.[55] Kalecki argued that a full employment policy of the kind that Keynesianism was proposing had to be understood in political terms as representing a fundamental shift in power between the owners of property and the owners of labour power. The loss of legitimacy by capitalist institutions in the 1930s meant that the only means by which capitalism could be made compatible with democracy was if major reforms were implemented to permit significant redistribution of wealth and an increase in economic and social security. These reforms were achieved in the Keynesian welfare state of the post-war period.

Hayek identifies this policy regime, particularly the commitment to full employment, the extension of state powers, the enhanced protection for organized labour, and the increase in collective welfare programmes as the policies that must be reversed if inflation is to be halted and the conditions for long-term prosperity created. He was always a market-restorer to the end.

Hayek never wavered in his opposition to the full employment policies and the welfare state established in the 1940s and 1950s. He insisted that ultimately inflation could only be halted by allowing unemployment to rise, and that in a market economy the employment problem was a wage problem, not a problem of demand:

> What is needed is that the responsibility for a wage level which is compatible with a high and stable level of employment should again be squarely placed where it belongs: with the trade unions ... the long-run problem remains the restoration of a labour market which will produce wages which are compatible with stable money.[56]

Public Spending

Yet, despite his opposition to the welfare state, Hayek always supported the case for some state intervention to provide minimum incomes and to improve opportunities for all citizens, so long as these were compatible with the rule of law and did not attempt to impose an artificial equality guided by notions of social justice. In *The Constitution of Liberty* he noted that the ideal of equality in classical liberalism had been

> a demand that all man-made obstacles to the rise of some should be removed, that all privileges of individuals should be abolished, and that what the state contributed to the chance of improving one's conditions should be the same for all. ... It was understood that the duty of government was not to ensure that everybody had the same prospect of reaching a given position but merely to make available to all on equal terms those facilities which in their nature depended on government action.[57]

A public minimum of provision is necessary, if only for the expedient reason that it helps to protect citizens against acts of desperation on the part of the needy. What he strongly opposed, however, was the monopolistic character of the welfare state, such that individuals were not simply required to pay compulsory insurance, but were compelled to pay it through an organization controlled by the state. Such arrangements violated his principle that monopolistic control by the state should be minimized as much as possible.

His other main objection to the welfare state was the use of social welfare programmes and the tax system to promote a redistribution of income: 'while in a free society it is possible to provide a minimum level of welfare for all, such a society is not compatible with sharing out income according to some preconceived notion of justice.'[58] He noted that the insurance principle in the provision of many benefits, such as pensions, was being lost, thereby storing up huge problems for the future. The more the welfare system became a playground for special interests and vote-catching, the greater the danger that the link between future benefits and personal contributions would be further eroded, with implications for conflict between generations in the future. For the same reason, he opposed the principle underlying the National Health Service, on the grounds that any service in which there is no link between the resources that individuals must make available for it and costs will cause demands to become unlimited, with no means of satisfying them.

Since he believes in the need for government, he also accepts the need for government coercion in the form of taxation. But the harmful effects of this coercion can be mitigated if certain principles are followed. He rejects the case for progressive taxation, since this is another way of seeking redistribution. Hayek argues that the only valid argument for progressive taxation is that it may compensate for the heavier proportional burden which indirect taxes place on lower income-earners. The principle which he favours is proportional taxation, with every individual paying the same proportion of tax on his or her income or property.

Once the principle of proportional taxation is abandoned, then there is no limit to the burdens which may be imposed. Fiscal policy becomes driven not by the most efficient means of raising revenue, but by the political objective of attempting to impose on society a pattern of distribution determined by majority decision. Such a policy wreaks havoc with the pattern established through market exchange, and leads to the gradual politicization of all activities in the market economy.

Hayek regrets the growth of a set of cultural attitudes which is hostile to large incomes and rewards, especially those which come from the taking of risks. The mentality of the employee, who believes that there is an appropriate level of income for every job and that no one should receive a reward outside this range, comes to influence taxation policy, with harmful effects on enterprise, initiative, innovation, the building up of new businesses, and social mobility. Hayek proposes that a reasonable system of taxation would be one in which the majority which determines through the ballot-box the total amount of taxation should also accept taxation at the maximum rate. In this way the burden of taxation would not be shifted disproportionately to the rich. A direct tax rate of 25 per cent on both individual income and national income Hayek regarded as the maximum which should be levied.[59]

The key to keeping taxation low is restraint in public spending. Hayek's main proposals for doing so focus on removing the harmful effects of overbidding and lobbying through the political process. But he is surprisingly interventionist in many areas, accepting the need for government programmes in housing, agriculture, and the environment. The main criterion is that they should be limited, and used only when markets are not working. But he does accept market failure and some public goods arguments. After arguing that civilization is inseparable from urban life, he argues that 'The general formulas of private property do not provide an immediate answer to the complex problems which city life raises'.[60] He also accepts the need for some conservation policies in respect to natural resources, but they should be treated as investments and judged by the same criteria as other investments. He accepts the case for a minimum education provided through the state on the orthodox collectivist grounds that there are significant benefits if all citizens acquire a common knowledge and set of beliefs, and that democracy is unlikely to work if people are illiterate. But he also argued that there was no need for educational institutions to be directly run by the government, particularly in higher education. In all his policy interventions, Hayek was chiefly concerned to find ways to reduce the monopolistic power of the state. If the funding for a particular good, such as insurance, was best provided through the coercive mechanism of the state, its actual supply should be organized through the private sector.

Restoring conditions for a market order, however, was still a perplexing business, given the way in which democracy operated and the lack of understanding of the principles of a market order among the electorate. Pressures for increased spending and for government programmes which interfered with the market order were always present. Hayek lived to see Keynesianism as a doctrine repudiated, but the institutional and political legacy of Keynesianism lived on.

8

The Iron Cage of Liberty

Libertarianism now faces a kind of political defeat, for while the Austrian school argument against socialism has been proven valid, libertarians may be unable to offer any internally consistent reason to oppose the welfare state; and even more clearly there seems to be no escaping the environmental state.

Jeffrey Friedman, *Critical Review*

This book has argued that underpinning all Hayek's work is a particular conception of modernity, which owes much to Max Weber. Hayek makes few references to Weber, but they had many ideas in common, particularly their scorn for socialism and their appreciation of the constraints which modern civilization imposed on human societies. The German intellectual tradition which nurtured Weber was preoccupied with the meaning of human history and the future of Western civilization. So was Hayek.

Max Weber was on the whole seen as an ally by the Austrian school, not as an opponent. Although strongly influenced by historical and institutionalist approaches, during the *Methodenstreit* he had been closer to the Austrian position than to the historicists, and just before his death in 1920 his critique of the feasibility of implementing a socialist organization of either the economy or the state was similar to that of Mises. But although he reognized the value of theoretical economics, his own methodology was aimed at developing a comparative analysis of social systems. In politics he was a national liberal, and supported a strong German state of the kind that was anathema to Hayek.[1]

Weber's sociological analysis of the social processes which constituted modernity established many of the terms of the twentieth-century debate. He identified rationalization and secularization as the key processes in the transition from traditional society, in which values were communal and relationships were primary and face-to-face, to modern society, in which values were individualist and relationships were secondary and impersonal. The image of traditional society which was so central to nineteenth-century sociology was drawn from a particular idealization of medieval society. Medieval forms of culture and community had provided individuals with a strong sense of belonging and identity, and it was these which were being undermined by the processes of rationalization and secularization.

Rationalization means the subordination of all values, all culture, and all social relationships to decisions made by centralized, impersonal, hierarchical organizations seeking to maximize efficiency. This form of organization, bureaucracy, is inevitable in the modern world, given the tasks that have to be performed in societies with rapidly increasing populations and dependent on an ever more complex division of labour.

Weber's vision of modernity is ultimately a tragic one. At first the process of rationalization meant applying utilitarian and liberal principles to established institutions and policies, sweeping away everything that could not be rationally justified. It resulted in a huge release of energy, a leap into freedom. But this sense of liberation depended on the continued existence of the old institutions and culture. As rationalization proceeded, so the old society was steadily undermined, and began to disappear. The new methods of organization associated with rationalization began to dominate, and as they did so, they ceased to be liberating. The new society increasingly locked individuals into vast impersonal, regimented organizations, destroying the individual's traditional sense of identity and the values of the old society and subjecting everything to a uniform utilitarian calculus. This process led to a disenchantment of the world, in which meaning was lost and human experience was devalued. Liberation from the constraints of traditional society brought enormous wealth and high standards of comfort, but also spiritual poverty and a pervasive restlessness and unease.

Weber saw the modern condition as an unhappy one, but one which there is no escaping. He strongly criticized those intellectuals who sought to deny the reality of the modern world by taking refuge in pre-modern systems of values and beliefs. The modern world was created by science and bureaucracy, and individuals must come to terms with them. Modern science meant that, in principle, there were no mysterious incalculable forces left in the universe. Everything could be explained and therefore controlled. But the consequence of this, Weber argued, is that no one any longer believes that science teaches us anything meaningful about the world or that it is a way to God. Science gives understanding, but cannot tell us which things are worthwhile. It has no answer to Tolstoy's questions: what shall we do, and how shall we live?[2]

In Weber's account, death is no longer a meaningful phenomenon for moderns, because the life of modern individuals has become an infinite progress of new experiences.[3] Since everything in the modern world is always provisional and never definitive, time is no longer understood cyclically as in pre-modern cultures, and therefore it is impossible for modern individuals ever to be satiated. The contrast with pre-modern cultures is marked. They assumed that experience was finite and that human beings who lived a full life could die knowing that they had experienced everything life had to offer. As Marcus Aurelius reflected:

> the rational soul . . . wanders round the whole world and through the encompassing void, and gazes into infinite time, and considers the periodic destruction and rebirths of the universe, and reflects that our posterity will see nothing new, and that our ancestors saw nothing greater than we have seen. A man of forty years, possessing the most moderate intelligence, may be said to have seen all that is past and all that is to come; so uniform is the world.[4]

No such happy fate awaits modern individuals. They may become tired and bored, but never satiated in the sense of achieving existential satisfaction.

The conclusion which Weber draws from this stark analysis of modernity is that the only way of coping with such an impersonal, disenchanted world is for individuals to invent their own values. They cannot rely on any kind of revealed truth, from either a god or a prophet. What they confront is a confusing situation in which there are numerous warring gods. What the individual has to do, argues Weber, is to choose which of the warring gods to serve. The basic values which can be adopted in life are irreconcilable, which means that in the modern world the struggle between them can never be brought to a satisfactory conclusion. The deadlock can be broken only by each individual making a decisive personal choice.[5]

Weber presents the modern world as an iron cage in which individuals are trapped. As rationalization proceeds, so meaning, individuality, and autonomy are all threatened, and the potential for a tyranny more extensive and more enduring than anything previously experienced is created. Rationalization removes the irrationality and superstitions of traditional society, and reduces the amount of coercion and exploitation in direct face-to-face relationships. But the cost is the erosion of mystery and enchantment, and genuinely communal and spiritual experience.

Hayek and Weber

Hayek too sees the modern world as an iron cage. He too contrasts traditional with modern society, and argues that there is no possibility of returning to an earlier era. Socialism belongs to traditional society, and is therefore, for Hayek, like one of Weber's archaic religions which is used as a refuge from the modern world. Socialism, in Hayek's view, is incompatible with the modern world. It seeks to impose a communal moral ethos in a world in which the only possible morality is derived from individual choices. It abolishes the only institutions which are capable of ensuring the rationality of economic calculation and therefore prosperity. And it sanctions so much power for the state that it prepares the way for totalitarianism.

Thus socialism is not a legitimate choice for Hayek. But why not? Is it not one of the warring gods among which individuals must choose in the modern world? Here there is a real gulf between Hayek and Weber. Weber also dismissed socialism as utopian, but primarily on the basis of consequentalist arguments – for example, that socialism in practice will fail to deliver what it promises, and may seriously compromise the efficiency of modern society.

Hayek goes further than this. In his eyes, modernity has certain unavoidable, irreversible features – including the extended division of labour, impersonality, a loss of community, and personal responsibility. Hayek believes that each individual must make a definitive choice in favour of liberal values and scientific truth. Both Weber and Hayek made such a choice, although what they understood by liberal values differed. But for Weber the commitment is essentially arbitrary. It has no objective basis. It is the choice which injects meaning into the world for him, but he acknowledges that other people will choose different goals and values. But for Hayek, there is only one god that can be chosen. All other choices lead to disaster. If others choose different goals, the reason is intellectual error. They choose wrongly, because they do not understand that there really is no choice if civilization is to survive. Weber anticipated Schumpeter's argument that the outcome of modern development might well be socialism, understood as the complete bureaucratization of society. Such an outcome would extinguish what few possibilities remained in the modern world for genuine autonomy and individuality, but it would still constitute a viable social system.

Hayek's understanding is different. He too regards only one form of institutional structure as sustainable in the modern world, but he fiercely rejects the idea that liberty could be extinguished and modern civilization still survive. For him, Western civilization is inconceivable without liberty. Science and organization are important, but so too are individualism and the unintended spontaneous orders which have evolved to form the framework of modern society. The capacity to evolve further resides not in bureaucracy, organization, and planning, but in the constant experimentation and competition that liberal institutions encourage.

Hayek's evolutionary ideas, which became ever more pronounced in his later writings, are close in some respects to those of Herbert Spencer.[6] But again, there is an important difference. Spencer thought that it was possible to identify evolutionary laws, and on this basis argued that the final destination of human societies, their highest stage of development, was *laissez-faire*. Hayek shared this goal (although he always disliked the term *laissez-faire*), but disagreed that it was inevitable. For him, no single destination lay at the end of contemporary social development. Liberal civilization might destroy itself. In this he agrees with Rosa Luxemburg that the future offers a choice. For her it was a choice between socialism and barbarism. For Hayek, the achievement of socialism represents barbarism, so the choice is not between socialism and barbarism but between capitalism and barbarism.

The structures of modern civilization, in Weber's view, constantly erode and marginalize individual freedom and autonomy. For Hayek, however, these structures, properly understood, are the expression of liberty. He is more optimistic than Weber about the prospects for Western civilization. Since he is so often regarded as a pessimist, a Cassandra repeatedly appearing before the public with dark warnings of apocalypse, this needs some explaining. The reason is that, unlike Weber, he sees the problems of modern society as stemming not from the core structures and modes of social action that define it, but from a perversion of those structures. It follows that what is needed is a purge of the body politic and of intellectual culture. If bad ideas can be driven out and discredited, then the distinctive quality of Western civilization can be preserved, and it can continue to grow and develop.

Much of Hayek's work, as we have seen, is devoted to this task. His division of liberalism into two camps, the true and the false, and his denunciation of constructivists and rationalists for being completely wrong in their perception of the world are all part of it. It is an aspect of Hayek which many commentators have found difficult to accept. If the problems of modern Western civilization are due to intellectual error, how has this error arisen? Hayek's evolutionary arguments desert him at this point. The constructivist rationalists have existed for at least as long as Hayek's true liberals, the critical rationalists, but they show no sign of being sidelined by the normal evolutionary process. Should not evolution have discarded them by now? Instead, in the twentieth century their influence has increased, and even after the failure of the Soviet experiment it is far from spent.

Hayek's argument is at its weakest here. Having committed himself so strongly to evolutionary arguments, it seems perverse to dispense with such arguments on this crucial question. But this reflects the fundamental tension in Hayek's thought, which he is unable to resolve. The source of his difficulty lies in his refusal to accept so much of the Western intellectual tradition as an authentic part of that tradition. Constructivist rationalism has been a central part of this tradition for the past four hundred years, yet Hayek implies that it has no right to exist. Standing aside, however, from internal ideological struggles, what is striking about the Western tradition of political thought is how much its different strands have in common, rather than how irreconcilable they are. It is recognizably one tradition.

The End of History

Hayek's attempt to delegitimize one side of the Western tradition is one of the most significant ideological closures in his work. It prevents him from seeing the close ties which exist between liberalism and socialism. Far from being the negation of liberalism, socialism can plausibly be seen as part of the same project as liberalism, even as its fulfilment. Hayek considered socialism an atavistic reactionary creed which dominated the 'socialist century' of 1848–1948, but which, in the second half of the twentieth century, had been in headlong retreat. In the twenty-first century he expected it to become a historical curiosity, a discarded experiment, from which only negative lessons could be learned.

Hayek is not alone in proclaiming the end of socialism at the end of the twentieth century. This has been a common refrain on both Left and Right with the ending of the Cold War, the collapse of communism, and the disappearance of serious alternatives in the world order to capitalist forms of economic organization. The best-known statement of this position is Francis Fukuyama's essay on the end of history.[7] But there is a considerable difference between the positions taken by Hayek and Fukuyama. Hayek thinks that socialism has disappeared because it has been discredited finally, whereas Fukuyama argues that it has disappeared because it has been surpassed. All that is legitimate and valuable in socialism has been incorporated in contemporary forms of liberal capitalism and social democracy.

Fukuyama puts forward four main theses in his original article: economic and political liberalism have triumphed; viable alternatives to capitalism no longer exist; the final point in humanity's ideological evolution has been achieved; and democratic government and free market capitalism have been universalized. His argument is based on an explicit revival of a liberal historicism, the project of a universal history. After a long period in which historicism and its doctrine of progress were associated with Marxism, Fukuyama argues that history does have a direction, but not the one that Marx suggested. Hegel proclaimed that history was at an end after the Battle of Jena in 1806, because Napoleon's victory meant the triumph of the ideals of the French Revolution, liberty and equality, the quintessential principles of modernity.

Fukuyama claims that these basic principles of the liberal democratic state were impossible to improve upon. Two centuries of ideological conflict have finally confirmed that there is indeed no way of improving them. Markets and private property are indispensable for the organization of the economy. Similarly, democratic institutions are essential, to give individuals public recognition and identity as citizens.

Fukuyama states that liberal capitalism has triumphed, but he does not regard its institutional form as fixed or invariant. A range of institutions are compatible with its basic principles of organization. From Hayek's standpoint, such a claim concedes a large part of the argument against socialism, since Fukuyama is arguing that capitalist economies with large public sectors and universalist welfare programmes are as legitimate as those with minimal state intervention. He regards the form of contemporary capitalism that has emerged to be a case of Hegel's universal homogenous state, in which all contradictions are reconciled and all human needs satisfied. There is no longer any issue which cannot be handled within the institutional framework which has been established; hence there is no need to explore alternative socioeconomic systems. History and ideological debate are at an end in this sense. All that remains is for increasingly prosperous and satisfied societies to solve the detailed, practical problems they face. Politics becomes administration, not the expression of fundamental values.

Fukuyama's vision is much more optimistic than either Weber's or Hayek's. He believes that democratic institutions and capitalist institutions are so strong that there is no danger of rationalization leading to totalitarianism in either the political or the economic system; and he is happy to accept a pluralism of institutional forms. Social democracy and the mixed economy, welfare programmes, industrial strategies, public services, and redistributive fiscal policies are all legitimate ways of organizing modern industrial societies. Rationalization and secularization have proceeded with many of the effects which Weber predicted. The world has been thoroughly disenchanted, but it has not succumbed to authoritarianism.

Fukuyama's complacency, as his critics have pointed out, depends on his having restricted his gaze to the handful of prosperous developed states in the global political economy. Nevertheless, Fukuyama's vision is a powerful testimony to the success which liberal capitalism has had in establishing itself as the only viable model of political and economic development, even if its ability to ensure development in the rest of the world has declined. Hayek has no real answer to Fukuyama. He continued to believe to the end that no compromise is possible, and that the welfare state poses as great a long-term danger to the survival of individualist Western civilization as central planning and state socialism.

The Modern State

The problem, as some perceptive libertarian critics like Jeffrey Friedman have pointed out,[8] is that the Austrian critique worked

very well against central planning, but it has been much less successful against the welfare state. Friedman turns Fukuyama upside
down, and in doing so, goes to the heart of some of the unresolved
tensions in Hayek. He argues that history did not end in 1991, but
in 1921. The failure of war communism and the announcement of
the New Economic Policy marked the decisive moment when the
Communist experiment in the Soviet Union failed and the attempt
to launch a real experiment entailing an alternative to capitalism
was abandoned. Friedman, however, regards these events not just
as a defeat for communism but also as a defeat for liberalism, on
the grounds that the goals of the Communist revolutionaries were
the ultimate expression of the aspirations of egalitarian individualism, and hence the logical culmination of the modernist project
initiated by the French Revolution. The defeat of communism is
not a vindication of liberalism, therefore, as Fukuyama imagines,
but a sign of deep dislocation within the modernist project. Western
civilization has reached a point where it 'depends for its continued
existence on a system of production and exchange that is fundamentally at odds with its deepest moral precepts'.[9]

Prominent among these moral precepts are notions of the sanc-
tity and moral equality of each individual. The first is associated
with the ideas of individual conscience and individual autonomy,
the second with the idea that if individuals are considered to be
equally worthy of respect, they should have equal rights. The joining
of these two notions makes egalitarianism inseparable from individualism, and helps to explain why it has always been so difficult
to confine liberty to negative liberty. Realization of the principle of
moral equality always involves positive liberty as well, not merely
the protection of a sphere for each individual, but the creation of
conditions in which individuals can fully enjoy such a sphere and
develop their full potential. Egalitarian individualism has always,
as a result, meant the raising of new demands and the generation
of new entitlements.

Friedman argues that the attempt to confine liberalism to negative liberty and proscribe other forms, as Hayek tries to do, is a
hopeless task, which misconstrues the character of the cultural and
ideological project of modernity. Negative liberty cannot be limited to property-owners. Once individual freedom becomes an end
in itself, the principles of self-determination and self-realization
become central. Self-interest is condemned as being narrow and
restrictive. True freedom is conceived as liberation from the selfish
appetites which lead to materialism and inequality. The ideal of a
community of citizens who are all responsible agents and moral

equals is thus not rooted, as Hayek thinks, in some atavistic pre-modern impulses. It lies at the heart of the project of modernity which has developed within Western civilization.

Yet it seems that this ideal is unrealizable. History ended in 1921, because the attempt to move towards this ideal collapsed. In Friedman's view, we have been living in the twilight ever since. In the post-historical era since 1921, the egalitarian-individualist ideal has been 'permanently half-fulfilled' in the successful capitalist societies of the West through the welfare state and consumerism. The welfare state, like the former Soviet economy, is a compromise, a form of distorted capitalism and market economy, which acknowledges, but fails to realize, the deepest values of Western civilization.

Friedman offers a different version of the iron cage of modernity. The deepest desires of the Western tradition are unattainable; but so too is Hayek's dream that individuals might in future be content to think of themselves simply as property-owners and restrict their hopes and aspirations to property rights. What has emerged in all societies in the era of mass democracy is the demand for welfare programmes which express the moral equality of all citizens. Friedman considers the culture of Western civilization to be highly unstable, because the statist solution of welfare programmes does not provide a true moral community, and entails many dangers, from moral hazard, the creation of dependence, and the influence of special interests. Yet there seems no way of either creating a moral ethos for capitalism which abandons egalitarianism or launching a new attempt to realize a communist utopia. The result is a society which has lost its moral bearings and its moral purpose. Its politics, its civil society, and its public institutions all decay as a result of individual acquisitiveness, on the one hand, and state dependency on the other.

Society after the end of history is one of postmodern stalemate, in which the socialist and liberal projects characteristic of modernity cannot be realized. The iron cage has triumphed. Far from ushering in Fukuyama's society of contentment, blandness, prosperity, and peace, however, it has created a restless, unstable, centrifugal culture, in which private agendas come to dominate public ones. Postmodernism throws up cultural rebellions against the imperatives of modernity, but does not transcend them.

Hayek correctly diagnosed that the iron cage of modernity would frustrate the realization of socialism. But the greatest failure of his analysis stems from his refusal to accept that part of the iron cage consists of the structures of the modern state, especially its security, surveillance, and welfare apparatuses. He encouraged a liberal utopianism, suggesting the possibility of bringing the ideology and culture of modern society into harmony with its economics, built on a moral community of property-owners. The political implications of attempting to realize this utopia, however, involve an assault upon the realities of modern life just as great as does the socialist utopianism he criticized.

Hayek's thought does not reach its full potential because of this ideological closure. He remains trapped in a discourse which sets up liberalism and socialism as polar opposites, with the result that he never acknowledges how much the two doctrines have in common and the insights that both contribute to an understanding of modernity. Yet there is in Hayek a reaching beyond the particular modernist straitjacket in which he has imprisoned himself. His most fruitful insights on spontaneous orders lead to an affirmation of the value of particular knowledges and the importance of individual differences which provide a bridge with postmodernist concerns and discourses in ways that are often subversive of his original intentions.

Conservatism and Liberalism

Many commentators on Hayek have noted a change in emphasis over the years in the way he justifies the market order. In *The Constitution of Liberty*, written in the 1950s, the balance of his argument is consequentialist (based on the outcomes of policies and institutions) but also at times deontological (based on what is morally binding). The concept of spontaneous order is at the forefront of his analysis. In *Law, Legislation, and Liberty*, written in the 1970s, the balance has moved towards evolutionary arguments, typified by the claim that the ultimate justification of the market order is that it supports a higher population. But Hayek's evolutionism is always ambiguous. Although he becomes increasingly cautious about recommending any changes or reforms, which makes his work take on a strongly conservative tone, this does not extend to his attitude to the extended state. His recommendations on trade union legislation and on monetary policy, for example, are both precise and sweeping. No caution is evident in his advocacy of the immediate repeal of all the complex laws which had evolved to govern industrial relations in the twentieth century. This attitude reflects a deep vein of rationalist constructivism in his thinking, which keeps surfacing throughout his work. In *Law, Legislation, and Liberty* it is most evident in his proposals for reconstructing democratic institutions to restore limited government.[10]

Hayek's constructivism keeps him from ever becoming a true Conservative. This explains the distaste which many Conservatives continued to feel for him. As noted in chapter 5, the gulf between him and Oakeshott is critical. They drew on many of the same figures in the Anglo-Irish and Anglo-Scottish traditions, especially Burke and Hume, for their conceptions of the nature of the English tradition, which, particularly on civil association, were remarkably similar. But ultimately they diverge, and the source of this divergence can be traced to their quite opposite evaluations of Hobbes.[11] For Oakeshott, Hobbes is the most important English political philosopher, who saw more clearly than any other the nature of political reality in the modern era. For Hayek, Hobbes is anathema, a supreme rationalist whose arguments justified state power without limits. For Hobbes, individuals have no rights, only obligations once the state has been formed. Oakeshott admired the absolutism of Hobbes's account. The founding of a state required an absolute commitment, which simultaneously fixed the character of the state. There could be no compromise between the state as a civil association and the state as an enterprise association. A state was either one or the other. Oakeshott's point was that the identity of the English state as a civil association existed prior to any democratic legitimation. Democracy threatened this identity by making possible the development of political parties and programmes which sought to transform the English state from a civil to an enterprise association.

Oakeshott's thought is liberal in its endorsement of the civil association of the English and Scottish liberal traditions, but conservative in its rejection of democracy. The legitimacy of the English state and its institutions and the obligations they impose on citizens do not derive from any outcomes which flow from the kind of order that is established. Although he supports limited government, Oakeshott does not seek to justify it in either of the two classical liberal ways: in terms of individual rights existing prior to the formation of government or in terms of the outcomes it produces.

Hayek's thought is conservative in its distrust of experiment and in its increasing reliance on the authority of tradition, but it remains liberal in its basic conception and justification of the state. Although Hayek, like Oakeshott, is a strong critic of democracy and is very aware of its dangers, and, again like Oakeshott, was prepared to support authoritarian government in certain circumstances, he is never prepared, as are Oakeshott and Hobbes, to give unlimited authority to the state as an association. Hayek's thought is anti-political; government is an evil, to be minimized as much as possible. What are valuable for Hayek are the spontaneous exchanges made possible by the market order. The state is always a dead hand, a burden, however necessary, on the creativity and energy of civil society. The legitimacy of the market order is ultimately not a political matter at all, understood as one entailing the self-determination of a community, but depends rather on the flow of benefits it makes possible. Hayek's fundamental liberalism consists in this. He is never willing to grant a particular pattern of political organization an absolute authority. He refuses to recognize that there can be overriding social or political obligations for the individual which derive from the way in which a social and political order is constituted. His conception of the state is that it exists to protect civil association, not that the state itself must be understood as a civil association.

For Oakeshott, to understand the state as a civil association means that the state has no purpose of its own. It is not an enterprise association. For Hayek, by contrast, the state is always an enterprise association. The only question is which purposes it pursues, not whether it has a purpose.[12] Hayek argues that its powers must be kept strictly limited, so that it sustains the market order rather than supplants it. But this is a liberal, consequentialist view. For conservative thinkers like Oakeshott, the authority and continuity of the institutions of the state always come first, because they are the guarantees of order and identity. Liberalism has always been rejected for its celebration of the rights and purposes of the individual above the maintenance of authority and order.

Hayek rejects arguments based on the need for authority. He was always a strong critic of the powers which states claimed for themselves through the doctrines of popular sovereignty or nationalism. He supported federalism both at national and international levels.[13] His reasoning was always pragmatic. He favoured any arrangement which tended to reduce and disperse the powers of governments. His proposals for constitutional reform are driven by that same underlying goal.

The ideological cast of his thought, however, means that on several questions he fails to pursue some of his most important arguments and insights. These closures include his failure to apply his concept of evolution to the expanding role of the state and to democracy,[14] to apply his concept of coercion to the subordinate position of workers in factories, and to apply his concept of dependency to the organization of industry. Yet his concepts often push beyond the confines of the ideological closures he imposes on his work, for example, in his theory of knowledge and spontaneous order. Although his evolutionary theories have been much criticized for other reasons, one of the main problems with them is their selectivity.

Hayek's greatest failure is his neglect of the problem of private power. All his efforts go into the denunciation of state power, but he has little to say about private coercion. He endorses negative liberty over positive liberty, and defines negative liberty almost wholly in terms of the liberty of property-owners. Since on his own account the majority of citizens in the market order cannot be property-owners, and since he proposes no measures to enable them to become so, he appears to accept that there can be no return to the kind of liberal order which he favours.

The Future of Socialism

Whatever the chances of restoring liberalism, Hayek was at least confident that the intellectual and practical basis of socialism had been destroyed. But the future of socialism may be rather different from how he pictured it, and, paradoxically, his own work may assist in the emergence of new forms of socialism in the future.

Perry Anderson has recently argued that while the eclipse of socialism at the end of the twentieth century is undeniable, there is a range of possible futures for socialism.[15] He lists them as oblivion (Hayek's hope), transvaluation, mutation, and redemption. Anderson explores each possibility through historical analogies with the fate of other social experiments in the modern period. The first two possibilities, oblivion and transvaluation, entail a complete historical break. In the case of oblivion, no significant legacy would remain for the future, or would ever be recovered. The example taken by Anderson to illustrate this is the community which the Jesuits organized in Paraguay, which lasted for more than a hundred years until it was suppressed by the Spanish authorities. It is now known only as a historical curiosity. Will the socialist societies and movements of the twentieth century, he asks, come to be seen in the same light, as bizarre attempts in distant lands to overturn economic and social realities?

A second possibility is transvaluation. Here again, there is a sharp break in continuity, following complete defeat and demoralization and the disappearance of the original movement. But at a much later date some of the same ideas and principles re-emerge in a new form. Anderson cites the fate of the Levellers' radical programme in the British civil war of the seventeenth century, which was suppressed at the time and left no legacy or memory behind it. (The Putney debates on representation and the suffrage, for example, were not rediscovered until the end of the nineteenth century.) But the basic ideas and principles later re-emerged in the altered form of the socialist movements of the nineteenth century.

A third possibility is mutation. Here historical continuity is maintained to some extent, and memory and tradition are not entirely lost, so something is handed on directly to later generations. But although the later movement acknowledges its links with the earlier one, it is substantially different. The French Jacobins were ousted from power in the Thermidor *coup*, but their example started a tradition of revolutionary organization which forms a direct link with many of the revolutionary socialist organizations of the nineteenth and twentieth centuries. But the programmes and tactics of these later movements, although they owed something to Jacobinism, were also different from it in several crucial respects, particularly in their attitude to private property.

A final possibility is redemption. At the nadir of its fortunes, socialism might be reborn, just as liberalism recovered from its decline and defeat between 1914 and 1945 to re-emerge as the dominant doctrine and idea of the post-war world. Anderson speculates that some new world crisis might make socialism also once more relevant and necessary; only, like liberalism before it, this would be a socialism purged of many of its past flaws and enriched by its borrowings from other traditions.

Knowledge, Co-ordination, and Institutions

Socialism will have a future, because, as Robin Blackburn has argued, there are common conditions of human existence which can be sustained only by collective and democratic means, and individuality and self-determination, if they are to be enjoyed by more than a small minority, require collective action to establish and maintain the conditions that make them possible.[16] For these reasons, the core ideas and ideals of socialism are unlikely to lose their relevance or their power. Egalitarian individualism has not yet run its course. There remain many aspects of the structures of modern societies, including race and gender, where individuals have not yet achieved equal rights, and are constrained in developing their potential as individuals. The problem of poverty both within and relatively between societies has not remotely been solved. In several respects the gap is widening, and this raises issues of social cohesion for both national and global societies of a most intractable kind. Finally, new problems, particularly those associated with the environment and sustainability, present collective action problems on a scale which could eventually force a reconstruction of the global political economy and the evolution of new forms of regional and international co-operation.

Hayek has much to contribute to the renewal of the socialist project. His fundamental importance for social science was in directing attention to the way in which institutions form as a means of co-ordinating the myriad decisions and preferences of individual agents. He directed attention to the dispersed nature of knowledge, the problems of co-ordination, the appropriate level for planning, the unintended consequences of social action, and the importance of spontaneous orders in human affairs. Although he sometimes resisted them, the implications of his theories are towards decentralized, local forms of governance, enabling rather than command structures, and the need to reinforce (and if necessary create) institutions which can co-ordinate the information and decisions of individual agents and lead to outcomes that benefit the whole society.[17]

Hayek's research programme in economics is likely to live longer than his anti-socialist polemics, because it directs attention to many of the problems which need to be resolved if economies are to perform more effectively. His understanding of the institutions which make possible regulation and co-ordination of economic and social action remains central to any form of political economy and public policy.[18]

Hayek's subtle and complex understanding of the interplay between institutions and agency focuses attention on the kind of problems which a post-constructivist economics and social science need to address.[19] One of the key theoretical questions underlying his economic research programme was how the plans of individual agents are co-ordinated in a way that creates and sustains an economic order. Such co-ordination depends on the information and knowledge which individuals possess. Knowledge is inherently dispersed and fragmented, so co-ordination cannot be imposed.

One obvious but trite answer to the co-ordination problem was simply to assume it away. In his conception of the price system as a discovery procedure, Hayek posed a series of fundamental questions about the relationship between preferences, prices, and information. Meghnad Desai has argued[20] that in his later writings after 1945, however, Hayek turned away from investigating these questions, and tended to assume that the solution to the problem of fragmented knowledge was to ensure that prices were determined freely. But in some of his writings in the 1930s he hinted at a much more interesting answer, focusing on the way in which expectations and preferences interact with prices, shaping them and being shaped by them. Instead of treating preferences as fixed and unalterable, and deriving purely formal, timeless equilibria in the manner of mainstream neoclassical economics, he directs his inquiry towards the institutional structure which shapes individuals' knowledge and preferences and which individuals reproduce through their choices and actions.[21]

On this conception of co-ordination there is always uncertainty. The order that is created is not a perfect order, but an order that is always capable of being improved. The pattern of co-ordination is created through rules and institutions. Many of these have evolved spontaneously. No one can stand outside this society and impose a pattern which will improve on what already exists. But once this pattern and how it has come into existence have been grasped, there are numerous opportunities for improving and shaping it.[22] The identification of co-ordination failures and of the institutional changes, such as the supply of knowledge and forms of governance, which might remedy them offer a rich and varied agenda both for social science research and for political action.

Conceiving social interaction as a discovery process puts the emphasis on the way in which new needs and new opportunities can emerge. Institutions arise as a solution to problems of co-ordination, but a range of different institutions expressing different values is possible. There is no reason to be narrowly prescriptive in the way in which Hayek sometimes seeks to be.[23]

One of the implications of a Hayekian analysis of knowledge, co-ordination, and institutions, however, is that the most effective forms of social organization are likely to be decentralized and democratic. Hayek's old liberal anti-democratic and elitist views led him to support an institutional pattern which was highly centralized, hierarchical, and despotic for most of the people involved in it. But on his own assumptions, such a pattern is highly unlikely to be the most effective or fruitful pattern for the future development of human societies. Hayek's approach has much to offer both liberals and conservatives, but ironically, perhaps most to socialists, as they seek to rethink ways of reforming institutions so as to achieve their historic aims of liberty, equality, and solidarity. Hayek might not have approved, but he would hardly have been surprised. As he himself said at the end of his life:

> The evolution of ideas has its own laws and depends very largely upon developments which we cannot predict. I mean, I'm trying to move opinion in a certain direction, but I wouldn't dare to predict what direction it will really move.[24]

Notes

Chapter 1   Introduction: Rethinking Hayek

1   F. A. Hayek, *Hayek on Hayek*, ed. S. Kresge and L. Wenar (London: Routledge, 1994), p. 51.
2   Ibid., p. 89.
3   Lichtheim wrote under the pseudonym G. A. Arnold in *Twentieth Century*, Aug. 1960, p. 107.
4   J. Birner and R. van Zijp (eds), *Hayek, Coordination and Evolution* (London: Routledge, 1994).
5   Two of the best studies of Hayek which explore the contradictions of his thought are C. Kukathas, *Hayek and Modern Liberalism* (Oxford: Clarendon Press, 1989), and R. Kley, *Hayek's Social and Political Thought* (Oxford: Clarendon Press, 1994).
6   A. V. Dicey, *Lectures on the Relation between Law and Public Opinion in England during the Nineteenth Century* (London: Macmillan, 1926).
7   K. Polanyi, *The Great Transformation* (Boston: Beacon Press, 1957), p. 23
8   Ibid., p. 249.
9   J. Schumpeter, *Capitalism, Socialism, and Democracy* (London: Allen and Unwin, 1950), p. 61.
10 See the account in R. Cockett, *Thinking the Unthinkable: Thinktanks and the Economic Counter-Revolution, 1931–1983* (London: Fontana, 1995), pp. 9–13.
11 D. Bell, *The End of Ideology* (Glencoe, Ill.: Free Press, 1960); E. Shils, 'The End of Ideology?', *Encounter*, 5 (1955), 52–8.
12 S. M. Lipset, *Political Man* (London: Mercury, 1960), p. 406.
13 See Cockett, *Thinking the Unthinkable*, and A. Denham, 'Thinktanks of the New Right: Theory, Practice, and Prospects', Ph.D. diss., Southampton, 1992.

14   F. A. Hayek, *New Studies in Philosophy, Politics, Economics and the History of Ideas* (London: Routledge, 1978), p. 305.

15   For an account of Vienna before the First World War see C. Schorske, *Fin-de-Siècle Vienna* (Cambridge: Cambridge University Press, 1961).

16   F. A. Hayek, *The Sensory Order: An Enquiry into the Foundations of Theoretical Psychology* (London: Routledge, 1952).

17   J. Gray, *Hayek on Liberty* (Oxford: Blackwell, 1986). See also R. P. de Vries, 'The Place of Hayek's Theory of Mind and Perception in the History of Philosophy and Psychology', in Birner and van Zijp (eds), *Hayek, Coordination and Evolution*, pp. 311–22, and M. Forsyth, 'Hayek's Bizarre Liberalism', *Political Studies*, 36/2 (June 1988), 235–50.

18   Hutchison suggests that under the influence of Mises, Hayek adopted a praxeological approach in his early writings, but that later, after reading Popper, he became a critical rationalist. See T. W. Hutchison, *The Politics and Philosophy of Economics: Marxians, Keynesians, and Austrians* (Oxford: Blackwell, 1981). Gray argues convincingly against this interpretation in *Hayek on Liberty*. See also Kley, *Hayek's Social and Political Thought*.

19   On Hayek's Kantianism see Gray, *Hayek on Liberty*, and Kukathas, *Hayek and Modern Liberalism*.

20   See F. A. Hayek, 'Friedrich von Wieser', in *The Fortunes of Liberalism*, vol. 4, *Collected Works* (London: Routledge, 1992), pp. 108–25.

21   See F. A. Hayek, 'Ludwig von Mises', in *Fortunes of Liberalism*, pp. 126–59.

22   Mises remained an important influence throughout Hayek's life. Many of Hayek's ideas were derived from Mises. But there were also important differences between them, particularly in their methodological approach to economic analysis and the concept of knowledge. Mises was a more rigid, less original thinker than Hayek.

23   The term 'methodological individualism' was coined by Joseph Schumpeter. For a searching critique of its limitations in economic explanation see G. Hodgson, *Economics and Institutions* (Cambridge: Polity, 1988).

24   Subsequently published as *Prices and Production* (London: Routledge, 1931). For assessments of Hayek's impact and his contribution as an economist see B. McCormick, *Hayek and the Keynesian Avalanche* (Hemel Hempstead: Harvester Wheatsheaf, 1992) and G. R. Steele, *The Economics of Friedrich Hayek* (London: Macmillan, 1993).

25   Hayek, *Hayek on Hayek*, p. 78.

26   See McCormick, *Hayek and the Keynesian Avalanche*, and Steele, *Economics of Friedrich Hayek*. McCormick points out that the distinction between Mengerian and Walrasian analysis was not appreciated by economists in the 1930s, who imagined they shared common assumptions. As a result of Hayek's work, the differences between the two approaches, particularly in their assumptions about knowledge and

equilibrium, became much clearer (McCormick, *Hayek and the Keynesian Avalanche*, p. 136).

27 F. A. Hayek (ed.), *Collectivist Economic Planning: Critical Studies on the Possibility of Socialism* (London: Routledge, 1935).
28 F. A. Hayek, 'Economics and Knowledge', *Economica*, 13 (Feb. 1937), 33–54.
29 Hayek, *Hayek on Hayek*, p. 80.
30 See M. Desai, 'Equilibrium, Expectations, and Knowledge', in Birner and van Zijp (eds), *Hayek, Coordination and Evolution*, 25–50.
31 An excellent example of this is the radio discussion between Hayek, Maynard Krueger, and Charles Merriam on 22 April 1945, reproduced in *Hayek on Hayek*, pp. 108–23.
32 See especially Gray, *Hayek on Liberty*.
33 This is not to deny the major tensions in his thought. As noted earlier, both Chandran Kukathas and Roland Kley have explored these at length, although they have differing conceptions of Hayek's project. Kukathas concentrates on Hayek's attempt to combine Kantian and Humean ethical claims in a coherent moral theory of liberalism, while Kley argues that Hayek's project is defined principally by an instrumentalist, rather than a moral, justification of liberalism which links a traditionalist argument derived from a theory of cultural evolution with a proceduralist argument derived from a theory of spontaneous order. Both studies conclude that Hayek's ambitious project fails. See Kukathas, *Hayek and Modern Liberalism*, and Kley, *Hayek's Social and Political Thought*.
34 Hayek, *New Studies*, p. 304.

Chapter 2   Morals

1 Roland Kley points out that Hayek's argument is instrumentalist, because it assumes that liberalism and socialism share the same values and the same ultimate ends but differ only on the means to achieve them. The superiority of liberalism over socialism is demonstrated primarily through the relative success of liberal and socialist institutions in producing outcomes which correspond to those ends. See R. Kley, *Hayek's Social and Political Thought* (Oxford: Clarendon Press, 1994).
2 F. A. Hayek, *The Constitution of Liberty* (London: Routledge, 1960), ch. 3.
3 Even Karl Popper, who became a close friend and associate of Hayek, confessed in his autobiography that for many years he was a socialist, and that 'if there could be such a thing as socialism combined with personal liberty I would be a socialist still. For nothing could be better than living a modest, simple, and free life in an egalitarian society. It took some time before I realised this as no more than a beautiful dream' (*Unended Quest* (London: Routledge, 1992), p. 36).

4 F. A. Hayek, *Knowledge, Evolution, and Society* (London: Adam Smith Institute, 1983).

5 Adam Smith, *An Inquiry into the Nature and Causes of the Wealth of Nations* (London: Methuen, 1950), p. 18.

6 Hayek, *Knowledge, Evolution, and Society*, p. 31.

7 Smith, *Wealth of Nations*, p. 18.

8 Ibid., p. 26.

9 Hayek, *Knowledge, Evolution, and Society*, p. 47.

10 Ibid.

11 Hodgson has provided one of the most searching accounts of Hayek's theory of evolution, in particular his oscillation between ontogenetic theories of evolution based on eighteenth-century notions of evolution and philogenetic theories using a concept of natural selection. He demonstrates that the key weakness of Hayek's evolutionary theory is that it fails to identify a mechanism of natural selection to explain the outcomes of the evolutionary process. See G. Hodgson, *Economics and Evolution* (Cambridge: Polity, 1993), chs. 11 and 12.

12 Hayek comes close here to endorsing Spencer's arguments, although in other respects, as Hodgson notes, his position is very different from Spencer's: e.g., Hayek's theory of evolution is a theory of group, not individual, selection, and does not posit immutable laws of development. See Hodgson, *Economics and Evolution*, and E. F. Paul, 'Liberalism, Unintended Orders, and Evolutionism', *Political Studies*, 36/2 (1988), 251–72.

13 This may seem paradoxical because of Hayek's depiction of the evolution of the rules of conduct which constitute the Great Society as a natural process, not planned or intended by anyone. But the end result of this natural evolution is a situation which is unnatural, because human societies have moved so far from their origins. The Great Society is viable only if human beings learn to behave in ways which are contrary to their deepest emotional and instinctual promptings.

14 L. von Mises, *The Free and Prosperous Commonwealth* (New York: Van Nostrand, 1962), p. 85.

15 For Hayek's thoughts on Mandeville see esp. 'Dr. Bernard Mandeville', in *New Studies in Philosophy, Politics, Economics and the History of Ideas* (London: Routledge, 1978), ch. 15. See also the discussion of Mandeville's influence on Hayek in Hodgson, *Economics and Evolution*.

16 Hayek, *Constitution of Liberty*, p. 61.

17 Ibid.

18 Hayek, *Knowledge, Evolution and Society*, p. 53.

19 Hayek, *Constitution of Liberty*, ch. 4.

20 F. A. Hayek, *Law, Legislation and Liberty* (London: Routledge, 1982), vol. 1, p. 36. For a discussion of Hayek's concept of spontaneous order see S. Brittan, 'Hayek's Spontaneous Social Order', in *Capitalism with a Human Face* (London: Edward Elgar, 1995), 113–26.

21 Hayek's failure to apply his insights about the necessarily limited and fragmented character of knowledge to centralized, hierarchical organizations is explored by Hilary Wainwright in *Arguments for a New Left* (Oxford: Blackwell, 1994).
22 See Hayek, 'The Confusion of Language in Political Thought', in *New Studies*, pp. 71–97.
23 Hayek, *Law, Legislation, and Liberty*, vol. 1, p. 42.
24 Hayek, *Knowledge, Evolution, and Society*, p. 19.
25 See the discussion in Kley, *Hayek's Social and Political Thought*, pp. 122ff. He lists five arguments that Hayek uses for spontaneous orders, but argues that there are many circumstances, such as the response to epidemics, public goods, and neighbourhood effects, where reliance on spontaneous orders will not provide the best solutions. Another problem which Kley highlights is that Hayek's concept of order is often vague. When does a particular network of interaction constitute an order rather than a disorder? At times Hayek too easily assumes that spontaneity will produce harmonious co-ordination.
26 Hayek, *Constitution of Liberty*, p. 61.
27 Hayek, *Law, Legislation, and Liberty*, vol. 3, p. 165.
28 Hayek, *Constitution of Liberty*, p. 11.
29 Ibid., p. 14.
30 Ibid., p. 20.
31 Ibid., p. 136. See the criticism by R. Hamowy, 'Hayek's Concept of Freedom: A Critique', *New Individualist Review*, 1 (1961), 28–31, and the discussion in C. Kukathas, *Hayek and Modern Liberalism* (Oxford: Clarendon Press, 1989), ch. 4.
32 Hayek, *Constitution of Liberty*, p. 77.
33 Ibid., p. 80.
34 F. A. Hayek, *The Road to Serfdom* (London: Routledge, 1944), p. 101.
35 Ibid., p. 151.
36 Ibid., pp. 151–2.
37 Hayek, *Law, Legislation, and Liberty*, vol. 1, pp. 32–3.
38 Ibid., p. 33.
39 Ibid., p. 67.
40 Ibid., p. 11.
41 Ibid., p. 99.
42 Ibid., p. 30.
43 Ibid., p. 6. See the important discussion of this point in R. Plant, *Modern Political Thought* (Oxford: Blackwell, 1991), ch. 3.
44 Hayek, *Constitution of Liberty*, p. 235.
45 Hayek, *Law, Legislation, and Liberty*, vol. 2, p. 39.
46 As Kley notes, however, there are other, non-market institutions which Hayek acknowledges to be necessary for a successful market order, which include the state, the family, religion, and a particular set of moral attitudes and dispositions. See Kley, *Hayek's Social and Political Thought*.

47 Hayek, *Law, Legislation, and Liberty*, vol. 2, p. 77.
48 One way in which the market is not a game or a lottery is that the winnings tend to be cumulative. Individuals do become equal again, as at the beginning of a new round of a game. See Kley, *Hayek's Social and Political Thought*, ch. 4. A market order that periodically and randomly redistributed life chances would resemble the lottery described by Borges in 'The Lottery in Babylon', in *Labyrinths* (London: Penguin, 1970).
49 Hayek, *Law, Legislation, and Liberty*, vol. 2, p. 94.
50 Ibid., p. 74.
51 L. Doyal and I. Gough, *A Theory of Human Need* (London: Macmillan, 1991).
52 M. Walzer, *Spheres of Justice* (Oxford: Blackwell, 1983).
53 See the discussion by N. Barry, 'Hayek on Liberty', in J. Gray and Z. Pelzcynski (eds), *Conceptions of Liberty* (Oxford: Clarendon Press, 1990), pp. 263–86.

Chapter 3   Markets

1 B. McCormick, *Hayek and the Keynesian Avalanche* (Hemel Hempstead: Harvester Wheatsheaf, 1992).
2 For Hayek's comments on the *Methodenstreit* see especially F. A. Hayek (ed.), *Collectivist Economic Planning* (London: Routledge, 1935), p. 10.
3 See B. Semmel, *Imperialism and Social Reform* (London: Allen and Unwin, 1960).
4 On the Austrian school see W. Grassl and B. Smith (eds), *Austrian Economics* (London: Croom Helm, 1986); and N. Barry, *On Classical Liberalism and Libertarianism* (London: Macmillan, 1986). On contemporary Austrian analysis see A. Shand, *The Capitalist Alternative: An Introduction to Neo-Austrian Economics* (Brighton: Wheatsheaf, 1984).
5 See G. R. Steele, *The Economics of Friedrich Hayek* (London: Macmillan, 1993).
6 G. Hodgson, *Economics and Institutions* (Cambridge: Polity, 1988), ch. 3.
7 See Hodgson, *Economics and Institutions*. The problem with methodological individualism is that it gives no good reason why explanation should stop at the individual. The individual is eminently deconstructible into the conflicting pressures which shape attitudes and preferences and structure experiences. Hodgson notes Nozick's observation that an injunction to methodological institutionalism is equally as plausible as an injunction to methodological individualism, and would be similarly flawed.
8 This theme is taken up in the last chapter.
9 Hayek (ed.), *Collectivist Economic Planning*, p. 10.

10 Ibid., p. 17.
11 L. von Mises, *Socialism: An Economic and Sociological Analysis* (London: Cape, 1936), p. 19.
12 Ibid., p. 22. Mises describes his book as a scientific enquiry, not a political polemic. What a polemic from him would be like certainly stretches the imagination.
13 Mises, e.g., wrote: 'Every attempt to realise a socialist, interventionist, agrarian socialist, or syndicalist society must necessarily prove unsuccessful. Neurotics who could not bear this truth have called economics a dismal science. But economics and sociology are no more dismal because they show us the world as it really is than the other sciences are – mechanics, for instance, because it teaches the impracticability of perpetual motion, or biology because it teaches us the mortality of all living things' (*The Free and Prosperous Commonwealth* (New York: Van Nostrand, 1962), p. 90. This was first published in 1927).
14 D. Lavoie, *Rivalry and Central Planning: The Socialist Calculation Debate Reconsidered* (Cambridge: Cambridge University Press, 1985).
15 J. Schumpeter, *Capitalism, Socialism, and Democracy* (London: Allen and Unwin, 1950), p. 185.
16 J. Kornai, *The Socialist System* (Oxford: Clarendon Press, 1992), pp. 476–7.
17 Another early sign of the breadth of his concerns was his Inaugural Lecture at the LSE, 'The Trend of Economic Thinking', later published in *Economica*, 13/2 (1933), 121–37. See J. Tomlinson, *Hayek and the Market* (London: Pluto, 1990), p. 7: 'It would not be an exaggeration to say that the agenda of issues Hayek was to spend most of the rest of his life working on was raised in this 1933 article.'
18 Reprinted in Hayek (ed.), *Collectivist Economic Planning*.
19 Ibid., p. 105.
20 Ibid., p. 24.
21 Ibid., p. 17.
22 Mises, *Socialism*, p. 120.
23 Ibid., p. 138.
24 Ibid., p. 130.
25 N. Bukharin, *The Economics of the Leisure Class* (New York: Monthly Review Press, 1972).
26 The key articles can be found in Hayek (ed.), *Collectivist Economic Planning*. The best review of the debate is provided by Lavoie, *Rivalry and Central Planning*. See also N. Barry, *Hayek's Social and Economic Philosophy* (London: Macmillan, 1979); K. I. Vaughn, 'Economic Calculation under Socialism: The Austrian Contribution', *Economic Inquiry*, Oct. 1980, pp. 535–54. Commentaries from non-Austrian perspectives include A. Nove, *The Economics of Feasible Socialism* (London: Allen and Unwin, 1983); G. Hodgson, *The Democratic Economy* (Harmondsworth: Penguin, 1984); R. Blackburn, 'Fin-de-Siècle:

Socialism after the Crash', *New Left Review*, 185 (1991), 5–67; and Tomlinson, *Hayek and the Market*.

27 This point was made by Maurice Dobb in comments he made on the debate in *Political Economy and Capitalism* (London: Routledge, 1937). See A. Gamble, 'Capitalism or Barbarism: The Austrian Critique of Socialism', *Socialist Register*, 1985–6, pp. 355–72.

28 F. A. Hayek, 'The Use of Knowledge in Society', *American Economic Review*, 55/4 (1945), 519–30.

29 Ibid., repr. in *Individualism and Economic Order* (London: Routledge, 1948), p. 78.

30 Barry, *Hayek's Social and Economic Philosophy*, ch. 3.

31 Kornai, *Socialist System*, ch. 21.

32 A point emphasized by Lavoie in *Rivalry and Central Planning*.

33 Blackburn, 'Fin-de-Siecle'.

34 Hayek quotes Trotsky's comment that 'economic accounting is unthinkable without market relations', in 'The Use of Knowledge in Society', in *Individualism and Economic Order*, p. 89.

35 See Nove, *Economics of Feasible Socialism*, and D. Miller, *Market, State, and Community: The Theoretical Foundations of Market Socialism* (Oxford: Clarendon Press, 1989).

36 Blackburn, 'Fin-de-Siècle'; H. Wainwright, *Arguments for a New Left* (Oxford: Blackwell, 1994), esp. ch. 2.

37 F. A. Hayek, *The Constitution of Liberty* (London: Routledge, 1960), pp. 264–6.

Chapter 4 Politics

1 F. A. Hayek, *The Road to Serfdom* (London: Routledge, 1944), p. 3.

2 Ibid., p. 5.

3 Ibid., p. 3.

4 Ibid., p. 1.

5 See R. Cockett, *Thinking the Unthinkable* (London: Fontana, 1995). Clement Attlee was quick to link the broadcast with the sinister influence of 'Professor von Hayek', cynically drawing attention to his nationality and ignoring the fact that Hayek had been living in Britain for fourteen years and had taken British citizenship.

6 Hayek, *Road to Serfdom*, p. 9.

7 Ibid., p. 10.

8 Ibid., p. 9.

9 Ibid.

10 Ibid., p. 10.

11 Ibid., p. 12.

12 Ibid., p. 13.

13 Ibid.

14 Ibid., p. 15.
15 Ibid.
16 K. Mannheim, *Man and Society in an Age of Reconstruction* (London: Routledge, 1940), p. 175.
17 Hayek, *Road to Serfdom*, p. 16.
18 Ibid., p. 31.
19 See Geoff Hodgson's discussion of 'the impurity principle' in *Economics and Institutions* (Cambridge: Polity, 1988), ch. 11.
20 Hayek, *Road to Serfdom*, p. 37.
21 Ibid., p. 42.
22 Ibid., p. 94. Although Hayek hardly ever refers to Herbert Spencer, there is a clear echo of his categories in the use of the terms 'commercial' and 'military' society. On similarities between the evolutionary ideas of Spencer, Hayek, and also Sumner, see E. F. Paul, 'Liberalism, Unintended Orders and Evolutionism', *Political Studies*, 36/2 (1988), 251–72.
23 Hayek, *Road to Serfdom*, p. 100.
24 Ibid., p. 101.
25 Ibid., p. 127.
26 Ibid., p. 131.
27 Ibid., p. 139. Carl Schmitt was one of the leading theoreticians of the Nazi regime.
28 This is an argument which has been revived in the 1990s. See A. Gamble and A. Payne (eds), *Regionalism and World Order* (London: Macmillan, 1996).
29 Hayek, *Road to Serfdom*, p. 148.
30 Ibid., p. 149.
31 F. A. Hayek, *The Constitution of Liberty* (London: Routledge, 1960), p. 106.
32 F. A. Hayek, *Law, Legislation, and Liberty*, vol. 3 (London: Routledge, 1982), p. 39.
33 J. L. Talmon, *The Origins of Totalitarian Democracy* (London: Secker and Warburg, 1952).
34 Hayek, *Constitution of Liberty*, p. 104.
35 M. Friedman, *Capitalism and Freedom* (Chicago: University of Chicago Press, 1962).
36 Hayek, *Constitution of Liberty*, p. 106.
37 Ibid., pp. 107–8.
38 F. A. Hayek, *Individualism and Economic Order* (London: Routledge, 1948), p. 22.
39 Hayek, *Constitution of Liberty*, p. 105.
40 Ibid., p. 106.
41 Ibid., p. 109.
42 See ch. 6.
43 Hayek, *Constitution of Liberty*, p. 112.

44 Ibid., p. 114.
45 Ibid., p. 153.

Chapter 5   Conservatism

1 M. Forsyth, 'Hayek's Bizarre Liberalism: A Critique', *Political Studies*, 36/2 (1988), 235–50.
2 See esp. N. Barry, *The New Right* (London: Croom Helm, 1987); D. Green, *The New Right* (Brighton: Wheatsheaf, 1987); N. Bosanquet, *After the New Right* (London, Heinemann, 1983); R. Levitas, *The Ideology of the New Right* (Cambridge: Polity, 1986); K. Hoover and R. Plant, *Conservative Capitalism in Britain and the United States* (London: Routledge, 1989).
3 See also F. A. Hayek, 'The Road to Serfdom after Twelve Years', in *Studies in Philosophy, Politics, and Economics* (London: Routledge, 1967), pp. 216–28.
4 See his discussion of the liberal tradition in 'Liberalism', in *New Studies in Philosophy, Politics, Economics, and the History of Ideas* (London: Routledge, 1978), pp. 119–51.
5 F. A. Hayek, *The Constitution of Liberty* (London: Routledge, 1960), p. 397.
6 Ibid., p. 398.
7 Ibid.
8 Ibid., p. 400.
9 Ibid.
10 Ibid., p. 401.
11 Ibid.
12 Ibid., p. 405.
13 Ibid., p. 410.
14 Ibid.
15 Ibid., p. 411.
16 H. Gissurarson, *Hayek's Conservative Liberalism* (New York: Garland, 1987), p. 11.
17 Hayek asserts that the operations of the invisible hand are benign, but he does not explain why this should be so or the circumstances in which it might not be so. Nor does he consider the possibility that the workings of the invisible hand might create disorder rather than order.
18 W. H. Greenleaf, *The British Political Tradition*, vol. 1: *The Rise of Collectivism* (London: Methuen, 1983), pp. 15–20.
19 R. Scruton, *A Dictionary of Political Thought* (London: Macmillan, 1982), p. 271.
20 Murray Rothbard, *Power and Market* (Kansas: Sheed, Andrews and McMeel, 1977), pp. 1–2.
21 Ibid., p. 2.

22 Ibid.
23 Ibid., ch. 3. For a commentary on anarcho-capitalism see N. Barry, *On Classical Liberalism and Libertarianism* (London: Macmillan, 1986).
24 Rothbard's main opposition is to any form of state action. But he does not favour unbridled individualism. In recent times he has given strong backing to the fundamentalist Christian Right, arguing that on moral questions there is a strong agreement between Christians and libertarians. See *Conservative Chronicle*, 17 Mar. 1993. I am indebted to Martin Durham for pointing out this reference to me.
25 Rothbard, *For a New Liberty: The Libertarian Manifesto* (New York: Collier–Macmillan, 1978), p. 24.
26 R. Nozick, *Anarchy, State, and Utopia* (Oxford: Blackwell, 1974).
27 I. Kristol, 'Capitalism, Socialism, and Nihilism', in R. Kirk (ed.), *The Conservative Reader* (New York: Viking, 1982).
28 Ibid., p. 633.
29 Ibid., p. 637.
30 See the argument in R. Kley, *Hayek's Social and Political Thought* (Oxford: Clarendon Press, 1994), pp. 203–4.
31 J. Schumpeter, *Capitalism, Socialism, and Democracy* (London: Allen and Unwin, 1950), p. 143.
32 Particularly in his evolutionary writings, Hayek too stresses the institutional foundations inherited from the past on which a capitalist order relies, which are in danger of being eroded by modern rationalism.
33 M. Oakeshott, *Rationalism in Politics* (London: Methuen, 1962), p. 21.
34 The confession comes in Cowling's famous essay on the British New Right, 'The Sources of the New Right', in *Encounter*, Nov. 1989, pp. 3–13, which received an equally famous rejoinder from Hugh Trevor-Roper, one of its targets, in the *Independent*, 9 Dec. 1989.
35 F. A. Hayek, 'The Confusion of Language in Political Thought', in Hayek, *New Studies*, p. 89.
36 M. Oakeshott, *On Human Conduct* (Oxford: Clarendon Press, 1975).
37 Disraeli, speech at Crystal Palace, 24 June 1872.
38 Schumpeter, *Capitalism, Socialism, and Democracy*, p. 229.
39 N. O'Sullivan, 'Conservatism, the New Right, and the Limited State', in J. Hayward and P. Norton (eds), *The Political Science of British Politics* (Brighton: Wheatsheaf, 1986), pp. 21–36.
40 R. Scruton, *The Meaning of Conservatism* (Harmondsworth: Penguin, 1980), p. 24.
41 Ibid.
42 Ibid., p. 15.
43 Ibid., pp. 15–16.
44 O'Sullivan, 'Conservatism, the New Right'.
45 S. Letwin, 'On Conservative Individualism', in Maurice Cowling (ed.), *Conservative Essays* (London: Cassell, 1978), p. 62.
46 Ibid., p. 57.

47　Ibid.
48　J. H. Grainger, 'Mrs Thatcher's Last Stand', *Quadrant*, Dec. 1980, p. 5.
49　Ibid., p. 6.
50　J. Gray, *The Undoing of Conservatism* (London: Social Market Foundation, 1994).

Chapter 6　A Constitution for Liberty

1　See R. Cockett, *Thinking the Unthinkable* (London: Fontana, 1995), pp. 9–12.
2　Hayek's success with *The Road to Serfdom* was rivalled only by Karl Popper's *The Open Society and its Enemies* (London: Routledge, 1945), which Hayek helped to get published in 1945. These two books became the classic texts in the liberal revival after 1945. Mises' book, which received much less attention but which had a similar theme to *The Road to Serfdom*, was entitled *Omnipotent Government* (New Rochelle, N.Y.: Arlington House, 1964). It was also published in 1944.
3　F. A. Hayek, *The Fortunes of Liberalism*, vol. 4, *Collected Works* (London: Routledge, 1992), p. 204.
4　Ibid.
5　Ibid., pp. 206–7.
6　Ibid., p. 208.
7　Ibid., p. 209.
8　Ibid., p. 211.
9　Ibid., p. 216.
10　Ibid., p. 212.
11　Ibid., p. 214.
12　Ibid., p. 238.
13　The feeling of isolation of so many of these intellectuals and their resulting pessimism is well caught by these remarks of Mises: 'Occasionally I entertained the hope that my writings would bear practical fruit and show the way for policy. Constantly I have been looking for evidence of a change in ideology. But I have never allowed myself to be deceived' (*Notes and Recollections* (South Holland, Ill.: Libertarian Press, 1978), p. 115).
14　Hayek, *Fortunes of Liberalism*, p. 238.
15　Ibid., p. 243.
16　Ibid., p. 244.
17　Ibid., p. 259.
18　S. M. Lipset, *Political Man* (London: Heinemann, 1960), pp. 404–5.
19　In *Hayek's Social and Political Thought* (Oxford: Clarendon Press, 1994), Kley lists six legitimate roles for the state which can be found in Hayek's writings: the enforcement of the rules of just conduct, the adaptation of existing rules to social and technological changes,

enabling the operation of market processes, restraint of the destructive features of markets, the provision of public goods, and counter-cyclical intervention. This is quite a list.

20 Victor Vanberg has argued that Hayek's theory of social evolution contradicts his methodological individualism, and argues strongly in favour of the latter. See V. Vanberg, 'Spontaneous Market Order and Social Rules: A Critical Examination of F. A. Hayek's Theory of Cultural Evolution', *Economics and Philosophy*, 2 (1986), 75–100.

21 F. A. Hayek, *The Road to Serfdom* (London: Routledge, 1944), p. 53.

22 See the discussion in ch. 4.

23 F. A. Hayek, *The Constitution of Liberty* (London: Routledge, 1960), p. 165.

24 Ibid., p. 167.

25 See Oakeshott's Introduction to his edition of Hobbes, *Leviathan* (Oxford: Blackwell, 1946).

26 See F. Mount, *The British Constitution Now* (London: Heinemann, 1992).

27 The hollowing out of the British constitution is explored in ibid. One of the ironies of the Thatcher Government in Britain was that its programme of radical institutional reform was greatly facilitated by the uninhibited use of the centralized powers of the British state. The doctrine of unlimited parliamentary sovereignty enabled the Government to disregard opposition and impose its preferred policies. The authoritarianism which Hayek had earlier discerned in British constitutional arrangements was used to try to re-establish a free economy.

28 Hayek, *Constitution of Liberty*, p. 180.

29 Ibid., p. 184.

30 The same kind of thinking underlay his opposition to basing sovereignty on nationality. He quotes Acton approvingly against Mill's argument that the boundaries of governments should coincide with nationalities, that 'co-existence of several nations under the same state is a test, as well as the best security of its freedom. It is also one of the chief instruments of its civilisation' (Hayek, *Fortunes of Liberalism*, p. 213).

31 For a discussion of this point see D. Beetham, *The Legitimation of Power* (London: Macmillan, 1991).

32 Hayek, *Constitution of Liberty*, p. 197.

33 Ibid., p. 240.

34 F. A. Hayek, *Law, Legislation, and Liberty*, vol. 3 (London: Routledge, 1979).

35 Hayek, *Constitution of Liberty*, p. 207.

36 Ibid., p. 105. This argument would have applied to apartheid in South Africa.

37 Hayek, *Law, Legislation, and Liberty*, ch. 17. One of the most searching critiques of Hayek's constitutional doctrines, including the rule of law, and the difficulties of applying them to the contemporary capitalist societies is provided by R. Bellamy, ' "Dethroning Politics":

Liberalism, Constitutionalism, and Democracy in the Thought of F. A. Hayek', *British Journal of Political Science*, 24 (1994), 419–41.

38 Particularly James Buchanan and the Virginia school. See e.g. J. Buchanan, *The Limits of Liberty* (Chicago: University of Chicago Press, 1975).

39 Hayek, *Law, Legislation, and Liberty*, vol. 3, p. 109.

40 Ibid., p. 113.

Chapter 7 The Economic Consequences of Keynes

1 Hayek, 'Reflections on the Pure Theory of Money of Mr. J. M. Keynes', *Economica*, 11 / 33 (1931), 270–95. J. M. Keynes, *A Treatise on Money: The Pure Theory of Money*, in *Collected Writings*, vol. 5 (London: Macmillan, 1971).

2 J. M. Keynes, 'A Pure Theory of Money: A Reply to Dr. Hayek', *Economica*, 11 / 34 (1931), in *Collected Writings*, vol. 13 (London: Macmillan, 1972), p. 243.

3 Quoted in R. Skidelsky, *John Maynard Keynes: The Economist as Saviour 1920–1937* (London: Macmillan, 1992), pp. 456–7.

4 P. Staffa, 'Dr. Hayek on Money and Capital', *Economic Journal*, 42 (1932), 42–53.

5 Skidelsky, *John Maynard Keynes*, pp. 458–9.

6 See Hayek, *Hayek on Hayek*, ed. S. Kresge and L. Wenar (London: Routledge, 1994), and 'Personal Recollections of Keynes and the "Keynesian Revolution"', in *New Studies in Philosophy, Politics, Economics and the History of Ideas* (London: Routledge, 1978), pp. 283–9.

7 Ibid., p. 283.

8 Ibid., p. 289.

9 J. M. Keynes, *The General Theory of Employment, Interest, and Money* (London: Macmillan, 1973), pp. 384–5.

10 Hayek, *New Studies*, p. 192.

11 Ibid., p. 287.

12 Ibid., p. 230.

13 Ibid., p. 218; id., *Choice in Currency: A Way to Stop Inflation* (London: Institute of Economic Affairs, 1976).

14 Ibid., p. 219.

15 Keynes, *Collected Writings*, vol. 27 (London: Macmillan, 1980), p. 385.

16 J. M. Keynes, *Essays in Persuasion, Collected Writings*, vol. 9 (London: Macmillan, 1972), pp. 296–7.

17 Ibid., p. 306.

18 Ibid., p. 297.

19 Ibid., p. 295.

20 Ibid.

21 Quoted by Hayek in *Law, Legislation and Liberty*, vol. 1 (London: Routledge, 1982), p. 26.

22 Hayek never seems to have suspected or known about Keynes's bisexuality until the publication of Michael Holroyd's biography of Lytton Strachey in 1967. These revelations about the Bloomsbury group, Hayek concluded, were 'probably a sufficient explanation of their revolt against ruling morals' (*New Studies*, p. 16).

23 J. M. Keynes, 'Tract on Monetary Reform', in *Collected Works*, vol. 4 (London: Macmillan, 1972), p. 65.

24 F. A. Hayek, *The Fatal Conceit: The Errors of Socialism, Collected Works*, vol. 1 (London: Routledge, 1988), p. 57.

25 Ibid. See the comments on Hayek's criticism by J. Tomlinson, *Hayek and the Market* (London: Pluto, 1990), p. 51.

26 Quoted by Skidelsky in *John Maynard Keynes*, p. 62.

27 Keynes, *Collected Writings*, vol. 27, pp. 387–8.

28 Ibid., p. 387.

29 J. M. Keynes, 'The End of *Laissez-Faire*', in *Essays in Persuasion*.

30 For Hayek's economics see B. McCormick, *Hayek and the Keynesian Avalanche* (Hemel Hempstead: Harvester Wheatsheaf, 1992); G. R. Steele, *The Economics of Friedrich Hayek* (London: Macmillan, 1993); and chapters by M. Desai, P. Rosner, and H. Garretsen, in J. Birner and R. van Zijp (eds), *Hayek, Coordination and Evolution* (London: Routledge, 1994).

31 Peter Jay revived this analysis in his account of inflation in the 1970s. See his *Employment, Inflation, and Politics* (London: Institute of Economic Affairs, 1976).

32 On Keynes see R. Skidelsky, *John Maynard Keynes: Hopes Betrayed 1883–1920* (London: Macmillan, 1983); *idem, Keynes: The Economist as Saviour 1920–1937*; and P. Clarke, *The Keynesian Revolution in the Making 1924–1936* (Oxford: Clarendon Press, 1988).

33 L. Robbins, *Autobiography* (London: Macmillan, 1971).

34 See Hayek, 'The Campaign Against Keynesian Inflation', in *New Studies*, pp. 191–231, and *idem, The Denationalisation of Money* (London: Institute of Economic Affairs, 1990).

35 J. Strachey, *The Coming Struggle for Power* (London: Gollancz, 1932); *idem, The Nature of Capitalist Crisis* (London: Gollancz, 1934). After 1945 Strachey became a Labour Minister, converted to Keynesianism, and wrote *Contemporary Capitalism* (London: Gollancz, 1956). For his career and ideas see H. Thomas, *John Strachey* (London: Harper Row, 1973).

36 Strachey, *Nature of Capitalist Crisis*, p. 113.

37 Ibid., p. 134.

38 See also L. Robbins, *The Great Depression* (London: Routledge, 1932).

39 Keynes, *General Theory*, p. 322.

40 Hayek, *Hayek on Hayek*, p. 143.

41 See esp. M. Desai, 'Equilibrium, Expectations, and Knowledge'; H. Garretsen, 'The Relevance of Hayek for Mainstream Economics'; and M. Bianchi, 'Hayek's Spontaneous Order: The "Correct" Versus the

"Corrigible" Society'; in Birner and van Zijp (eds), *Hayek, Coordination, and Evolution.*

42 Anthony Fisher was an ex-RAF pilot who read *The Road to Serfdom,* and contacted Hayek to ask what he could do. Hayek suggested founding an institute. Fisher recruited Harris and Seldon to organize the new institute. Subsequently the success of Fisher's business – Buxted Chickens – helped keep it afloat financially.

43 R. Cockett, *Thinking the Unthinkable* (London: Fontana, 1995), p. 142.

44 I. Gilmour, *Inside Right* (London: Hutchinson, 1977), and *idem, Dancing with Dogma* (London: Simon and Schuster, 1992). See esp. his comments on Hayek's 'Why I am not a Conservative' in *Inside Right,* pp. 115–19.

45 See Hayek, *Denationalisation of Money,* for an account of his differences with the monetarists.

46 W. Rees-Mogg, *The Reigning Error* (London: Hamilton, 1974).

47 F. A. Hayek, *Choice in Currency: A Way to Stop Inflation* (London: Institute of Economic Affairs, 1976), and *idem, Denationalisation of Money.*

48 C. A. E. Goodhart, *Money, Information, and Uncertainty* (London: Macmillan, 1989). The argument on free banking has been vigorously pursued by Kevin Dowd in several publications, including K. Dowd (ed.), *The Experience of Free Banking* (London: Routledge, 1992).

49 F. A. Hayek, *The Constitution of Liberty* (London: Routledge, 1960), p. 269.

50 Ibid., p. 274.

51 Ibid., p. 275.

52 Ibid., p. 284.

53 Ibid., p. 276.

54 Hayek, *Studies in Philosophy, Politics, and Economics* (London: Routledge, 1967), p. 281.

55 M. Kalecki, 'Political Aspects of Full Employment', *Political Quarterly,* 14 (1943), 322–31.

56 Hayek, *Studies,* p. 298.

57 Hayek, *Constitution of Liberty,* p. 92.

58 Ibid., p. 303.

59 Even with the principle of proportional taxation, the rich still pay more in absolute terms. Hayek was not prepared to advocate the more radical principle of a flat rate tax, levied on individuals. The Thatcher Government introduced such a tax, the community charge, to replace rates, the local property tax. It proved a costly fiasco.

60 Hayek, *Constitution of Liberty,* p. 341.

Chapter 8   The Iron Cage of Liberty

1 D. Beetham, *Max Weber and the Theory of Modern Politics* (London: Allen and Unwin, 1974).

2 M. Weber, 'Science as a Vocation', in H. H. Gerth and C. Wright Mills (eds), *From Max Weber* (London: Routledge, 1970), p. 143.

3 Modern ideas about death are explored by Z. Bauman, *Mortality, Immortality, and Other Life Strategies* (Cambridge: Polity, 1992).

4 Marcus Aurelius, *Meditations*, Book 11 (Harmondsworth: Penguin, 1964).

5 Weber, 'Science as a Vocation', pp. 152–3.

6 See the discussion in ch. 2 and the analysis in G. Hodgson, *Economics and Evolution* (Cambridge: Polity, 1993).

7 F. Fukuyama, 'The End of History?', *National Interest*, 16 (Summer 1989), 3–18. This article became the basis for *The End of History and the Last Man* (London: Hamish Hamilton, 1992).

8 See esp. J. Friedman, 'The New Consensus: I The Fukuyama Thesis', *Critical Review*, 3/4 (1989), 373–410, and 'The New Consensus: II The Democratic Welfare State', *Critical Review*, 4/4 (1990), 633–708.

9 Friedman, 'New Consensus: I' , p. 401.

10 This tension between his conception of society as a spontaneous order and his conception of it as the product of cultural evolution is dissected by R. Kley, *Hayek's Social and Political Thought* (Oxford: Clarendon Press, 1994).

11 This point is made in a brilliant essay by P. Anderson, 'The Intransigent Right at the End of the Century', *London Review of Books*, 24 Sept. 1992, pp. 7–11.

12 As he put it in *Individualism and Economic Order* (London: Routledge, 1948), p. 22: 'The state, the embodiment of deliberately organised and consciously directed power, ought to be only a small part of the much richer organism which we call society . . . the former ought to provide merely a framework within which free (and therefore not "consciously directed") collaboration of men has the maximum of scope.'

13 A minor irony, given the associations which the term 'federalism' had come to have in the debate on European Union in the Conservative party by the end of the 1980s, was that Hayek always strongly supported federalism, and in the 1930s had seen a federal structure in Europe as the best way of reducing nationalist conflicts between the European powers. See 'The Economic Conditions of Inter-State Federation', *New Commonwealth Quarterly*, 5/2 (1939), 131–49.

14 Why, e.g., cannot democracy and the state be analysed as spontaneous orders? See G. Dizerega, 'Democracy as a Spontaneous Order', *Critical Review*, 3/2 (1989), 206–40.

15 P. Anderson, 'The Ends of History', in *A Zone of Engagement* (London: Verso, 1992), pp. 279–375.

16 R. Blackburn, 'Fin-de-Siècle: Socialism after the Crash', *New Left Review*, 185 (1991), 5–67.

17 See Hilary Wainwright's discussion of this aspect of Hayek's thought in *Arguments for a New Left* (Oxford: Blackwell, 1994), ch. 2. Blackburn

in 'Fin-de-Siècle', also notes Hayek's argument that capitalism permits much broader participation in decision-making than any other social system. The strength of Hayek's critique of socialism for socialists, according to Blackburn, is that it questions whether members of society should plan for themselves or whether a benevolent government should impose plans on them.

18 Hayek's work has considerable relevance to some of the new institutionalist analysis using game theory to investigate co-ordination failures and information problems in markets. See M. Bianchi, 'Hayek's Spontaneous Order: The "Correct" versus the "Corrigible" Society', in J. Birner and R. van Zijp (eds), *Hayek, Coordination and Evolution* (London: Routledge, 1994), pp. 232–54; and S. H. Heap and Y. Varoufakis, *Game Theory: A Critical Introduction* (London: Routledge, 1995). See also R. Sugden, 'Naturalness and the Spontaneous Order of the Market', in S. H. Heap and A. Ross (eds), *Understanding the Enterprise Culture* (Edinburgh: Edinburgh University Press, 1992), pp. 161–81. These approaches are moving away from a traditional concern with the theory of the firm to a broader analysis of institutions, co-ordination, and information.

19 A number of strands in contemporary social science are converging to form a new political economy. See A. Gamble, 'The New Political Economy', *Political Studies*, 43/3 (1995).

20 M. Desai, 'Equilibrium, Expectations, and Knowledge', in Birner and van Zijp (eds), *Hayek, Coordination and Evolution*, pp. 25–50.

21 The assumption of fixed preferences is one of the greatest obstacles to the development of an adequate account of the relationship between structure and agency. See M. Harris and G. Kelly, 'Rethinking Preferences in Public Choice', in J. Lovenduski and J. Stanyer (eds), *Contemporary Political Studies 1995*, Proceedings of the PSA Annual Conference, pp. 676–84.

22 One example of the possibilities is G. Kelly, A. Gamble, M. Dietrich, and R. Germain, 'Regional Finance and Corporate Governance: Do We Need Regional Development Banks?', *New Economy*, 2/4 (1995), which uses the concepts of co-ordination failures and corporate governance to explore the potential for changing the relationship between banks and small and medium-sized enterprises.

23 See, e.g., the illuminating discussion by D. Elson, 'Market Socialism or Socialization of the Market?', *New Left Review*, 172 (1988), 3–44.

24 F. A. Hayek, *Hayek on Hayek* (London: Routledge, 1994), p. 155.

Bibliography

A comprehensive bibliography appears in John Gray, *Hayek on Liberty* (Oxford: Blackwell, 1986). The bibliography given below lists the main sources used in writing this book.

HAYEK: MAIN WRITINGS

Books

Prices and Production (London: Routledge, 1931).
(ed.) *Collectivist Economic Planning: Critical Studies on the Possibility of Socialism* (London: Routledge, 1935).
The Pure Theory of Capital (London: Macmillan, 1941).
The Road to Serfdom (London: Routledge, 1944).
Individualism and Economic Order (London: Routledge, 1948).
The Counter Revolution of Science (Glencoe: Free Press, 1952).
The Sensory Order: An Inquiry into the Foundations of Theoretical Psychology (London: Routledge, 1952).
(ed.) *Capitalism and the Historians* (London: Routledge, 1954).
The Constitution of Liberty (London: Routledge, 1960).
Studies in Philosophy, Politics, and Economics (London: Routledge, 1967).
Law, Legislation, and Liberty: A New Statement of the Liberal Principles of Justice and Political Economy (London: Routledge): vol. 1: *Rules and Order* (1973); vol. 2: *The Mirage of Social Justice* (1976); vol. 3: *The Political Order of a Free People* (1979).
New Studies in Philosophy, Politics, Economics and the History of Ideas (London: Routledge, 1978).
Collected Works (London: Routledge): vol. 1: *The Fatal Conceit: The Errors of*

Socialism (1988); vol. 3: *The Trend of Economic Thinking* (1991); vol. 4: *The Fortunes of Liberalism* (1992).
Hayek on Hayek, ed. S. Kresge and L. Wenar (London: Routledge, 1994).

Pamphlets

A Tiger by the Tail: The Keynesian Legacy of Inflation, ed. Sudha R. Shensy (London: Institute of Economic Affairs, 1972).
Full Employment at Any Price? (London: Institute of Economic Affairs, 1975).
Choice in Currency: A Way to Stop Inflation (London: Institute of Economic Affairs, 1976).
The Denationalisation of Money (London: Institute of Economic Affairs, 1976; rev. 1990).
1980s Unemployment and the Unions (London: Institute of Economic Affairs, 1980).
Knowledge, Evolution, and Society (London: Adam Smith Institute, 1983).

Articles

'The Trend of Economic Thinking', *Economica*, 13 (1933), 121–37.
'Economics and Knowledge', *Economica*, 13/2 (1937), 33–54.
'The Economic Conditions of Inter-State Federation', *New Commonwealth Quarterly*, 5/2 (1939), 131–49.
'The Use of Knowledge in Society', *American Economic Review*, 55/4 (1945), 519–30.

SECONDARY SOURCES AND COMMENTARIES

Anderson, P., *A Zone of Engagement* (London: Verso, 1992).
Arblaster, A., *The Rise and Decline of Western Liberalism* (Oxford: Blackwell, 1984).
Barry, N., *Hayek's Social and Economic Philosophy* (London: Macmillan, 1979).
—— *On Classical Liberalism and Libertarianism* (London: Macmillan, 1986).
—— *The New Right* (London: Croom Helm, 1987).
—— 'Hayek on Liberty', in J. Gray and Z. Pelczynski (eds), *Conceptions of Liberty* (Oxford: Clarendon Press, 1990), 263–86.
Bellamy, R., ' "Dethroning Politics": Liberalism, Constitutionalism, and Democracy in the Thought of F. A. Hayek', *British Journal of Political Science*, 24 (1994), 419–41.
Birner, J., and van Zijp, R. (eds), *Hayek, Coordination and Evolution* (London: Routledge, 1994).
Blackburn, R., 'Fin-de-Siècle: Socialism after the Crash', *New Left Review*, 185 (1991), 5–67.

Brittan, S., 'Hayek's Spontaneous Social Order', in *Capitalism with a Human Face* (London: Edward Elgar, 1995), 113–26.

Buchanan, J., *The Limits of Liberty* (Chicago: University of Chicago Press, 1975).

Butler, E., *Hayek* (London: Temple Smith, 1983).

Cockett, R., *Thinking the Unthinkable: Thinktanks and the Economic Counter-Revolution 1931–83* (London: Fontana, 1995).

Cowling, M., 'The Sources of the New Right', *Encounter*, Nov. 1989, pp. 3–13.

Denham, A., 'Thinktanks of the New Right: Theory, Practice, and Prospects', Ph.D. diss., Southampton, 1992.

Dicey, A. V., *Lectures on the Relation between Law and Public Opinion in England during the Nineteenth Century* (London: Macmillan, 1926).

Elson, D., 'Market Socialism or Socialization of the Market?', *New Left Review*, 172 (1988), 3–44.

Forsyth, M., 'Hayek's Bizarre Liberalism: A Critique', *Political Studies*, 36/2 (June 1988), 235–50.

Friedman, M., *Capitalism and Freedom* (Chicago: University of Chicago Press, 1962).

Fukuyama, F., *The End of History and the Last Man* (London: Hamish Hamilton, 1992).

Gilmour, I., *Inside Right* (London: Hutchinson, 1977).

Gissurarson, H., *Hayek's Conservative Liberalism* (New York: Garland, 1987).

Grassl, W., and Smith, B. (eds), *Austrian Economics* (London: Croom Helm, 1986).

Gray, J., *Hayek on Liberty* (Oxford: Blackwell, 1986).

—— *The Undoing of Conservatism* (London: Social Market Foundation, 1994).

Green, D., *The New Right* (Brighton: Wheatsheaf, 1987).

Greenleaf, W. H., *The British Political Tradition*, vol. 1: *The Rise of Collectivism* (London: Methuen, 1983).

Hamowy, R., 'Hayek's Concept of Freedom: A Critique', *New Individualist Review*, 1 (1961), 28–31.

Heap, S. H., and Varoufakis, Y., *Game Theory: A Critical Introduction* (London: Routledge, 1995).

Hicks, J. R., 'The Hayek Story', in *Critical Essays in Monetary Theory* (Oxford: Oxford University Press, 1967).

Hodgson, G., *Economics and Institutions* (Cambridge: Polity, 1988).

—— *Economics and Evolution* (Cambridge: Polity, 1993).

Hoover, K., and Plant, R., *Conservative Capitalism* (London: Routledge, 1989).

Kalecki, M., 'Political Aspects of Full Employment', *Political Quarterly*, 14 (1943), 322–31.

Kley, R., *Hayek's Social and Political Thought* (Oxford: Clarendon Press, 1994).

Kristol, I., 'Capitalism, Socialism, and Nihilism', in R. Kirk (ed.), *The Conservative Reader* (New York: Viking, 1982).

Kukathas, C., *Hayek and Modern Liberalism* (Oxford: Clarendon Press, 1989).

Lavoie, D., *Rivalry and Central Planning: The Socialist Calculation Debate Reconsidered* (Cambridge: Cambridge University Press, 1985).

Letwin, S., 'On Conservative Individualism', in M. Cowling (ed.), *Conservative Essays* (London: Cassell, 1978).

Machlup, F. (ed.), *Essays on Hayek* (New York: New York University Press, 1976).

McCormick, B., *Hayek and the Keynesian Avalanche* (Hemel Hempstead: Harvester Wheatsheaf, 1992).

Mises, L. von, *The Free and Prosperous Commonwealth* (New York: Van Nostrand, 1962).

Nozick, R., *Anarchy, State, and Utopia* (Oxford: Blackwell, 1974).

Oakeshott, M., *Rationalism in Politics* (London: Methuen, 1962).

—— *On Human Conduct* (Oxford: Clarendon Press, 1975).

O'Sullivan, N., 'Conservatism, the New Right, and the Limited State', in J. Hayward and P. Norton (eds), *The Political Science of British Politics* (Brighton: Wheatsheaf, 1986), 21–36.

Paul, E. F., 'Liberalism, Unintended Orders, and Evolutionism', *Political Studies*, 36/2 (1988), 251–72.

Plant, R., *Modern Political Thought* (Oxford: Blackwell, 1991).

Polanyi, K., *The Great Transformation* (Boston: Beacon Press, 1957).

Popper, K., *The Open Society and its Enemies* (London: Routledge, 1945).

Robbins, L., *The Great Depression* (London: Routledge, 1932).

—— *Autobiography* (London: Macmillan, 1971).

Rothbard, M., *Power and Market* (Kansas: Sheed, Andrews and McMeel, 1977).

—— *For a New Liberty: The Libertarian Manifesto* (New York: Collier–Macmillan, 1978).

—— *The Ethics of Liberty* (Atlantic Heights, NJ: Humanities Press, 1981).

Schumpeter, J., *Capitalism, Socialism, and Democracy* (London: Allen and Unwin, 1950).

Scruton, R., *The Meaning of Conservatism* (Harmondsworth: Penguin, 1980).

—— *A Dictionary of Political Thought* (London: Macmillan, 1982).

Shand, A., *The Capitalist Alternative: An Introduction to Neo-Austrian Economics* (Brighton: Wheatsheaf, 1984).

Shearmur, J., 'Libertarianism and Conservatism in the Thought of FA Hayek', Ph.D. diss., London, 1988.

Skidelsky, R., *John Maynard Keynes: The Economist as Saviour 1920–1937* (London: Macmillan, 1992).

Steele, G. R., *The Economics of Friedrich Hayek* (London: Macmillan, 1993).

Strachey, J., *The Coming Struggle for Power* (London: Gollancz, 1932).

—— *The Nature of Capitalist Crisis* (London: Gollancz, 1934).

Streissler, E., et al. (eds), *Roads to Freedom: Essays in Honour of F. A. Hayek* (London: Routledge, 1969).

Talmon, J. L., *The Origins of Totalitarian Democracy* (London: Secker and Warburg, 1952).

Tomlinson, J., *Hayek and the Market* (London: Pluto, 1990).

Vanberg, V., 'Spontaneous Market Order and Social Rules: A Critical Examination of F. A. Hayek's Theory of Cultural Evolution', *Economics and Philosophy*, 2 (1986), 75–100.

Vaughn, K. I., 'Economic Calculation under Socialism: The Austrian Contribution', *Economic Inquiry*, Oct. 1980, pp. 535–54.

Wainwright, H., *Arguments for a New Left* (Oxford: Blackwell, 1994).

Weber, M., 'Science as a Vocation', in H. H. Gerth and C. Wright Mills (eds), *From Max Weber* (London: Routledge, 1970).

Index

Made in United States
North Haven, CT
05 February 2023

32080969R00128